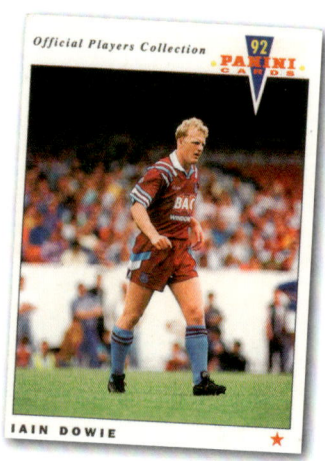

Conker Editions Ltd
22 Cosby Road
Littlethorpe
Leicester
LE19 2HF
Email: books@conkereditions.co.uk
Website: www.conkereditions.co.uk
First published by Conker Editions Ltd 2022
Text © 2022 Sid Lambert, Dave Walker and ExWHUEmployee.
Sid Lambert, Dave Walker and ExWHUEmployee have asserted their rights in accordance with the Copyright, Designs and Patents Act 1988 to be identified as the author of this work. All rights reserved. No part of this publication may be reproduced, stored in a retrieval system, or transmitted in any form or by any means, electronic, mechanical, photocopying, recording or otherwise, without the prior permission in writing of the publisher and the copyright owners, or as expressly permitted by law, or under terms agreed with the appropriate reprographics rights organisation. Enquiries concerning reproduction outside the terms stated here should be sent to the publishers at the UK address printed on this page.

The publisher makes no representation, express or implied, with regard to the accuracy of the information contained in this book and cannot accept any legal responsibility for any errors or omissions that may be made.

A CIP catalogue record for this book is available from the British Library.
13-digit ISBN: 978-1739770532
Design and typesetting by Gary Silke.
Printed in the UK by Mixam.

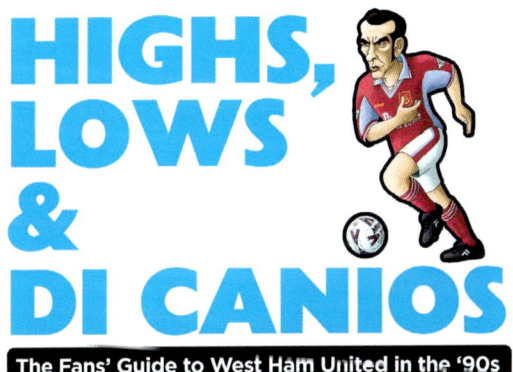

# HIGHS, LOWS & DI CANIOS
### The Fans' Guide to West Ham United in the '90s

**Sid Lambert, Dave Walker & ExWHUEmployee**

# Foreword

I miss Upton Park. What a place to play football. I'd heard the old saying about "playing under the lights," but it was only when I put on that Claret and Blue shirt and walked out of that tunnel – into the full glare of the floodlights – that I appreciated how glorious it was.

Even after all this time, I can still remember it so clearly. The sounds, the smells, the sheer electricity in the air. It was so special.

When I first signed for West Ham all I knew about was John Lyall and Billy Bonds. Billy was a player I really admired. I loved his never-say-die attitude. That was exactly my style of football. I rolled up my sleeves and gave it everything I had, every single week. I cared about losing, I cared about wearing the shirt. And this created an amazing relationship with you, the West Ham fans. For eleven years, over two spells at the club, you were a huge part of my life.

The '90s was an incredible time to be at this football club. When I got the chance to come back in 1994, it was the easiest decision I ever made. It gave me some memories that I'll treasure forever. I hope you enjoy reliving some of those moments in this book.

Sid, Dave and Ex have told the story from a supporter's perspective, which is really important. Because that's what a football club is. It's not a brand. It's not a badge. It's not the players or the manager. It's the people. That's what makes West Ham so special.

Enjoy.

**Julian Dicks**

# Introduction

When you're young, football clubs are magical places. I was lucky enough to watch West Ham in the '70s when we had players like Brooking and Bonds, who became my heroes. It was a fantastic time, and the first time I went to Upton Park I was hooked. By the time I was 12, I was doing a paper round for the princely sum of £1 per week, money that I used to go to as many away games as possible.

By the time I was 17 I was living the dream. Those heroes who I worshipped from the terraces had become my team-mates. I cherished every moment I played in the famous Claret and Blue. And I can remember almost every goal. When you've grown up like I did – an East End boy from an East End family that lived and breathed West Ham United – the feeling of scoring at the Boleyn Ground is indescribable.

I wish I had spent my whole career here and made myself a one-club legend like Trevor and Bonzo. It means that much to me. And it's why I jumped at the chance to come back. I'll be honest, I wasn't sure how I'd be treated after six years away. But West Ham is a family. And I was welcomed back with open arms, for which I am truly grateful.

Reading this book reminds you of what it's like to be part of this football club. You never know what's going to happen next, and the '90s was a perfect example. We started the decade languishing in the Second Division, and by the end we had qualified for Europe. Sid, Dave and Ex could have written ten books on what happened in-between. Whether it was the Bond Scheme, Harry and Billy, the ridiculousness of Raducioiu or the delight of Di Canio, life at Upton Park was always unpredictable.

Yet, despite the chaos, one thing stayed the same: the passion of the West Ham fans. I know exactly how you feel.

COYI.

**Tony Cottee**

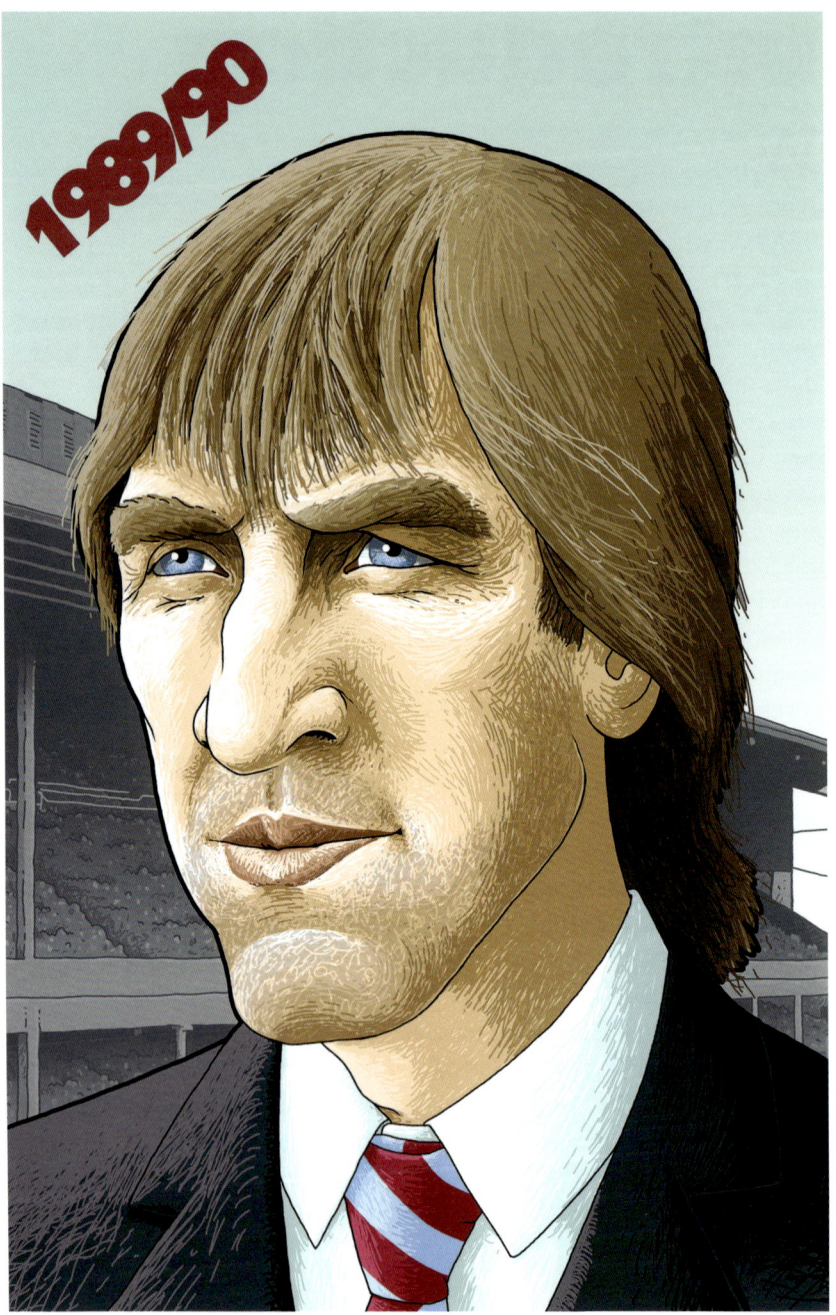

## A Brave Lou Dawn: Macari the New Man in Charge

In the summer of 1989 optimism was in short supply at Upton Park. Just three years earlier, the Irons had come within a whisker of winning the title. Now they'd slipped meekly out of the top flight, beloved boss John Lyall had been sacked and their best player, Paul Ince, wanted to leave. There were probably harder jobs in east London – the Krays' defence lawyer, or Dirty Den and Angie's marriage-guidance counsellor – but rejuvenating West Ham United was going to be no easy task.

Still, there was no shortage of contenders. According to the papers, former Everton boss Howard Kendall was interested in the hotseat, as was Peter Shreeves, assistant manager at Spurs. Closer to home, Tony Carr and Mick McGiven – loyal members of Lyall's coaching staff – had both expressed their ambitions to continue his legacy.

The overwhelming favourite though was possibly the only man who could match Lyall for his unadulterated love of Claret and Blue: the mighty William Arthur Bonds. For 21 years and 663 League games Billy Bonds had rampaged through the Saturday-afternoon battlefields of English football in defence of his beloved West Ham United. Rumour has it that when he ran along the beach at Leigh-on-Sea, the tide refused to come in. If anyone could drag this team up by its bootstraps and restore some pride to the ranks, it was 'Bonzo'.

The players knew it. The fans knew it. Everyone knew it. Everyone, that is, except the chairman. After watching Lyall's team slowly decline for three seasons, the board had decided that more of the same was not an option. What we needed was a shock to the system. It was time to shake up the dressing room, by throwing in a hand grenade. A hand grenade named Lou Macari.

The Scotsman had taken lowly Swindon from the fourth to the second tier in quick succession. But this was no fairy-tale rise through the ranks. Macari's Swindon were the stuff of nightmares: direct, in-your-face and ugly. Those are excellent qualities if you're a nightclub bouncer. But they were not terms you'd associate with the Academy of Football.

The reason West Ham fans had been so tolerant of Lyall's decline was that he represented the romanticism associated with our club. He'd taken us to the brink of glory and then back into despair, but he'd done it playing football the way he, Ron Greenwood, Bobby Moore and co. had taught us to play. The closest to romance Lou Macari had ever come was letting his wife switch on the heating on Valentine's Day.

So there were big question marks against his appointment. There had been games at Swindon where the ball was barely on speaking terms with the grass.

How would ball players like Liam Brady, Mark Ward and Alan Devonshire adapt to his style? And could he convince wantaway star Paul Ince that his future lay at Upton Park?

He wouldn't have long to address the latter. Unbeknownst to him, Paul Ince's agent – angling to get his client a move to a big club – had come up with a great idea for a photoshoot in *The Sun* newspaper. And before Lou Macari had even sat down for pie and mash in his new home, he was dealing with his first shitstorm of the season.

**EX:** I remember my dad absolutely fuming when he found out about the appointment. Like everyone else, he wanted Billy Bonds to get the job. When he told me that our new manager was Lou Macari, my first question was "Who's he?" He told me they managed Swindon, to which I replied, "Who are they?" That didn't improve his mood much.

Looking back, Lou had an almost impossible task in replacing a legend like John Lyall. It was a brave move by the board to bring in an outsider, but it felt like the wrong appointment at the time.

**DAVE:** Sacking John Lyall and hiring Lou Macari was like losing a tenner and finding a quid. It's just remarkable that he got the job in the first place. West Ham, especially at that time, placed a lot of value on history and tradition. It should have been someone who followed our philosophy, who understood how we played the game. Instead, we got Lou Macari, who was a very decent lower-league manager in his own right but played football in his own way. He was always going to struggle. Booting the ball downfield as far as possible wasn't going to win you many friends at Upton Park.

## Paul Gets Shirty: Ince Shows True Colours

"Hello, Guv'nor. It's your agent here. Yeah, sorry I didn't call you back earlier. I was busy working on a PR strategy for Pol Pot. He's struggling a bit with all this genocide stuff. Yeah, nasty business. We need to give his reputation a boost. So, the Khmer Rouge are going to bring out a Christmas album. You know, put a few smiles on people's faces. Reckon it's a real money-spinner. Anyway, enough about him. Let's talk about you, pal. I've come up with this cracking idea to get your move sorted…"

The whole world knew Paul Ince was unhappy. John Lyall had been like a father figure to him since he arrived at the club as a troubled teenage schoolboy. The young midfielder's rise from the youth ranks to the first team – even earning England Under-21 honours – had been one of the rare bright spots in the gloom of Lyall's latter years. The dismissal of his mentor had made Ince's decision to look for opportunities elsewhere an easy one. The only question was where he was going, and when.

Two clubs were known to be in the mix: Terry Venables' Tottenham and Alex Ferguson's Manchester United. In Ince's mind, there was only one winner: he wanted to go to Old Trafford, and trusted in his advisor to make it happen.

Now, even in the days before internet and social media, there were many tools at a football agent's disposal to get transfer deals done: clandestine meetings at motorway services, a quiet word with a journalist. Christ, you could even plant a vicious rumour on ClubCall and charge punters the princely sum of 49p a minute to hear it.

What you didn't do, under any circumstances, was pose in another club's kit before you'd signed on the dotted line. Which is exactly what Ince was persuaded to do. Days before the start of the season, a story appeared in *The Sun* that West Ham's prize asset was on his way to the Red Devils, accompanied by a picture of him in his new side's strip.

It was an unmitigated public relations disaster, one that Ince has since insisted was entirely of his agent's making. Apparently, the image wasn't meant to be used until the deal was done, and had been mistakenly published by an unwitting editor. Whatever the reason, it was the death knell for Ince's reputation with West Ham fans. Overnight he became Public Enemy Number One. And when his name was announced in the starting line-up at Stoke for Macari's first League game as manager, it was greeted with a chorus of boos.

Hardly the ideal start for the new gaffer. But unbelievably, things were about to get worse.

**DAVE:** *Even now, I look back at what Paul Ince did and think it was absolutely ridiculous. It's not like he was nine years old. He was an adult. A grown man. You'd think he'd have an ounce of common sense to ask somebody's opinion: "All right mate, my agent wants me to do this. What do you think?" But no, he didn't. He didn't fire up one of his brain cells and get some better advice. Instead, he posed with the United shirt and, in my opinion, he deserves every bit of stick he's got. The West Ham fans sent a message that day and every day since: "Don't take the piss out of our football club."*

**EX:** *I don't feel as strongly as Dave. I just think it was an incredibly stupid, emotional decision. Ince was traumatised by the way John Lyall left the club. John had been that father figure to him, who'd help him get through that rough upbringing and* become part of the first team at West Ham. He hated the board for the way they treated Lyall and was desperate to get out. But that doesn't excuse what he did. Posing in another team's shirt before you've signed was an incredibly naïve thing to do. He would have joined United anyway. There's no way West Ham would have turned down the money. All this did was make sure he was never welcome back.

## Mac Attack: Kamara Crocks Frankie

Frank McAvennie's return from Celtic hadn't quite been the fairy tale we had hoped for. In 1986 'Macca' had the world at his feet. A glut of goals had propelled us to third in the League, he'd scored his first international goal for Scotland, and an appearance on *Wogan* made him an overnight celebrity. And, boy, did Frankie love being famous.

It wasn't for everyone. Some footballers liked to clock off after training and go home to the family. Some liked a nice game of snooker or golf. McAvennie liked a bottle of champagne and a gaggle of glamour models to share it with. He soon became as lethal in Stringfellows as he was in the penalty area. And the press loved him for it. He was regularly pictured with a bevvy [*sic*] of busty Page 3 models, and as long as he was equally proficient on the pitch, no one really cared about his extracurricular exertions.

By 1989, after two chaotic but consistent years at Celtic, it was the lure of love that had motivated his move back to the capital. He'd been spending his weekends flying back to London to see his girlfriend, Page 3's own Jenny Blyth. A return to Upton Park suited all parties. The Scot got to spend his nights with his beloved. The Hammers welcomed back a hero to spearhead their fight against relegation.

However, it soon became clear that this was not the Frankie Mac of old. He looked unfit and off the pace. He looked like he'd left his shooting boots on the conveyor belt at Stansted. As someone who worshipped him and had his picture adorning my wall since my early days of fandom, it was heartbreaking to see. (Incidentally, I also had pictures of Optimus Prime in my bedroom. As much as it pains me to say, he would have been more f\*\*king use in those final eight games of the season.)

Still, relegation was a chance to hit the reset button for everyone. You wondered if the installation of a sergeant major like Macari as manager might be the kick up the backside that the striker needed to rediscover his former glories. A fighting-fit Frank McAvennie would be way too good for the Second Division, surely? He could score 20 goals by Christmas and we'd be halfway to promotion before he popped the cork on the champers at Peter Stringfellow's New Year piss-up.

It wasn't to be. A late block by Chris Kamara early in the second half folded

Frankie like an accordion. It didn't look any worse than 99% of the challenges that happened every Saturday afternoon, but by some cruel twist of physics and fate it tore his tibia to pieces. Unbelievable, Jeff.

Frank was whisked away to hospital where he later underwent three-and-a-half hours in surgery, getting eight pins and a metal plate to hold his bones in place. By the time he came round after his anaesthetic, his left ankle looked like it was sponsored by RoboCop.

Meanwhile, Lou Macari was 57 minutes into his career as West Ham boss. His best player was being booed by his own fans and his main striker's leg looked like a plate of spaghetti. Fortune's always hiding and all that.

**DAVE**: *I still feel sorry for Chris Kamara about what happened at Stoke. When you watch the tackle back, there was really nothing in it. But the list of injuries was incredible: broken ankle, broken leg, broken ligaments. It sounded like Frank had been in a car crash, not playing football on a Saturday afternoon. It was just so unlucky, and that goes for Kamara too. He had death threats from the ICF, and all the poor bloke had done was put his foot in. Football can be a cruel game sometimes.*

**EX:** *When Frank McAvennie got injured, it felt like the end of an era. Tony Cottee had gone, Phil Parkes was getting old, the likes of Alan Devonshire just couldn't get fit consistently. That group of players – from that famous season in 1986 – was slowly disbanding, and so much of it was due to injury. The level of physiotherapy in those days was nowhere near what we have now. Players routinely retired much earlier if they suffered a serious injury.*

## Stuart Slater: A Star Is Born

The season started to follow a frustrating pattern. Great one week, crap the next. Our defence had more leaks than the starboard side of the *Titanic*. When you're conceding three goals a game to relegation fodder like West Brom and Brighton, you've got to ask yourself a question.

The only consistent aspect was the form of young Stuart Slater. The youth-team graduate had been a rare bright spark in the misery of the previous season.

With Frank McAvennie trying to piece his leg back together and Leroy Rosenior spending nearly the entire season on the treatment table, the Suffolk-born striker was now our main threat from centre-forward. It made him the exception in a Second Division where the frontlines were populated by physically imposing target men. Slater weighed about 10 stone soaking wet, and looked like he'd lose an arm-wrestle with DangerMouse. If he got any f**king skinnier, Bob Geldof was going to get the band back together.

What he lacked in strength, he made up for in pure speed. Watching him run at a full-back was the sort of thing punters paid good money to see. West Ham fans have always enjoyed seeing one of their own make it to the first team, and whilst frustration grew with some of the more experienced members of the team, Slater's youth afforded him more patience from the terraces.

He rewarded them with one of the finest goals Upton Park had ever seen, during a midweek fixture with Sunderland, who were expected to be in the mix for promotion. We absolutely battered them. It was Macari's finest hour as a manager, and one of those nights that made you believe in the fabled lustre of those Upton Park floodlights. Slater was playing up front alongside fellow youth-team graduate and best pal Eamonn Dolan, who scored his first two home goals for the club. The young Irishman celebrated with a memorable jig of delight, and ordinarily his name would have commanded the headlines, were it not for Slater's moment of magic.

A big boot downfield from Phil Parkes was flicked on by Dolan, Slater controlled it on his chest and then walloped the ball on the volley into the top corner from 25 yards. Five seconds, four touches, and not a single blade of grass touched. It was Route One football at its best.

A 5-0 win put us fifth in the table. Two young guns were starting to fire up front. Maybe the Macari era might not be so bad after all.

**EX:** *I love Stuart Slater. He was the first player I ever idolised at Upton Park. I had a poster of him on my wall and it went everywhere with me. It didn't matter if we were going to a caravan park in Norfolk or to an apartment in Majorca, if I was going, then my Stuart Slater poster was coming too. At school, other kids were Arsenal, Spurs or United fans so they're all pretending they're Gazza or Merson in the playground. I was always Stuart Slater. He was my hero.*

**DAVE:** *When I think about Stuart Slater, he was the perfect fit for West Ham and how we played. He was skilful, he was bright. He took players on. He got the crowd off their seats. That goal against Sunderland is so underrated, it really is. The* *technique to execute that sort of finish is absolutely top-level. If Messi or Maradona scored that, we'd never hear the end of it. Instead it only exists in the heads of those who saw it live or watched it relentlessly on our end-of-season VHS review.*

## Justin Time? Fashanu Arrives on Loan

The enthusiasm didn't last long. Two wins from our next seven League games saw us lose ground in the promotion race.

Little did we know at the time, but Dolan had scored his last goals in West Ham colours, before being sold to Birmingham as part of the manager's ongoing transfer merry-go-round. That left us with a makeshift forward line of Slater and the much-maligned David Kelly. The latter had been John Lyall's marquee signing at the start of the 1988-89 season, a replacement for Everton-bound Tony Cottee. And more importantly, it meant I could tear down my beloved poster of TC from the bedroom wall – lovingly located between Frank McAvennie and Optimus Prime – and have a ready-made replacement.

The £750,000 recruit from Walsall, who had been linked with Liverpool before signing for Lyall, had made his debut in a 4-0 defeat at The Dell where he spent the majority of the 90 minutes face down in the dirt. To describe him as lightweight would have been generous. We'd have had more physical presence if we'd played Sooty and Sweep up front. Since that inauspicious start, Kelly's confidence had gradually crumbled under the deluge of criticism from the terraces. By springtime, I'd replaced his poster with one of Kevin Keen.

So Macari decided it was time for reinforcements. In came one of the more curious loan signings in recent history: Justin Fashanu. A decade earlier the big striker had been one of England's brightest talents. He became Britain's first £1 million black footballer and a fixture on *Match of the Day* credits thanks to an extraordinary goal against Liverpool.

By 1985 it seemed his career was over. A crippling knee injury sent him to the States in search of a miracle cure. Incredibly, the surgeon's knife did allow him to resume his career. And though he clearly wasn't the player of old, there were plenty of desperate football managers out there willing to take a punt on him. One of them was Lou Macari.

Fashanu made his debut as a substitute in a ferocious League Cup tie with Wimbledon, who featured his younger brother John. Despite his lack of match practice, Justin showed some neat touches and played a part in the winning goal. He then played a full 90 minutes in 5-4 loss at Ewood Park where our defence looked like they'd just met in the car park, before being subbed off in a depressing 2-1 defeat at Bradford a week later.

That was the last we saw of him. Three games, no goals. A man who looked like a shadow of his former self, doing his best despite obvious physical limitations. In that respect, he fitted in nicely with the rest of the squad. Fan favourites like Alan Devonshire and Phil Parkes were almost unrecognisable from the Boys of '86. The mind was always willing, the body wasn't. Cruel game, football.

As for Fashanu, he drifted around non-League before finally finding a permanent home at Torquay in 1991, arriving somewhat bizarrely with *Coronation Street*'s Julie Goodyear on his arm amidst a wave of publicity after coming out as gay in the press months earlier.

Fashanu's time at West Ham was a brief chapter in a story that would ultimately end in tragedy, and another footnote in a season that was veering from the sublime to the ridiculous on a weekly basis.

**DAVE:** *You can still find one clip on YouTube of an interview Justin did after the Wimbledon game, and what really strikes you is what a nice fella he was. It's hard to imagine the incredible pressure he must have lived his life under, given what an ignorant society we lived in back then. He didn't do much at West Ham, but I'm glad he found somewhere to play football after he left us.*

*As for David Kelly, the thing I always remember about him is that every time he hit the ball, he fell over. I'd never seen anything like it. He was like a newborn foal.*

**EX:** *Justin Fashanu would probably have been an icon in this day and age, but back then the terraces everywhere were much more hostile, and horrible places to be in terms of racism and homophobia. When Macari signed him, it was a classic attempt to get that big physical presence up front that he had built teams around before. That physical presence certainly wasn't David Kelly. He had a very decent career after West Ham at clubs like Wolves and Newcastle, but he wasn't up to the standard we needed, and definitely not a good enough replacement for Tony Cottee.*

## The Nightmare Before Christmas

At long last, December brought some consistency for Lou Macari's West Ham United. He'd brought in some new faces, said goodbye to some old ones, chopped and changed the team, fiddled with formations. Along the way there'd been some good results, some not-so-good and some downright awful. Now, with Christmas on the horizon, it finally felt like we had an identity: we were shite. Utter shite.

Games against Stoke, Bradford, Oldham, Ipswich and Leicester yielded one point and one goal in a month that ranks amongst the worst in the club's history. We were mid table in the second tier. Our squad of 'title contenders' were a soft touch in a division where you had to graft for three points every single week. Even our cup form, which had at least given the season some hope, deserted us. We lost 4-3 to Chelsea in the Zenith Data Systems Cup, a competition so tinpot that these days even Wikipedia barely acknowledges its existence. Of course, as it was a meaningless game in a meaningless competition, David Kelly scored.

As the decade came to an end, it was hard to imagine that the 1990 could be any worse. Things could only get better, surely?

**DAVE:** *This was relegation form, and a clear sign that the clock was ticking for Lou Macari. He'd made a lot of changes in a short space of time. And some of the young players were looking really promising for the future. But as a manager you need results now, not tomorrow. There was a core in the dressing room that didn't like him, didn't want to play for him, and that was always going to end one way.*

**EX:** *That month really felt like the writing was on the wall for Macari. You have to have respect in a dressing room, and the big personalities we had at the time didn't have that. The tales some players tell about Macari's love of horse racing are legendary. Apparently, he would often stop the team bus outside a betting shop so he could stick a few quid on. To go from a legend like John Lyall to someone who's sending one of the subs to find out what had happened at Aintree – sometimes in the middle of a game – is just not going to work.*

### Terrible in Torquay: An FA Cup F\*\*k-up

January is traditionally a time for a new start, and despite the December gloom there were reasons to believe that the New Year would bring new hope for West Ham's despondent fanbase.

With the crowd growing restless, Lou Macari dived straight back into the transfer market. In came Ian Bishop and Trevor Morley from Manchester City in a swap deal that meant it was time to say goodbye to Mark Ward. The combative winger, who had taken to the new manager's regime with the same zest Giant Haystacks took to the treadmill, couldn't get out of the door fast enough. A Lyall devotee, it was time for him to start afresh, and the more relaxed style of City boss Howard Kendall – who notoriously encouraged his players to spend pre-season in the boozer – felt like a natural fit.

Bishop and Morley weren't the only additions. Northern Ireland striker Jimmy Quinn joined from Bradford. At six-foot plus, he brought some physicality to our powder-puff front line and had scored a lot of goals for Macari at Swindon.

Whilst none of the three new signings had played at the top level, they were seasoned operators in the second tier. It felt like sensible business. Their nous would be crucial to turning our season around. And what better place to start than with a day by the seaside in the FA Cup?

Torquay may have been an area of outstanding natural beauty, but they were habitually around the Football League relegation zone. Sadly, it's one of football's great injustices that photogenic scenery isn't necessarily commensurate with football success, otherwise Antarctica would have won the World Cup by now.

So whilst the long coach trip to the arse end of the country felt arduous, at least there was the guarantee of some goals at the end of it. It was a new year and a new dawn (again) for West Ham United. When you're drawn against lower-league teams in the FA Cup there's a tendency, particularly when you're young, to assume that it's going to be a walkover. Even at eleven years old, I knew the competition's reputation for giant-killings and remembered the day non-League Sutton United knocked out Cup-holders Coventry City just two seasons before.

But Coventry didn't have the mighty Jimmy Quinn and Trevor Morley up front. The ignorance of youth and the nonsensical injection of optimism that comes with any new signing had me convinced that we'd stroll into the fourth round. I'd even recreated the fixture (playing for both teams) on my Subbuteo table that very morning, using Newcastle United as a substitute for the home side. We won 8-0 with debut hat-tricks for Quinn and Morley alongside a brace for George Parris. Admittedly, that last part did sound slightly dubious. Particularly when you take into consideration that a) George was one of my favourite players; b) both his goals could be attributed to keeper error, and c) I was acting as the Torquay keeper. Nonetheless, six goals seemed a more than reasonable return from our trip to the Riviera.

Of course, what I hadn't considered was West Ham's perennial ability to West Ham up even the easiest of opportunities.

I spent the afternoon furiously checking Ceefax for updates from Plainmoor. Whilst goals were raining in elsewhere, there was a curious silence from the south coast. Half-time came and went with the score goalless. My pre-game prediction started to feel a little iffy. Even with our fantastic new forward line, six goals in the second half was a lot to ask. Finally, after 77 excruciating minutes, there was an update from p302. Torquay went in front through a goal from Paul Hirons. We lost 1-0.

New Year. New team. Same old shite.

**EX:** *This was an early education for me on what life would be like as a West Ham fan. Whilst all my mates at school supported the big clubs, my dad had been convincing* me since I first showed any interest in football that this was the greatest team in the world – and I had to follow his example. I would proudly talk about being a West Ham fan whilst everyone else talked about United, Arsenal and Liverpool. Then we go and lose to Torquay. I'd never even heard of them. I didn't even know if Torquay was a place in England. It was a disaster.

**DAVE:** This was sheer embarrassment. But then again, it set my expectations just about right for every cup run after that. Getting done over by Torquay was the first in a series of crap FA Cup performances throughout the '90s. Sometimes you have to wonder if this club is cursed. The clue is in the anthem, I guess. 'Fortune's always hiding' epitomises the experience of supporting West Ham.

### Six of the Worst: Valentine's Day Massacre at Oldham

After the disaster in Devon, things picked up slightly. We managed a win, a loss and a draw in our next three League games. Jimmy Quinn was starting to find his feet in Claret and Blue. He'd scored twice already and, as expected, was proving a handful at this level.

With promotion looking unlikely, the last hope for any kind of salvation this season rested on the Littlewoods Cup semi-final. Bishop, Morley and Quinn were all cup-tied for the first leg at Oldham, which meant recalls for David Kelly and Gary Strodder.

As the season had progressed, my inquisitive eleven-year-old mind had started to notice a mathematical anomaly. West Ham + David Kelly = zero goals scored. West Ham + Gary Strodder = shitloads of goals conceded. Whilst It wasn't quite the sort of discovery that had Pythagoras reaching for his calculator, it did seem to have some merit.

This game would be the acid test for this unproven hypothesis. Oldham were becoming a decent team in the mix for the Second Division Play-off spots. They'd beaten us 2-0 at Upton Park during that dark month of December, and they had an ace up their sleeve in the form of their plastic pitch at Boundary Park. The '80s had been strewn with numerous shocking West Ham performances on the artificial surfaces at Luton and QPR. Much like Michael Jackson, our relationship with plastic wasn't always pretty.

Over two-legged cup ties, the general consensus is that the team that plays at home in the second leg has the advantage, as they know exactly what they have to do. What that doesn't account for is that same team producing such a monumental catastrof**k of a performance in the opening game that the return is essentially a dead rubber.

That is what West Ham United managed to achieve on the evening of February 14th, 1990. We lost 6-0, though that doesn't tell half the story. It was a performance that ended careers. At one stage poor Stewart Robson, whose knees were about as structurally sound as a packet of Skips, was outpaced by the corner flag. Phil Parkes looked every minute of his 39 years of age. And after being at fault for the second goal, Liam Brady looked ready to retire on the spot.

As for my mathematical thesis, I now had my answer. Strodder played his part in the defensive calamity, though he was by no means alone. These were six of the worst goals since records began. You'd have thought the Latics switched the ball with a hand grenade, such was the panic caused when it was lofted into the penalty area.

Up front, David Kelly was about as threatening as Bambi with a feather duster. He was nearing the finish line of his time at the club, provided he didn't f**king fall over before he got there.

The Great Reset under Lou Macari had stopped dead that night in the North West. The Hammers' board had taken a punt and paid the price. You wondered if they'd have the resilience to ride out the consequences. As it happened, they didn't need to. The Gaffer had been up to some gambling of his own.

**DAVE:** *My older brother was actually a steward for that game at Boundary Park and he maintains that it was one of the worst nights of his entire life. It was freezing f**king cold, pissing down with rain and we're getting stuffed 6-0. I'm glad I wasn't old enough to actually go along and see it myself. What a waste of time that would have been. Imagine being stuck in Oldham, soaked to your skin, and watching us slide all over the pitch like we're on roller skates.*

**EX:** *I have a vivid recollection of this night. My dad dropped me off at Cubs around 7pm and once again he was telling me how important it was to support West Ham, even after the embarrassment of Torquay. In the car, he told me this was a really big game, a semi-final, and if we lost 1-0 or 2-0 then that wouldn't be a disaster. He picked me up at half-time and, remembering how excited he was, I asked him what the score was. "Don't ask," he said. We were four down and getting battered.*

## All Bets Are Off: Macari Quits in Disgrace

When I read the headlines that Lou Macari was being accused by the FA of betting against his own team in a cup tie, that pathetic performance at Oldham suddenly began to make sense. Surely no group of footballers could manage to be so universally inept without some form of subterfuge.

In fact, the charge was related to Swindon where the Scot, in partnership with chairman Brian Hillier, had wagered a sizeable sum that the Robins would lose to Newcastle (they got pumped 5-0) in the FA Cup. Sadly there was no such skulduggery involved in the Littlewoods semi-final. We were just crap.

In any case, the revelations in the *Sunday People* made Macari's position untenable. He didn't show up for the team's next fixture (at Swindon, ironically) and the board announced that they had accepted his resignation the following day. His chaotic six-month reign was at an end.

The news was apparently greeted with much enthusiasm in the dressing room where the Scot had made himself about as popular as a fox in a henhouse. Whereas the criticism of Lyall had been that he was too soft and too slow to act, Macari had come in all guns blazing. His militaristic regime might have been the jolt to the arm that some players needed, however he made too many enemies too early, and his love of the horse racing made it hard to take him seriously. It's hard to preach about discipline and work ethic whilst you're stopping the team coach to put a one er on the 2.45 at Kempton.

Yet there had been some bright spots. His transfer policy had given the squad the shake-up it so desperately needed. Martin Allen – whose outstanding long-range shooting was proving a real asset to the team – alongside Colin Foster, Ian Bishop, Trevor Morley and Jimmy Quinn – looked like excellent value for money, and he had recently completed the signing of 6'4" Czech international keeper Ludek Miklosko from Banik Ostrava. These were the foundations of a good side.

Perhaps unfairly, there were few tears on the terraces after Macari's departure. We were 14th in the Second Division, and the Oldham defeat felt like the nail in the coffin, controversy or not. Whoever the next manager was, he had to be able to bring together a disparate squad and reignite a fanbase downtrodden by six months in the doldrums.

There was only one man up to the task.

**EX:** *I genuinely think that if you judge Lou Macari, you have to give him a lot of credit for what he did in the transfer market. When you think about players like Trevor Morley, Ian Bishop, Martin Allen and Ludo Miklosko, they were so important to the future of the club and how we established ourselves in the Premier League. If you were to judge him as Director of Football, he would have been amazing. It's hard to get signings right, and lots of his went on to become iconic players of the era. Unfortunately, as a manager he wasn't good enough in terms of results, and that's how you're always judged in the end.*

**DAVE:** When Lou Macari left, a black cloud had been lifted. You can be kind to him and say that he made good signings. I won't dispute that at all. You can't overlook the quality of players that he brought to the club, and they would all play an important part in our future. But, as I've said before, football isn't about the future. It's about the here and now, and our results were – sadly – nowhere near good enough. The football was shit, the team was a mess and the whole place needed a lift.

### Bonzo to the Rescue

Billy Bonds strolled to the dugout for the home game against Blackburn like a beloved King returning from the Crusades. In the monarch's absence the motherland had crumbled, the people had grown tired and weary. His arrival signalled the return of the good times.

The players believed so, too. From the first whistle they were unrecognisable from the ramshackle outfit that had tumbled down the League table. The passing was crisp. The tackling committed. We took the lead through Jimmy Quinn and hit the woodwork four times during the first half. This didn't look like the fabled new manager 'bounce', rather like he'd stuck a rocket up everyone's arse and told them to get on with it.

Despite our domination, the visitors scrabbled a late equaliser to deny Bonds his first win. He didn't have to wait long. A week later Martin Allen got the winner at Middlesbrough, and then there was the small matter of the return leg of the Littlewoods Cup semi against Oldham.

Three weeks had passed since that abomination at Boundary Park, during which my West Ham holdall had been consistently kicked across the school corridor and the 6-0 scoreline Tipp-Exed on to it for good measure.

I knew that a 7-0 win was about as likely as Iain Dowie being asked to pose for *Playgirl* magazine. All I wanted was redemption. Pride. And a chance to flick up the V sign to the Year Elevens from a safe distance.

With an hour on the clock we were 3-0 up. I knew Billy Bonds wasn't a miracle worker but, when David Kelly scored, I did wonder if he fancied his chances of tiptoeing across the Thames the following morning. Julian Dicks hit the bar with ten minutes to go. If that had gone in, then all bets were off (sorry, Lou). The scoreline stayed at three, and some degree of dignity had been restored.

An impressive run of form followed as we came within the proverbial whisker of making the Play-offs. The team had been transformed. Macari's signings had become cornerstones of the first team. Bishop strolled around midfield whilst Quinn and Morley were forming a strike partnership to be reckoned with.

Ten wins, three draws and four defeats from Bond's 17 League games in charge was an incredible return considering the mess he inherited. And whilst it wasn't quite enough to sneak us into the promotion picture, there was at least some romance to end the season.

The final home game against Wolves was to be Liam Brady's farewell. The Irish international, who had starred at Arsenal, Juventus and Inter before arriving in east London, had decided to call time on his storied career.

And that legendary left peg had one last moment of magic reserved for his special occasion. In the dying seconds, with the Irons 3-0 up, he marched forward from midfield before unleashing a 25-yard swerving pisswhistler of a shot into the top corner. Cue pandemonium as the crowd poured on to the pitch and hoisted Brady up on their shoulders.

It was a sensational end to a schizophrenic season. At least everyone could enjoy their summer holidays with a renewed sense of hope for next season. Billy Bonds' Claret and Blue Army was on the march.

**EX:** *There was a spiritual connection between Billy Bonds and the fans. He was one of our own and, unlike Macari, he commanded instant respect in the dressing room. Billy had high standards in terms of discipline and professionalism. In fact, he was still one of the fittest people at the club. So, the players knew they couldn't get away with anything less than 100% commitment. I don't think at that time anyone else could have come in and made the impact that he did on a team that was massively underperforming.*

**DAVE:** *Bonzo was the right man for the job all along, and the results proved it. He completely changed the trajectory of our season. Even though we eventually missed the Play-offs, at least we had a fairy-tale finish. As for Liam Brady, whilst he was in the twilight years of his career, it was a privilege to see him play for us. An icon of the sport was ending his career in Claret and Blue. I enjoyed that.*

## Football League First Division - 1989/90

| Date | Opponent | H/A | Score | Att. | Scorers |
|---|---|---|---|---|---|
| 19 August | Stoke City | A | 1–1 | 16,058 | Keen |
| 23 August | Bradford City | H | 2–0 | 19,914 | Slater (2) |
| 26 August | Plymouth Argyle | H | 3–2 | 20,231 | Kelly, Allen, Keen |
| 2 September | Hull City | A | 1–1 | 9,235 | Ward |
| 9 September | Swindon Town | H | 1–1 | 21,469 | Allen |
| 16 September | Brighton & H | A | 0–3 | 12,689 | |
| 23 September | Watford | H | 1–0 | 20,728 | Dicks (p) |
| 26 September | Portsmouth | A | 1–0 | 12,632 | Rosenior |
| 30 September | WBA | H | 2–3 | 19,842 | Dolan, Parris |
| 7 October | Leeds United | H | 0–1 | 23,539 | |
| 14 October | Sheffield United | A | 2–0 | 20,822 | Ward (2, 1 p) |
| 18 October | Sunderland | H | 5–0 | 20,901 | Allen, Slater, Keen, Dolan (2) |
| 21 October | Port Vale | A | 2–2 | 8,899 | Keen, Slater |
| 28 October | Oxford United | H | 3–2 | 19,177 | Parris, Slater, Dicks |
| 1 November | AFC Bournemouth | A | 1–1 | 9,979 | Strodder |
| 4 November | Wolverhampton W | A | 0–1 | 22,231 | |
| 11 November | Newcastle United | H | 0–0 | 25,892 | |
| 18 November | Middlesbrough | H | 2–0 | 18,720 | Slater, Dicks (p) |
| 25 November | Blackburn Rovers | A | 4–5 | 10,215 | Brady, Dicks (p), Slater, Ward |
| 2 December | Stoke City | H | 0–0 | 17,704 | |
| 9 December | Bradford City | A | 1–2 | 9,257 | Ward |
| 16 December | Oldham Athletic | H | 0–2 | 14,960 | |
| 26 December | Ipswich Town | A | 0–1 | 24,365 | |
| 30 December | Leicester City | A | 0–1 | 16,925 | |
| 1 January | Barnsley | H | 4–2 | 18,391 | Allen, Keen (2), Dicks (p) |
| 13 January | Plymouth Argyle | A | 1–1 | 11,671 | Quinn |
| 20 January | Hull City | H | 1–2 | 16,847 | Morley |
| 10 February | Brighton & HA | H | 3–1 | 19,101 | Quinn, Dicks |
| 18 February | Swindon Town | A | 2–2 | 16,105 | Quinn (2) |
| 24 February | Blackburn Rovers | H | 1–1 | 20,054 | Quinn |
| 3 March | Middlesbrough | A | 1–0 | 23,617 | Allen |
| 10 March | Portsmouth | H | 2–1 | 20,961 | Allen, Dicks (p) |
| 13 March | Watford | A | 1–0 | 15,683 | Morley |
| 17 March | Leeds United | A | 2–3 | 32,536 | Morley, Chapman (og) |
| 21 March | Sheffield United | H | 5–0 | 21,629 | Morley, Quinn (3), Allen |
| 24 March | Sunderland | A | 3–4 | 13,896 | Quinn (2), Morley |
| 31 March | Port Vale | H | 2–2 | 20,507 | Morley, Gale |
| 4 April | WBA | A | 3–1 | 11,556 | Quinn, Bishop, Keen |

| 7 April | Oxford United | A | 2–0 | 8,371 | Morley, Quinn |
| 11 April | AFC Bournemouth | H | 4–1 | 20,202 | Miller (og), Bishop, Dicks (p), Allen |
| 14 April | Barnsley | A | 1–1 | 10,344 | Morley |
| 17 April | Ipswich Town | H | 2–0 | 25,178 | Allen, Keen |
| 21 April | Oldham Athletic | A | 0–3 | 12,190 | |
| 28 April | Newcastle United | A | 1–2 | 31,496 | Dicks (p) |
| 2 May | Leicester City | H | 3–1 | 17,939 | Rosenior, Keen, Morley |
| 5 May | Wolverhampton W | H | 4–0 | 22,509 | Keen, Morley, Robson, Brady |

## FA Cup

| 6 January R3 | Torquay United | A | 0–1 | 5,342 | |

## League Cup

| 19 Sept R2 1L | Birmingham City | A | 2–1 | 10,987 | Allen, Slater |
| 4 October R2 2L | Birmingham City | H | 1–1 | 12,187 | Dicks |
| 25 October R3 | Aston Villa | A | 0–0 | 20,989 | |
| 8 November R3R | Aston Villa | H | 1–0 | 23,833 | Dicks |
| 22 November R4 | Wimbledon | H | 1–0 | 24,746 | Allen |
| 17 January QF | Derby County | H | 1–1 | 25,035 | Dicks |
| 24 January QFR | Derby County | A | 0–0 | 22,510 | |
| 31 January QF2R | Derby County | H | 2–1 | 25,166 | Slater, Keen |
| 14 February SF1L | Oldham Athletic | A | 0–6 | 19,263 | |
| 7 March SF 2L | Oldham Athletic | H | 3–0 | 15,431 | Martin, Dicks (p), Kelly |

|    |                 | P  | W  | D  | L  | GF | GA | GD  | Pts |
|----|-----------------|----|----|----|----|----|----|-----|-----|
| 1  | Leeds United    | 46 | 24 | 13 | 9  | 79 | 52 | +27 | 85  |
| 2  | Sheffield Utd   | 46 | 24 | 13 | 9  | 78 | 58 | +20 | 85  |
| 3  | Newcastle Utd   | 46 | 22 | 14 | 10 | 80 | 55 | +25 | 80  |
| 4  | Swindon Town    | 46 | 20 | 14 | 12 | 79 | 59 | +20 | 74  |
| 5  | Blackburn Rov   | 46 | 19 | 17 | 10 | 74 | 59 | +15 | 74  |
| 6  | Sunderland      | 46 | 20 | 14 | 12 | 70 | 64 | +6  | 74  |
| 7  | West Ham Utd    | 46 | 20 | 12 | 14 | 80 | 57 | +23 | 72  |
| 8  | Oldham Ath      | 46 | 19 | 14 | 13 | 70 | 57 | +13 | 71  |
| 9  | Ipswich Town    | 46 | 19 | 12 | 15 | 67 | 66 | +1  | 69  |
| 10 | Wolves          | 46 | 18 | 13 | 15 | 67 | 60 | 7   | 67  |
| 11 | Port Vale       | 46 | 15 | 16 | 15 | 62 | 57 | +5  | 61  |
| 12 | Portsmouth      | 46 | 15 | 16 | 15 | 62 | 65 | –3  | 61  |
| 13 | Leicester City  | 46 | 15 | 14 | 17 | 67 | 79 | –12 | 59  |
| 14 | Hull City       | 46 | 14 | 16 | 16 | 58 | 65 | –7  | 58  |
| 15 | Watford         | 46 | 14 | 15 | 17 | 58 | 60 | –2  | 57  |
| 16 | Plymouth Arg    | 46 | 14 | 13 | 19 | 58 | 63 | –5  | 55  |
| 17 | Oxford Utd      | 46 | 15 | 9  | 22 | 57 | 66 | –9  | 54  |
| 18 | Brighton & HA   | 46 | 15 | 9  | 22 | 56 | 72 | –16 | 54  |
| 19 | Barnsley        | 46 | 13 | 15 | 18 | 49 | 71 | –22 | 54  |
| 20 | WBA             | 46 | 12 | 15 | 19 | 67 | 71 | –4  | 51  |
| 21 | Middlesbrough   | 46 | 13 | 11 | 22 | 52 | 63 | 11  | 50  |
| 22 | Bournemouth     | 46 | 12 | 12 | 22 | 57 | 76 | –19 | 48  |
| 23 | Bradford City   | 46 | 9  | 14 | 23 | 44 | 68 | –24 | 41  |
| 24 | Stoke City      | 46 | 6  | 19 | 21 | 35 | 63 | –28 | 37  |

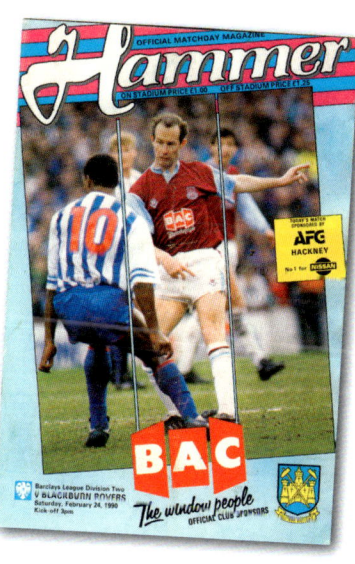

## Morley, Macca and Jimmy the Tree

After the sensational end to the season, West Ham were immediately installed as favourites alongside Oldham for automatic promotion. Billy Bonds felt so confident in his squad that he didn't even invest in additions over the summer. With Frank McAvennie returning from injury, the gaffer felt he had enough in the arsenal to get out of the division – and the early results proved him right.

We were solid, if unspectacular. We started the season with a couple of draws, then a late Julian Dicks penalty vs Watford got us our first win. This was a side that personified Bonds. There was a steel and a quiet confidence about our performances.

The main difference with the previous season was that we also had options up front. In McAvennie, Morley and Quinn we had players who brought something different to the side, and Bonds regularly rotated the trio depending upon the opposition.

McAvennie's return from injury was as welcome as it was unexpected. The nonsense in the papers about a potential legal case against Chris Kamara had disappeared, thankfully. If players were going to get arrested and sentenced for bad tackles, then Julian Dicks would have spent more time behind bars than the Yorkshire Ripper.

Considering that a year earlier his right leg had looked like it was made of Meccano, Frankie was surprisingly sharp in his early outings. The pace and movement of the blue-eyed boy who tore the League up in '86 had long gone, but he was still as lively around the penalty area as he was at the Page 3 Girls' Christmas party.

Morley was the main focal point of the side and clearly the striker Bonds had most confidence in. His intelligent hold-up play was crucial to bringing our wide players like Keen and Slater into the game, and his work rate made him immediately popular with the fans.

The outlier in the three was Quinn, who'd become affectionately known as 'Jimmy the Tree' on the Chicken Run. The reason for his new moniker was simple: he didn't move. Not a single bastard inch. And if by some act of divine intervention he did break into a trot, he was slower than a goldfish in treacle. Honestly, he'd lose a foot race with Big Ben would Jimmy, but his lack of mobility didn't bother the Big Fella, nor Bonds, nor anyone really. We all knew why Jimmy was there: head the ball, chest the ball, trap the ball. Simple. If you played the ball in front of him, he'd have to jump in a cab to have any chance of reaching it.

The variety of options proved their worth in a midweek home fixture against Ipswich. We were 1-0 down on the hour mark when Bonds withdrew an ineffective McAvennie and threw the big Irishman into the mix. It changed the game completely. Bishop equalised, Quinn put us in front with a diving header and Morley sealed the points during an electric last 30 minutes under the lights at Upton Park.

We were unbeaten, winning games from losing positions and ticking along nicely without even getting into second gear. Whisper it quietly: it felt like this might be our year.

**DAVE:** *I can understand why Billy didn't invest over the summer because, looking back, he had a fantastic group of players, especially for the Second Division. It was great to see Frank back and I really liked Jimmy, but for me Trevor was crucial to us that season, and I used to love watching him play. The only disappointment for me was, that year seemed to be the end of his incredibly impressive moustache! Why they never made replicas to buy in the club shop is anyone's guess.*

**EX:** *This was my first season ticket. My first game was a fairly insignificant 1-1 draw with Portsmouth. I was completely mesmerised by the whole experience. Upton Park felt magical under the lights. I can even remember the smell as you walked in: burgers, hot dogs, ciggies, cigars. We sat in the East Stand Upper and I felt like I was immediately accepted into the family. I was hooked from that point. And it helped that we started to put in some brilliant performances, especially after the disappointment of the previous year.*

**DAVE:** *There was so much excitement and expectation. The fact that Billy demanded more from the players – despite being undefeated for the first ten games – speaks volumes about the amount of talent we had available, and his leadership. He had that winning mentality that players need to drive them on.*

### Stevie Potts and the Worst Goal You've Ever Seen

The win against Ipswich was followed up by two away draws against fellow promotion chasers Newcastle and Sheffield Wednesday. The game at Hillsborough also produced our worst 45 minutes of the season as the Owls tore us apart from the first minute. David Hirst put them ahead, and we could have been 4-0 down were it not for the heroics of Ludek Miklosko.

The giant Czech thwarted the home side on numerous occasions as we did our best to make Wednesday look like Platini's Juventus during a wretched first-half display. It took a monumental half-time bollocking from Bonds and a deflected equaliser from Julian Dicks to salvage our unbeaten start.

If we needed further proof that Lady Luck might be wearing Claret and Blue, then it came on the afternoon of Saturday 6th October at Upton Park. Hull City were the visitors, and after a rare mistake from Miklosko gifted the Tigers an equaliser, Steve Potts took centre stage.

Yes, you read correctly. Steve Potts. The unassuming West Ham right-back who'd made himself a first-team regular without anyone really noticing. Now, Stevie was good at a lot of things: tackling, heading, running, marking; but shooting on goal was not one of them. Frankly, if Steve had been sat on that grassy knoll at Dallas, he'd have missed Kennedy and shot Nixon instead.

So when he ran forward in acres of space with the scores level and the Chicken Run urged him to "SHOOOOOOOT!" no one expected him to take it seriously. It was a bit like when Jim Bowen asked the audience for advice on *Bullseye*. They were always going to say "Gamble" because, at the end of the day, they didn't give two shits whether a pair of plumbers from Toxteth won a speedboat or not.

Similarly here, telling our shot-shy full-back to have a pop with that wayward right peg could only have minor consequences. We were going to beat Hull anyway. So if some poor sod in the West Stand got a black eye because Steve Potts momentarily mistook himself for Carlos Alberto, then it was worth it.

Except two things happened that day that the universe could not have predicted. Firstly, Steve Potts managed to get a shot on target. Admittedly it was a shot with such a pathetic lack of force behind it that you wondered whether it would reach the penalty spot, let alone the goal.

Secondly, Hull keeper Iain Hesford – a fairly accomplished performer in the lower leagues – lost the use of all his limbs. These two statistical anomalies, up there with Frank McAvennie staying indoors for a quiet one on a Saturday night, combined on this otherwise unremarkable October afternoon to produce a moment that will be marked forever in the record books.

Steve Potts took a shot, the ball rolled apologetically towards goal, Iain Hesford's motor functions temporarily deserted him, and the ball trickled between his legs before nestling cosily into the net. Cue delirium at Upton Park. In hindsight, it's hard to do justice to moments like this. No amount of pageantry could ever have done it justice. We could have had fireworks, a Red Arrows fly-by, or Elton John writing a charity single in celebration, and it wouldn't have been enough. Steve Potts had scored a f**king goal. What a time to be alive.

In the event, we stuffed Hull 7-1. It was the sort of performance that had been brewing all season. We put the rest of the League on notice: Billy Bonds' West Ham meant business.

**EX:** *I can remember the moment so clearly. I was sat in line with Pottsy as he set up to shoot. The ball must have bobbled at least five times, knocking ants off grass leaves. It's poetic that it was his only goal in a West Ham shirt, because when I look back Pottsy was one of our most underrated players of that era. He was reliable. He read the game so well, especially when he converted to centre-back, and that compensated for his lack of height (5'7" was pretty short back then for a centre-half). I never understood why he wasn't a US international. Bizarrely, one of my dad's friends had an irrational hatred of Steve Potts and would regularly pepper the Upton Park skyline with shouts of "POTTS, YOU'RE SHIT!" which always baffled me. How could anyone dislike Stevie Potts?*

**DAVE:** *Believe it or not, this was the first game I ever went to, and if ever there was a game to set a kid's expectation of what's to come as a West Ham fan, this wasn't it! Despite an incredible performance from the boys, the game will always be remembered for something that was as rare as rocking-horse shit: a goal from Stevie Potts. For some reason, he's decided to hit it from about 300 yards, and I can only assume that Ian Hesford temporarily died as it's coming towards him. Considering he then went on to concede another five, he probably wished he had. The fact that George Parris then scored against him, whilst wearing the number nine shirt, was just taking the piss. I reckon even Ludo could have got himself on the scoresheet if he was a bit more adventurous. That was a special day for me, one I'll never forget.*

### Trevor Morley and the Best Goal You've Never Seen

Ancient Chinese philosophers spoke of the concept of *yin* and *yang*, dual forces that keep the cosmos in balance. It has influenced Asian culture for thousands of years, providing the basis for philosophy, science and some of the most noted literary works in the history of humankind.

Though Lao Tzu may disagree, there was no finer example of *yin* and *yang* than the Barclays League Division Two in November 1990. With the universe still reeling from the shockwaves of Steve Potts entering the scoring charts, drastic action was needed to restore order. Step forward Trevor Morley to do just that.

West Ham travelled to Meadow Lane in early November on a three-game winning streak, one of the few teams in the country still unbeaten in the League that season. A visit to Neil Warnock's Notts County was going to be a real test of our mettle. It wasn't a day for the beautiful game. It was a day when you put your foot in and your elbows out, the Second Division's version of the hokey-cokey.

Bonds had dipped into the transfer market to bolster his squad for days like these. After Julian Dicks suffered a crippling knee injury that could have consequences for his entire career, Chris Hughton had arrived on loan from Spurs. Meanwhile, on the other flank, Bonds paid £600,000 to bring in Tim Breacker from Luton. The tall right-back had been an impressive performer against us for years. Bounding up and down the flank for 90 minutes, he looked like he was sponsored by Duracell, and was a welcome addition to the ranks.

Both men started against County as Bonds opted for a change of formation in a game where the ball was likely to be little more than an innocent bystander. Anticipating a midfield dogfight, he played Trevor Morley as a lone striker. And that's all we needed.

After an hour of some of the poorest association football since records began, Morley conjured up an unlikely Goal of the Season contender. Chasing the ball down the flank, and with two County defenders in close attendance, he flicked the ball up off the mud, twisted and planted a 25-yard volley into the opposite top corner. It was an astonishing moment of skill and technique in game that had otherwise been devoid of both. In later years, Thierry Henry would score a similar one for Arsenal vs Manchester United, a goal that has been eulogised by the Premier League ever since. You can keep your Va-va-voom, I'll have Morley at Meadow Lane any day of the week.

The striker's confidence, much like the team's, was sky-high. He was scoring world-class goals, and we won every game in November. In fact, we didn't lose a League game until a shock 1-0 defeat at Barnsley arrested a run of eight wins in nine. That proved to be a small blip as Morley and Slater inspired a 2-0 win over our title rivals Oldham on Boxing Day at Upton Park. As 1990 ended, our League form was sensational, and attention switched to the FA Cup.

**DAVE:** *This goal doesn't get the credit it deserves. No one talks about it! It's like that worldy from Stan Lazaridis at St James' Park later in the decade. A forgotten treasure. Why are goals like that just erased from the mainstream media? If Trevor had scored that goal as an Italian playing for Chelsea we wouldn't hear the f\*\*king* end of it. Maybe if he kept that moustache he would have had half a chance? Not only was it a cracking goal, but it was an important one. Notts County finished fourth that season, so to get the win away from home and keep a clean sheet was a massive result for us.

**EX:** That goal summed up the phenomenon that is Trevor Morley. He was so good. A clever, clever centre-forward with underrated technical ability. The only thing he didn't have, by his own admission, was pace. But he made up for that with his work rate, which was absolutely phenomenal. The quality and quantity of goals he scored, particularly in those early days, was remarkable. I was really fond of him. Not Stuart Slater fond, but pretty close. What a prize it was to get Bishop and Morley in that single deal. They both played such a significant role in our history.

## Slater for England

An FA Cup third-round draw against Aldershot should have been the perfect opportunity to exorcise the ghosts of Torquay. It had been a long 12 months since that pathetic performance at Plainmoor, and the madness of the Macari era felt like ancient history as Billy Bonds marched us towards promotion.

However, no matter who's in charge, there's one thing that no manager can ever quite compensate for at Upton Park: the propensity for West Ham to absolutely West Ham up even the most glorious of opportunities. Cash-strapped Aldershot had foregone home advantage as they looked to extract every penny from a game they'd given up before the first whistle. Yet somehow, with all the odds in our favour, we managed to conjure up our worst performance of the season in a drab 0-0 draw.

Thankfully, order was restored in the replay as we hammered them 6-1, before embarking on a curious Cup run that lurched from the sublime to the ridiculous. A scrappy 1-1 draw at Luton in the next round was followed by us dishing out a 5-0 thrashing in the replay. To add to the chaos, George Parris scored in both ties. What a time to be alive.

We then nicked a gloriously undeserved 1-0 at Crewe thanks to Jimmy the Tree, to set up a plum tie with Everton in the quarter-final. The game was screened on little-known station BSkyB, who were dipping their toes into the water for live football. It meant a bizarre Monday-night kick-off. It might be a fixture of the football calendar these days, but in 1990 Monday evenings were the home of *Wogan*, *Coronation Street* and *The Krypton Factor*. It was not the place for association football.

The unfamiliar kick-off was perhaps the perfect setting for an equally unfamiliar sight: a goal by big Colin Foster. And an absolute belter at that. When a cross from the right-hand side floated towards Fozzie's right foot, the Everton defence breathed a sigh of relief. The big centre-half was many things on a football pitch, but a technician he was not. He'd used that 6'4" frame to great effect all season: heading, blocking, heading, then blocking some more. There were games when you wondered if his feet had been made redundant. So it was quite the surprise when he decided that an FA Cup quarter-final against Everton, on a niche satellite station, was the opportune moment to reveal his inner Roberto Baggio.

Twisting in mid-air, he uncorked a laser-guided volley into the corner past Neville Southall to put us in front. Typical of Foster's luck, he scored the goal of his career and it was almost immediately forgotten.

The reason for that was the performance of Stuart Slater. The youngster had been electric since switching to the wing under Bonds, and this night was no exception. Everton's Neil McDonald looked like he was having an existential crisis on the pitch: was he a reliable top-flight right-back, or was he in fact a glorified training cone? Slater ran round him at will. At one stage it seemed like Everton had eleven men marking him, and they still couldn't stop him.

When Slater dribbled past three men to arrow a shot into the bottom corner, *Match of the Day*'s John Motson said it was the finest individual performance he'd seen all season. It felt like just praise. As the final whistle blew on a 2-1 win, the cries from the terraces were "Slater for England." This was his finest hour in a West Ham shirt, and the 28,162 in attendance stood to applaud him.

We'd outplayed a First Division side, we had the most exciting young player in the country, and we were on our way to an FA Cup semi-final.

Even West Ham couldn't West Ham this up, surely?

**EX:** *This was honestly one of the most magical games I can ever remember. And it felt like vindication for all those hours, days and weeks I'd spent telling my mates how good Stuart Slater was. They all supported Liverpool or Arsenal, and they would shout me down by claiming Slater wasn't in the same class as John Barnes or David Rocastle. That game was the confirmation that I was right. The headlines the next day in the national newspapers were all about Stuart Slater. He had arrived – and his life changed overnight. He went from being an unknown gem, hidden in the second tier, to a household name.*

**DAVE:** *Any West Ham fan or player will tell you that there was nothing like a night game at Upton Park: the lights, the atmosphere, the sights and the smells. It was special, and the quarter-final against Everton was one of the most iconic* nights. When you get to that stage of the competition, you can start dreaming. But as a Second Division side drawn against a top-flight Everton, I think all you have is hope. However, we also had Stuart Slater – and to this day his individual performance that night was one of the best I have ever seen. What a player. What a win.

## Morley's Poorly

"Hello, is that Mr Bonds?"

"Yes, who's calling?"

"It's the Met Police here, Mr Bonds. Unfortunately, there's been an incident involving one of your players."

"Here we go again. Look, Officer, Frankie's always been a ladies' man. They just throw themselves at the poor lad's feet. Whoever her husband is, just tell him we'll sling him a couple of tickets and pay for a slap-up meal for him and his beloved. No harm done."

"No, it's not Frank McAvennie, Mr Bonds."

"Ah right, listen Officer. Julian's always had a temper on him. I'm sure once the other fella's wounds heal up and the stitches are out, he'll realise that it's six of one and half a dozen of the other. Besides, it's a nice story to tell your mates about how you've been booted in the face by the best left-back in England."

"No, it's not Julian Dicks, Mr Bonds."

"Really? Then who is it?"

"It's Trevor Morley, Mr Bonds."

"Trevor Morley? Our top scorer Trevor Morley, who's in the form of his life and spearheading our march to Second Division and FA Cup glory? That Trevor Morley?"

"Yes. That Trevor Morley, Mr Bonds."

"What's he done?"

"He's been stabbed, Mr Bonds. He's in A&E as we speak."

"Ah, bollocks."

You can go on all the training courses and do all the coaching badges you like. There are some things that you can never prepare for as a football manager. Somewhere high up on that list is your star striker being stabbed by his wife in a domestic, and now recovering from his injuries in the emergency room. Yet that's what faced Billy Bonds on a spring morning in 1991.

Morley had become the first name on the team sheet, with McAvennie and Quinn rotating as his strike partner. His absence had an immediate effect on the team as we managed just two points from our next four League games, including a thumping at home from Sheffield Wednesday who were breathing down our necks on the promotion trail. Though we managed to get the win against Everton without Morley, thanks primarily to the superpowers of Stuart Slater, it was clear we'd need some reinforcements if we were going to get through Easter.

**EX:** *I was so gutted when I heard the news about this. As a kid, these things are so shocking. I asked my dad question after question. I just couldn't believe it. I think I was genuinely disturbed. You might read on Teletext that your star striker had a tight hamstring, or a sore knee, but a stabbing? Then came all the nonsense rumours about him and Ian Bishop. They were everywhere. And from that moment on, I couldn't mention either of them at school without someone saying Bishop and Morley were lovers. It was distressing for me, but it must have been a thousand times worse for the players having unfounded rumours affecting their home lives.*

**DAVE:** *The funniest story to come from this absolute nightmare is that when Trevor was released from hospital, he went to stay with Bish and his wife in Chigwell to keep his head down for a while (in hindsight, probably not the best decision he's ever made). One morning, Ian's wife went to make a cup of tea for everyone. Whilst she had the kettle on, Trevor went up and sat next to Bish on the bed to read the morning papers, which were no doubt plastered with the ridiculous rumours of their alleged affair. He'd been there a matter of minutes when, out of nowhere, the f\*\*king window cleaner appeared and saw the pair of them in bed with each other! You couldn't make it up!*

### Dowie to the Rescue: Bonds Looks for Bouncebackability

The '90s were a glorious time for transfer rumours. With no internet and no rolling news coverage, newspapers and ClubCall were your best sources of information. Which was like relying on Duncan Goodhew for tips on haircare.

There's nothing wrong with what they were doing. After all, they were selling football's most popular currency: hope. It's what keeps fans going through the tough times. The hope that sometime things will get better, that there's light at the end of the tunnel.

When West Ham fans read: NEW SIGNING ON HIS WAY! on the Teletext pages advertising ClubCall, thousands willingly dialled 0898 to bolster their reserves of hope, which were dwindling after our poor run since Morley's injury extended to one win in seven games. We needed a hero, and the exorbitant cost of 49p per minute was a price worth paying to discover his identity. We found out that Bonds was after a target man (Mick Harford?) with a proven goalscoring pedigree (Kerry Dixon, maybe?) and all would be revealed soon.

Heroes comes in all shapes and sizes. Few more distinctive than Iain Dowie. When the Northern Ireland striker was announced as West Ham's new star striker, there was a collective shrug of the shoulders from the fanbase. You didn't need to be a rocket scientist (which Dowie was, actually, courtesy of his university studies) to know that a goal ratio of one in four games in League football was hardly prolific. Plus, he was hardly the poster-boy star striker that we'd been hoping for.

No kid wanted a picture of Iain Dowie on their bedroom wall. Certainly not if they wanted to sleep at night. Bless him, he was hardly an advertiser's dream. Unless he was selling balaclavas.

Still, he was an extra body, albeit an ungainly one, and that's what we needed. Dowie made his debut in an April Fool's Day fixture against struggling Barnsley and, for the best part of an hour, it looked like we'd been the butt of some cruel joke. We were 2-0 down after a rotten first-half display, and Dowie had an absolute stinker. His first touch was like a fridge freezer. Thankfully, he warmed up in the second half, presumably after a roasting from his new gaffer, and a thumping header brought the scores level before Fozzie headed in a late winner. We got another welcome three points at Port Vale – where Ian Bishop hit a 25-yard screamer on a pitch like a rice pudding – and, with our League form back on track, it was time for the FA Cup semi-final.

Though we were up against a solid cup team in Brian Clough's Forest, we still fancied ourselves for a result at Villa Park. Our ticket allocation had sold out in double-quick time. And though we were underdogs, perhaps that raucous following could be the twelfth man we needed to cause an upset.

Unfortunately, what we didn't know was that Forest had a twelfth man of their own. And the bastard was wearing black.

**DAVE:** *I liked Iain Dowie, and think he did a decent job when Trevor Morley was injured. Whilst he wasn't a prolific goalscorer, he was a workhorse and the type of player that could defend from the front and create opportunities for other players around him. I think the fans appreciated his work ethic, which was shown during his second spell with us when he came second to Dicksy for Hammer of the Year.*

*But, f\*\*k me, he wasn't the prettiest, bless him. Don't think I've ever seen a face like his to this day. Poor bloke looked like he'd been chasing parked cars.*

**EX:** *To be fair to Ian Dowie, I was a little surprised that we sold him so quickly. He came in, he did a good job and he worked his socks off. There were question marks about his quality – his touch and vision weren't of the same calibre as Morley – but he really did put a shift in. I plastered every inch of my bedroom with West Ham posters. And sometimes I'd put some up in my sister's room just to annoy her. I thought briefly about replacing her picture of River Phoenix with one of Iain Dowie, but I think she would have absolutely battered me.*

### Hackett the Villain of Villa Park

No one will ever dispute that refereeing is a difficult occupation. From the moment the first whistle blows, you're the most unpopular human being in the stadium. Fans are convinced you're blind, coaching staff are convinced you're biased, and you're frequently referred to as a man who enjoys self-pleasuring himself whilst in uniform.

Nonetheless, there are certain things you can do to mitigate even the unfairest of circumstances. Even in an era where referees were moonlighting from their day jobs as headteachers, traffic wardens or tax assessors, following these rules might at least offer you some respite from the daily humiliation:

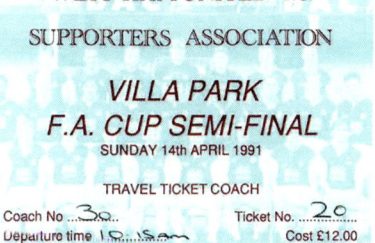

i) Stay in shape;
ii) Keep calm under pressure;
iii) Make sure you know the f\*\*king rules.

Sadly, on the afternoon of April 14th, 1991 Keith Hackett ignored all of the above and made himself the focal point of what should have been a fantastic football occasion.

The semi-final, live on the BBC, was loud and boisterous from the off. Earlier in the day, Paul Gascoigne's heroics had helped Spurs beat Arsenal. The prospect of a day at Wembley against our fiercest rivals added a little extra spice to the occasion, and the West Ham fans were in fine voice.

Our sizeable travelling contingent was also buoyed by the return of Trevor Morley to the starting line-up. Trevor had somehow pushed his recuperation schedule to ensure he was fit for the Villa Park showpiece. His body had recovered, even if his marriage hadn't. There are some things counselling can help with – "I just don't feel we talk about our feelings enough and never connect on a truly emotional level" – and then some that just can't – "She stabbed me with a f\*\*king kitchen knife."

With our best striker back, we started brightly. There were 40,000 packed into the ground and it felt like 39,999 of them were wearing Claret and Blue. Man for man, we were matching Forest comfortably, until Hackett intervened.

After a scramble on the halfway line, the ball broke and Gary Crosby engaged in a tussle with Tony Gale to get there first. The two tangled and fell to the ground. It was a fairly innocuous foul and, when the portly Hackett started to scribble in his notebook, Gale looked aggrieved that he was going to get the yellow card. When the referee produced red, he was absolutely crestfallen.

It was an appalling decision. Anyone with any hint of geography could see that this wasn't a clear goalscoring opportunity. Crosby was 30 yards out and heading diagonally away from goal when the contact took place. If he carried on that trajectory he was going to end up at New Street Station rather than Ludo Miklosko's net. Then there was the small matter of the covering defenders, with both Bishop and Parris closing in.

The rest of the game should, in theory, have been a walkover for Forest. But roared on by the crowd, we refused to lie down. With the first half ticking down, George Parris walloped a shot against the post, and even when Crosby (of course) put Forest ahead, Stuart Slater hit the woodwork at the other end. Despite our falling behind, the celebrations of the red half of the ground were drowned out by the chants of "Billy Bonds' Claret and Blue Army," which had been relentless since the restart.

To this day, that atmosphere remains unforgettable. I watched the game on TV and could barely hear John Motson and Bobby Charlton in the commentary box. You don't get organic fan reactions like this any more. These days, nothing is natural. Anger is commercialised. Fans in grounds film themselves celebrating, grown men film themselves throwing hissy fits to get more clicks on their fan channels.

With ten minutes of that game left, we were 4-0 down, a man down and our Wembley dream had been ruined by the referee. No one left the ground to beat the traffic. No one booed the referee. Instead, 20,000 supporters sang longer and louder than they ever had before.

It made you proud to be a fan. Proud to be part of a club so steeped in history. We lost the game, but we showed the viewers at home: *We are Billy Bonds' Claret and Blue Army. And we will not lie down.*

*Now let's go and win the f\*\*king League.*

**EX:** This was the first away game I ever went to. My dad hired a minibus with his mates and we drove to a local hotel, where we hired a function room to watch the Spurs-Arsenal semi-final before heading to the ground. I remember the carnival atmosphere. A random bloke gave me a West Ham flag but stewards took the stick out, so I ended up waving it like a handkerchief during the game.

Despite Hackett's disgraceful decision, we drowned out the Forest fans. I don't think any club will ever experience an atmosphere like that again. We were 4-0 down and we kept getting louder and louder. These days, people would be preoccupied having meltdowns on social media. That's a problem in modern football. People demand success instantly. No one tolerates hardship any more.

From that point on, I knew there was no turning back. I was so proud to be a West Ham fan.

**DAVE:** That decision from Hackett wasn't just an error of judgement, it was an unforgivable mistake! As much as I hate the technology, if VAR was around at the time it could have changed history for us. Forest had a good side, but so did we. We also had a winning mentality and a twelfth man in the stands. Many years later at a football conference, Martin Allen spotted Hackett and was giving him dirty looks for the duration of the event. At the end of the seminar, Hackett approached 'Mad Dog' and said, "From the bottom of my heart, I'm genuinely sorry. I made a mistake." Mad Dog's reply was less courteous: "Thanks Keith. But you can shove that apology up your arse, you f**king useless c***!"

That day though will always belong to the West Ham fans. They gave the rest of English football one example as to why we're the best in the world.

## Winning the League the West Ham Way – By Not Actually Winning It

There are moments as a football fan that make you burst with pride and some that make you cringe with embarrassment. For a West Ham fan, these moments can often be days – or hours – apart.

My most embarrassing moment came during a home game with Bristol City towards the end of this season. We'd won 1-0 thanks to a Tony Gale free-kick and, busting for the toilet ahead of a drive home, I joined the queue that snaked out of the men's bogs.

Unfortunately, as a wafer-thin eleven-year-old who wouldn't say boo to a goose, I lacked the physical authority to manoeuvre myself into a prime position by the medieval trough that passed for a urinal at Upton Park. As I unleashed all 330ml of the can of Tizer I'd consumed during the second half, I realised that my lack of gravitas with the match-going geezers around me had cost me dear. I'd undershot the distance by about six inches and, as such, was now emptying the majority of my bladder on to my own shoelaces. Thankfully, no one around me noticed. Puddles of piss were part of the matchday experience in the West Stand.

Nonetheless, I would rather that humiliation than what befell the pitch invaders on the hallowed turf on the final fixture of the Second Division season.

Beforehand, the equation was a simple one: win the game, win the title. We'd secured promotion thanks to a home win over Swindon three weeks prior, when Iain Dowie had rifled in a 20-yard screamer to seal the points. Even the most hopeful of season-ticket holders couldn't have expected to see both Steve Potts and Iain Dowie score from outside the box in the same season. In terms of probabilities, that's up there with walking into your front room and finding Lord Lucan playing Connect 4 with Shergar.

Since that game, our form had been patchy at best. Some might say it was the cumulative effort of a long, hard season on the promotion trail. Others would suggest it was the result of the players spending three weeks in the boozer. Whatever the reason, our lead over Oldham had shrunk to just three points.

Nonetheless, a win against Neil Warnock's Notts County would make us champions. Warnock had hardly endeared himself to Hammers fans during his spell as a TV pundit at Villa Park by claiming we were an average team reliant on the excellence of Miklosko for our League position. Sticking it to the County boss – and stopping his team's Play-off ambitions whilst securing the silverware for ourselves – would be a heartwarming end to a delightful first season under Bonds' stewardship.

As had been the case during the run-in, we looked a little sluggish from the first whistle. County eased into the lead through Mark Draper and, when he scored again in the second half, it looked like curtains for our title chances. Typical West Ham. Stealing defeat from the jaws of victory. Thankfully, there was good news filtering through on the transistor radios from Hillsborough, where Sheffield Wednesday were beating Oldham. When George Parris pulled a goal back it sparked a siege on the Notts County goal, and Ian Bishop hit the bar with a late header that would have been enough to win the trophy.

As the final whistle blew, we were beaten but not unbowed. The Oldham game was in injury-time and our rivals were still behind. They needed two unlikely goals to steal the title from our grasp. So the fans invaded the pitch and began the celebrations in style. The sun was shining, the fans were on the pitch and West Ham United were going back to the Promised Land as Second Division champions.

We hadn't West Hammed the whole thing up, after all.

Until we did.

News filtered through from Yorkshire that Oldham had equalised. That still wasn't enough to deny us top spot, but there were a few nervous glances around the masses of topless males in bootcut denim who had been marching triumphantly across the centre circle moments earlier.

Those nerves turned to full-on dread when the unthinkable happened. Unthinkable, that is, if you were a fan of a normal club. For West Ham United, this should have been completely expected. Oldham had scored in the last minute of injury time to secure three points and the Second Division title.

The smiles of the fans on the pitch disappeared instantly. They couldn't have looked more awkward if they'd accidentally wandered in on their dad's vasectomy. The stadium fell silent, and everyone meandered off the turf to witness the most sheepish lap of honour since records began. What should have been a glorious season finale had become the dampest of squibs.

Typical West Ham.

**EX:** *We were sat in the East Stand Upper, and I was annoyed that my dad wouldn't let me go on to the pitch with everyone else. It was an amazing scene. People were going mental: signing, cheering, swinging their shirts over their heads. And then it came through on the Tannoy: that dreaded* ding-dong *of the old Upton Park public-address system: "Bad news, everybody. Oldham have scored in the last minute and we have finished second." The atmosphere dropped like a stone, and you could hear this huge collective sigh of disappointment. It was classic West Ham. There has to be a twist or turn. Things can never go smoothly. This was another painful part of my education.*

**DAVE:** *What a rollercoaster of emotions! I think everyone believed that we would go up as champions on the last day, and it was a shame that we didn't. But, ultimately, we got promoted and that was the most important thing. It was an incredible season where we only lost seven games out of 46, and got to an FA Cup semi-final. You can't ask for much more than what they gave, and I was very proud of the boys that year. We were back in the top division, where we belong.*

## Football League First Division - 1990/91

| Date | Opponent | H/A | Score | Att. | Scorers |
|---|---|---|---|---|---|
| 25 August | Middlesbrough | A | 0–0 | 20,680 | |
| 29 August | Portsmouth | H | 1–1 | 20,835 | McAvennie |
| 1 September | Watford | H | 1–0 | 19,872 | Dicks (p) |
| 8 September | Leicester City | A | 2–1 | 14,605 | James (og), Morley |
| 15 September | Wolverhampton W | H | 1–1 | 23,241 | Martin |
| 19 September | Ipswich Town | H | 3–1 | 18,764 | Bishop, Quinn, Morley |
| 22 September | Newcastle United | A | 1–1 | 25,462 | Morley |
| 29 September | Sheffield Wed | A | 1–1 | 28,786 | Dicks |
| 3 October | Oxford United | H | 2–0 | 18,125 | Foster, Morley |
| 6 October | Hull City | H | 7–1 | 19,472 | Quinn (2), Potts, Dicks (2, 1 p), Parris, Morley |
| 13 October | Bristol City | A | 1–1 | 16,838 | McAvennie |
| 20 October | Swindon Town | A | 1–0 | 13,658 | McAvennie |
| 24 October | Blackburn Rovers | H | 1–0 | 20,003 | Bishop |
| 27 October | Charlton Athletic | H | 2–1 | 24,019 | Allen (2) |
| 3 November | Notts County | A | 1–0 | 10,871 | Morley |
| 10 November | Millwall | A | 1–1 | 20,591 | McAvennie |
| 17 November | Brighton & HA | H | 2–1 | 24,019 | Slater, Foster |
| 24 November | Plymouth Argyle | A | 1–0 | 11,490 | McAvennie |
| 1 December | WBA | H | 3–1 | 24,753 | Parris, Morley, McAvennie |
| 8 December | Portsmouth | A | 1–0 | 12,045 | Morley |
| 15 December | Middlesbrough | H | 0–0 | 23,705 | |
| 22 December | Barnsley | A | 0–1 | 10,348 | |
| 26 December | Oldham Athletic | H | 2–0 | 24,950 | Morley, Slater |
| 28 December | Port Vale | H | 0–0 | 23,603 | |
| 1 January | Bristol Rovers | A | 1–0 | 7,932 | Quinn |
| 12 January | Watford | A | 1–0 | 17,172 | Morley |
| 19 January | Leicester City | H | 1–0 | 21,652 | Parris |
| 2 February | Wolverhampton W | A | 1–2 | 19,454 | McAvennie |
| 24 February | Millwall | H | 3–1 | 20,503 | McAvennie (2), Morley |
| 2 March | WBA | A | 0–0 | 16,089 | |
| 5 March | Plymouth Argyle | H | 2–2 | 18,933 | Marker (og), Breacker |
| 13 March | Oxford United | A | 1–2 | 8,225 | Quinn |
| 16 March | Sheffield Wed | H | 1–3 | 26,182 | Quinn |
| 20 March | Bristol City | H | 1–0 | 22,951 | Gale |
| 23 March | Hull City | A | 0–0 | 9,558 | |
| 29 March | Oldham Athletic | A | 1–1 | 16,932 | Bishop (p) |
| 1 April | Barnsley | H | 3–2 | 24,607 | McAvennie, Dowie, Foster |
| 6 April | Port Vale | A | 1–0 | 9,658 | Bishop |

| 10 April | Brighton & HA | A | 0–1 | 11,904 | |
| 17 April | Ipswich Town | A | 1–0 | 20,290 | Morley |
| 20 April | Swindon Town | H | 2–0 | 25,944 | Parris, Dowie |
| 24 April | Newcastle United | H | 1–1 | 24,195 | Dowie |
| 27 April | Blackburn Rovers | A | 1–3 | 10,808 | Dowie |
| 4 May | Charlton Athletic | A | 1–1 | 16,137 | Allen |
| 8 May | Bristol Rovers | H | 1–0 | 23,054 | Slater |
| 11 May | Notts County | H | 1–2 | 26,551 | Parris |

**FA Cup**

| 5 January R3 | Aldershot | A | 0–0 | 22,929 | |
| 16 January R3R | Aldershot | H | 6–1 | 21,484 | Morley (2), Slater, Parris, Bishop, Quinn |
| 26 January R4 | Luton Town | A | 1–1 | 12,087 | Parris |
| 30 January R4R | Luton Town | H | 5–0 | 25,659 | Parris, Bishop, McAvennie, Morley (2) |
| 15 February R5 | Crewe Alexandra | H | 1–0 | 25,298 | Quinn |
| 11 March R6 | Everton | H | 2–1 | 28,161 | Foster, Slater |
| 14 April SF | Nottingham Forest | N | 0–4 | 40,041 | |

**League Cup**

| 26 Sept R2 1L | Stoke City | H | 3–0 | 15,870 | Dicks (p), Keen, Quinn |
| 10 October R2 2L | Stoke City | A | 2–1 | 8,411 | Allen (2) |
| 31 October R3 | Oxford United | A | 1–2 | 7,528 | Morley |

| | P | W | D | L | GF | GA | GD | Pts |
|---|---|---|---|---|---|---|---|---|
| 1 Oldham Ath | 46 | 25 | 13 | 8 | 83 | 53 | +30 | 88 |
| 2 West Ham Utd | 46 | 24 | 15 | 7 | 60 | 34 | +26 | 87 |
| 3 Sheffield Wed | 46 | 22 | 16 | 8 | 80 | 51 | +29 | 82 |
| 4 Notts County | 46 | 23 | 11 | 12 | 76 | 55 | +21 | 80 |
| 5 Millwall | 46 | 20 | 13 | 13 | 70 | 51 | +19 | 73 |
| 6 Brighton & HA | 46 | 21 | 7 | 18 | 63 | 69 | –6 | 70 |
| 7 Middlesbrough | 46 | 20 | 9 | 17 | 66 | 47 | +19 | 69 |
| 8 Barnsley | 46 | 19 | 12 | 15 | 63 | 48 | +15 | 69 |
| 9 Bristol City | 46 | 20 | 7 | 19 | 68 | 71 | –3 | 67 |
| 10 Oxford Utd | 46 | 14 | 19 | 13 | 69 | 66 | +3 | 61 |
| 11 Newcastle Utd | 46 | 14 | 17 | 15 | 49 | 56 | –7 | 59 |
| 12 Wolves | 46 | 13 | 19 | 14 | 63 | 63 | 0 | 58 |
| 13 Bristol Rovers | 46 | 15 | 13 | 18 | 56 | 59 | –3 | 58 |
| 14 Ipswich Town | 46 | 13 | 18 | 15 | 60 | 68 | –8 | 57 |
| 15 Port Vale | 46 | 15 | 12 | 19 | 56 | 64 | –8 | 57 |
| 16 Charlton Ath | 46 | 13 | 17 | 16 | 57 | 61 | –4 | 56 |
| 17 Portsmouth | 46 | 14 | 11 | 21 | 58 | 70 | –12 | 53 |
| 18 Plymouth Arg | 46 | 12 | 17 | 17 | 54 | 68 | –14 | 53 |
| 19 Blackburn Rov | 46 | 14 | 10 | 22 | 51 | 66 | –15 | 52 |
| 20 Watford | 46 | 12 | 15 | 19 | 45 | 59 | –14 | 51 |
| 21 Swindon Town | 46 | 12 | 14 | 20 | 65 | 73 | –8 | 50 |
| 22 Leicester City | 46 | 14 | 8 | 24 | 60 | 83 | –23 | 50 |
| 23 WBA | 46 | 10 | 18 | 18 | 52 | 61 | –9 | 48 |
| 24 Hull City | 46 | 10 | 15 | 21 | 57 | 85 | –28 | 45 |

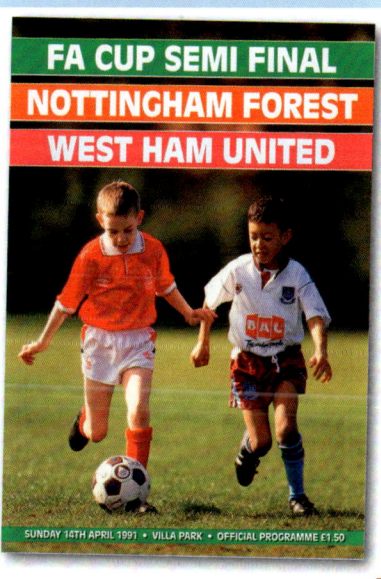

FA CUP SEMI FINAL
NOTTINGHAM FOREST
WEST HAM UNITED

SUNDAY 14TH APRIL 1991 • VILLA PARK • OFFICIAL PROGRAMME £1.50

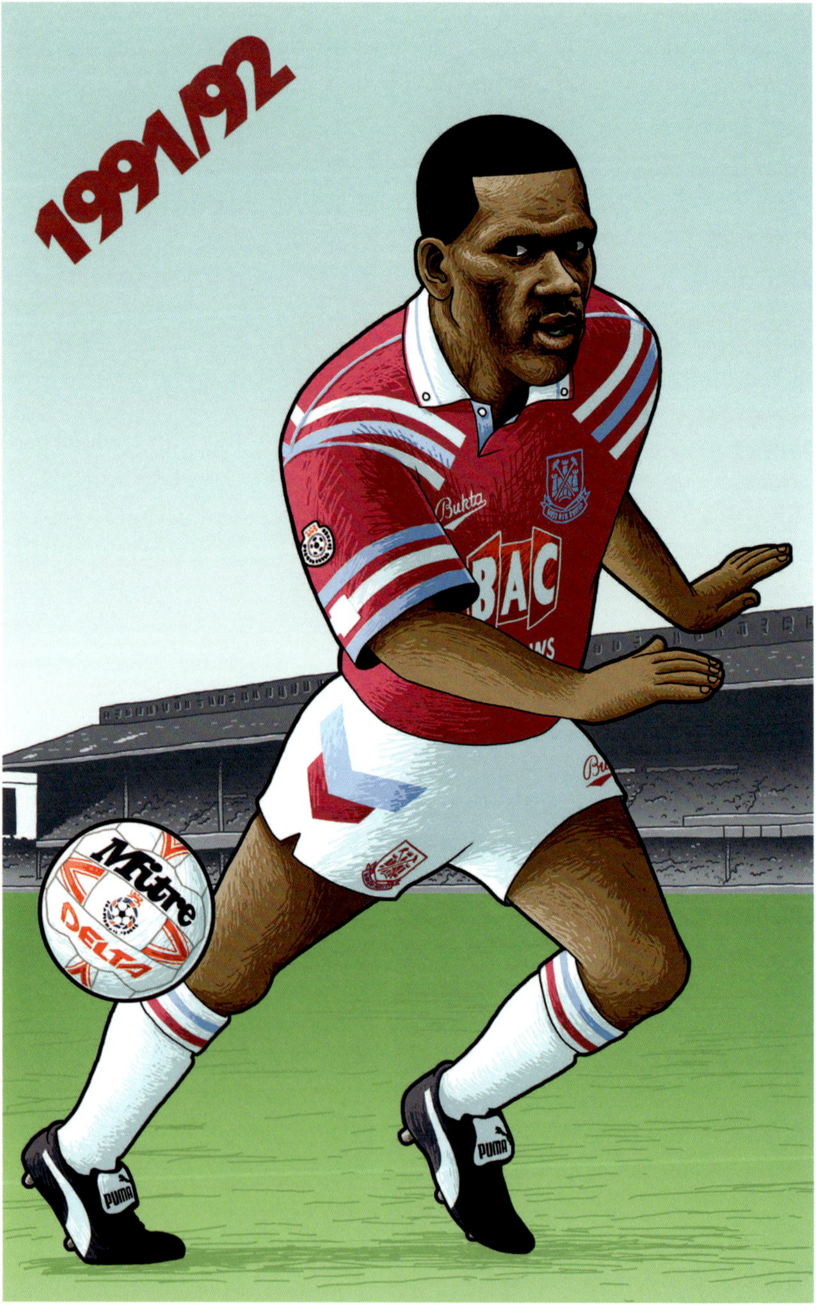
1991/92
Bukta
BAC
Mitre
DELTA
PUMA
PUMA

## Bargain Basement

There's nothing like a summer break to rekindle your hopes for the football season. With no international tournaments to speak of – Graham Taylor had taken his new-look (and mostly shite) England team on a curious tour to the Southern Hemisphere where they played like they were still on Greenwich Mean Time – we had the whole of the summer months to look forward to First Division football returning to Upton Park. Yes, the previous campaign had a somewhat cringeworthy conclusion. But facts were facts: West Ham United were back in the big time. Billy Bonds had taken us to the Promised Land in his first full season in charge. Now the big question was: could he keep us there?

The bookies didn't think so. We were immediately installed amongst the favourites for the drop. Our commendable FA Cup showings had done little to convince the pundits that we had a squad capable enough of competing at the top level. And, in fairness, many of us shared the same concerns. Whilst Oldham had been blowing teams away, helped no end by their plastic pitch, we had relied heavily on our watertight defence to get promotion. Up against international strikers, we'd surely be breached more often, and clearly needed strengthening at both ends of the pitch.

Unfortunately, our notoriously penny-pinching board disagreed. They approached our return to top-flight football with the same sort of ambition as a chicken strolling into a slaughterhouse. Our transfer budget was meagre compared to our rivals', and Bonds had to do some wheeling and dealing to bring in new faces.

Out the door went Ray Stewart after a distinguished service in east London. 'Tonka' had a place secure in West Ham folklore. His penalty-taking technique, which involved substituting his right foot for a grenade launcher just before striking the ball, was amongst the very best in British football. Unfortunately, the Scot's injury record over the past few seasons made it look like he was auditioning for a role in *Casualty*, and it made sense for him to return to his homeland for the twilight years of his career.

Sadly, Bonds also decided that Jimmy The Tree would never reach the dizzy heights of the Barclays First Division. It seemed a strange decision. Quinn's knack of crucial goals would surely come in handy, even if just as an impact substitute. Bonds, a notorious fitness fanatic, disagreed. Playing at the pinnacle of your profession required a certain level of athleticism. And having a man with the acceleration of Jabba the Hutt in the squad was not an option.

There were some new arrivals, however. Quinn's place up front was taken by Mike Small, a £250,000 signing from Brighton where he'd notched 20+ goals for the Seagulls last season. The big striker had scored against us at Upton Park and had the nuisance factor you'd associate with a man of his frame, even if at times he had the same first touch as a yo-yo.

Joining him in the ranks was the more familiar face of Mitchell Thomas, from Spurs, where he had carved out a respectable reputation as a utility man. Good in the air, a decent reader of the game and versatile enough to play across the back four or even in midfield, he seemed a solid enough acquisition. However, neither of the new faces felt like they were quite enough to address the deficiencies in the squad. Still, Bonds had worked wonders with a small group of players so far, and though we knew it was going to be a hard season, maybe his management and a bit of luck would be enough to steer us clear of the drop zone.

We had entered the Makita International Tournament, which was screened on ITV as part of the pre-season preparation. Traditionally staged at Wembley, it involved a select group of teams from across the continent honing their skills and fitness levels in front of the cameras. With English clubs still serving a ban from European competition, it was also a chance to see exotic foreign talents and how they fared against a bit of four-four-f**king-two.

This year's festivities would take place at Highbury, and alongside the hosts we were pitted against newly crowned Serie A champions Sampdoria and fellow title winners Panathinaikos. On paper, it seemed a slightly intimidating line-up, and possibly not the ideal way to boost confidence heading into the new season.

Our worst fears proved correct. In the baking sun at Highbury, we got our first glimpse of the dark days ahead.

**DAVE:** *It wasn't only the bookies that were writing us off, it was the national press too, and maybe that started to affect the players psychologically. So, in pre-season, what did we do to rebuild that confidence and self-belief? We play Sampdoria, winners of Serie A and undoubtedly one of the best teams in the world at the time – with the likes of Roberto Mancini and Gianluca Vialli in their starting line-up. Whose f**king idea was this? Surely they realised we were going to get absolutely obliterated.*

**EX:** *Mitchell Thomas was a bit of a strange signing. And one that it was hard to get excited about. When you look at his career, he was reasonably consistent everywhere else. But joining West Ham from Spurs brings extra pressure. And I think you need to be a really good player to get over that rivalry.*

*Still, I was looking forward to the season, especially as the Makita Tournament was going to be a rare televised game. I remember it was a beautiful, sunny day.*

*We were playing in that amazing Argentina strip, which is still one of my all-time favourites. Sampdoria were in that classic ERG strip. No matter that we hadn't made any major signings. West Ham were back in business, and I was excited about it… at least until the whistle blew.*

## Lamped by Samp

We're always told that results in pre-season don't mean anything. It's all about fitness levels, sharpness and rebuilding team cohesion after the summer break. Perhaps that's what Billy Bonds consoled himself with as the referee blew his whistle as the first fixture of the two-day Makita International Tournament drew to a close. We'd been thumped 6-1 by a Sampdoria side that was so utterly imperious, they could have been playing in flip-flops.

The likes of Cerezo, Lombardo and Mancini had ripped us to pieces. And reserve striker Renato Buso had scored four goals (the same total he managed in the entirety of the previous season) on an afternoon when you could have parked a bus in the gaps between our defenders.

There were some small mercies. The game was only 80 minutes long due to a quirk of the tournament that meant teams had to play two fixtures in two days. If we'd played regulation time, then TV commentator Brian Moore might have had to get his calculator out to keep score.

It was absolutely dire stuff, the culmination of a terrible set of performances, including a full-strength side losing 2-1 at non-League Wycombe Wanderers, that made you wonder whether we'd spent pre-season in Hooters. Though we restored some pride with a draw with Panathinaikos, we were duly tonked 4-1 by lowly Gillingham in our final meaningful fixture before the new season.

You didn't need the sensory awareness of Sherlock Holmes to sniff that we might be in trouble here.

**DAVE:** *Mental and physical preparation going into a new season is so important,* *especially when you're going into a higher league. You want to feel confident and ready to build some early momentum. Our pre-season was an absolute car crash. It got a point where we even played our best players against non-League opposition just to remind ourselves of what winning feels like, and we f\*\*king lost! After those early results, alongside a lack of investment and no hope from the mainstream media, the excitement of promotion was being replaced by fear of relegation... and the season hadn't even started.*

**EX:** *I remember buying the league ladders edition of* Shoot! *magazine that season, where you could change teams' positions in the table using the cardboard tabs. Initially, in my prediction of how the League would have finished, I had us in a relatively comfortable mid-table position. Then, as pre-season results got progressively worse, I gradually moved us further down the League until I had us rooted in the bottom three.*

### Small Makes a Big Impression

If there was one ray of sunshine, it was that we hadn't technically fielded our strongest team, as neither Mike Small nor Mitchell Thomas had appeared in pre-season. Hammers fans would get their first glimpse of the duo in Claret and Blue on the opening day when the fixture generator had afforded us a distinctly winnable game against Luton.

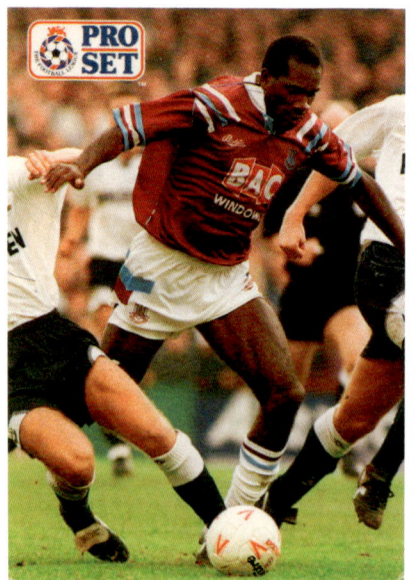

Small, in particular, was a curious sort of footballer, mainly because he didn't seem very good at it. His record wasn't particularly impressive. He started at Bromsgrove, didn't make the grade at Luton, then began a nomadic spell in Belgium, Greece and Holland, where he finally found some semblance of form at the wonderfully named Go Ahead Eagles.

Aged 28, he pitched up back on English shores at Brighton. In the '90s the south coast was the perfect place to revitalise your career if you'd exhausted all options on the continent. Little did we know that, 25 years later, avocados would do the very same thing.

Small's debut against Luton was hardly the stuff of fairy tales. There were moments when he played like a dream, and others when he seemed to be in a deep, cryogenic sleep. In the same passage of play, he could be a hustling, bustling nightmare for centre-halves then, seconds later, control the ball with the technical acumen of a duck wearing army boots. Still, he was one of our more dangerous players in a 0-0 draw with the Hatters where both sides lived down to their predictions as relegation favourites.

Big Mike got off the mark on only his second appearance, a Tuesday-night trip to Sheffield United. It was a strike that would later become The Essence of Small. A goal so undeniably terrible it looked better on Ceefax, yet he celebrated like it was the decider in a World Cup final.

A hopeful Ian Bishop cross drifted into the box where it caused mass panic amongst the gaggle of professional footballers awaiting its arrival. At one stage the ball became an innocent bystander, watching in a mixture of terror and disbelief as ten burly men pushed, shoved and fell on their arses to no discernible purpose. On Green Street in the '90s, they used to call that 'closing time'. In the Barclays First Division, that passed for a set piece.

As the smoke cleared, a lone limb appeared from the mass of humanity to poke the ball apologetically over the line. It belonged to Mike Small. To add insult to injury, he was probably offside (a position he would later spend most Saturday afternoons). Nonetheless, he celebrated with the massed ranks of the away end like he'd just lifted the Jules Rimet Trophy.

His first home goal came two weeks later in a fixture against perennial bogey team Aston Villa. The Midlanders had gone in front through Tony Daley and the Irons, still winless after three games in the top flight, were on the rack. Up stepped Upton Park's new hero. Small burst on to a through-ball to bury a left-foot zinger past Nigel Spink.

A minute later he went from the sublime to the ridiculous. A punt downfield from Tim Breacker found Small in the penalty area. He made two clumsy attempts to control the ball, failing miserably, before the third bounced off his arm beautifully into the path of an onrushing Leroy Rosenior to put us ahead. In 60 seconds, his chaotic contribution had completely changed the game. We had a crucial first three points of the season.

A derby against Chelsea neatly summed up everything about the enigmatic striker. With confidence high, he bullied the Blues' defence from the first whistle. Twice he hit the woodwork in the first half, initially with a scorching drive that deserved better, then missing a toe-poke from close range that you'd have backed Dot Cotton to score. In the second half he got the goal his industry deserved, bundling home roughly 10cm from goal after Colin Foster hit the post.

With the Hammers in the ascendancy, Small unwittingly let our rivals back into the game. Holding the ball up on the edge of the area, he had numerous options to play in a team-mate. Inexplicably, he passed it straight to a blue shirt, much to the dismay of the terraces. Seconds later, Chelsea had raced downfield and equalised. Three points turned to one. Small had gone from hero to zero in the space of ten minutes.

At this stage it was hard to say whether he was actually good, lucky or entirely in the wrong job as a top-flight footballer.

What couldn't be denied was his effectiveness. And over seven glorious days of winter he would write himself into West Ham folklore.

**EX:** *I couldn't believe how well Mike Small started, especially as I'd never really heard of him. I absolutely loved seeing his name on the top scorers list on Teletext, ahead of proven top-tier strikers like Gary Lineker, David Hirst and Ian Rush. We hadn't had that since Tony Cottee left. When Mike Small exploded on to the scene, I honestly thought we'd signed a world-beater.*

**DAVE:** *Players like Mike Small are an enigma. You're never quite sure what they're going to do. I suppose that unpredictability makes them a constant threat, in a strange way. There must have been a lot of pressure on Mike that season. He'd never played at this level before, and he'd really come from nowhere to be the first-choice centre-forward for West Ham United. You could see the relief in his celebration after his first goal against Sheffield United. And then he was off to the races. He just grew in confidence and couldn't stop scoring. It was unbelievable.*

## Kings of the North

Doubtless expecting us to be marooned in the relegation zone, the First Division fixture generator had a treat in store for us in late October: a home game against Gary Lineker's Spurs, followed by a trip to Highbury.

Football is a game steeped in superstition and habit. We've all worn a 'lucky' shirt, walked a 'lucky' route or eaten a 'lucky' pre-match meal in the misguided belief that it will somehow affect the cosmos and tilt the hand of fate in our favour. And despite the fact that subsequent results have proven all of those gestures to be utterly futile, we persevere. Just in case.

West Ham's defence was by no means impervious to such flawed rituals. Particularly when it came to Gary Lineker. England's skipper and goalscorer supreme had long enjoyed a fruitful record against us, whether it was for Everton or arch-rivals Tottenham. And the more it happened, the more you started to suspect that it was for reasons outside of traditional footballing logic.

Our main tactic seemed to be to leave the penalty-box poacher in the sort of unlikely space a dog shit might enjoy on an otherwise crowded dancefloor. As soon as a ball entered the box, our defenders would flee to far corners, leaving Lineker with ample time and space to tuck in a hatful of goals.

And it happened again on this October afternoon. Five minutes had gone when a straight pass found the Spurs striker completely alone on the penalty spot. Tony Gale couldn't have looked any more flat-footed if he were sitting on the porcelain curling out some pre-match carbohydrates. Anyway, Lineker finished expertly and we were behind.

What happened next sums up the magic of Mike Small. In fact, both of our new signings. A Mitchell Thomas mishit from the edge of the area unintentionally bisected the entire Spurs defence and found West Ham's top scorer minding his own business in acres of space. Caught somewhat by surprise, because the odds of a pass reaching him from Thomas's position were a million to one, he scuffed his shot into the ground and it bobbled apologetically into the far corner. It was a dreadful, dreadful goal. But those were the goals Big Mike specialised in. And besides, no one cared. Thomas scored the winner and we marched on to Highbury in good spirits.

Those who made the trip to North London witnessed West Ham's two pre-season signings combine again to great effect, only this time there was no doubting their intentions. The floodlights at Highbury bore witness to some iconic sights over the years, but surely none as unlikely as Mitchell Thomas striding forward like Beckenbauer in his pomp, evading tackle after increasingly desperate Arsenal tackle. The ball shifted right, then inside, where Small was waiting. He took a touch, left England's Tony Adams for dead, and hit an unstoppable 20-yarder past David Seaman with his weaker foot. The Arsenal keeper was by now establishing a reputation as the best shot-stopper around. He didn't get a sniff of it. We won the game 1-0.

By this time, Small had an astonishing 13 goals in 19 starts. He was the hottest striker in the country. There was even talk of him being called up to the England squad, and on reflection it's a mystery that it didn't happen. Small was a physical specimen who surely lacked anywhere near the technical expertise to operate at the very highest level. Yet those were precisely the hallmarks of a Graham Taylor international player. Just ask Carlton Palmer.

In the space of seven days, a season that had started with fears of relegation had given us unexpected hopes of mid table. We'd beaten two of our biggest rivals and our star striker was on the biggest hot streak since Lucifer ordered an extra-spicy chicken vindaloo.

   What could possibly go wrong?

**DAVE:** *This was just so typical of West Ham. So far, the season had seen us to lose to the likes of Wimbledon, Notts County, Norwich and Coventry – then we go and get six points from Arsenal and Tottenham. John Cleese once famously said, "I can take the despair, it's the hope I can't stand," and that is so relatable to West Ham! That said, after these two wins, that's exactly what we had... hope. Maybe we could stay in this division, after all.*

**EX:** *It was massive to beat those two teams, bowling into school two weeks in a row taking the piss out of Spurs and then Arsenal fans. I felt like a king, like the absolute bollocks. I was a proud West Ham supporter. We'd beaten our biggest rivals, and we had the top striker in the country playing in Claret and Blue. When you're a kid, you have a basic appreciation of the game. You concentrate on who scored, and that's it. I had no clue about Mike Small's technical limitations. And, to be honest, I wouldn't have cared. To me, he was invincible. A certainty for the England squad.*

### Breaking a Bond

With West Ham's season in danger of teetering towards positivity, the board took drastic action. Or, more specifically, Peter Storrie took drastic action. In November 1991, Storrie was hired as West Ham's first managing director, having spent a year on the board in a non-executive role.

   Like anyone in a fancy new job, Storrie was keen to make an immediate impact. He did all the usual stuff – shaking hands with the security staff, offering to make the secretaries a cup of tea, etc. And then he got down to more serious business: alienating the entire fanbase and collapsing the club from within.

   Storrie was the public face of the Bond Scheme, a desperate attempt to raise circa £15 million of funds required for Upton Park to comply with the recommendations of the Taylor Report, the post-Hillsborough paper that outlined English football's roadmap to all-seater stadia. That sort of renovation required serious investment, and boardrooms across the land were rippling with panic about how on Earth they were going to raise the money.

   These were the days before Murdoch's millions. The top-flight TV deal was worth a pittance and there was barely one televised game a week, plus two minutes of highlights on *Saint & Greavsie*. Frankly, with the shadow of '80s hooliganism still looming over the domestic game, broadcasters would rather show live colonoscopies from Whipps Cross than First Division football. The money was going to have to come from elsewhere.

Thankfully, Peter Storrie had an ace in his pocket. Or rather, our pockets. He was going to charge West Ham fans a 'bond' of around £500 which gave them the right to purchase a season ticket for the next 50 years. Yes, you read that correctly. That best part of a grand didn't get you a ticket. It gave you the 'opportunity to buy' a ticket. No bond, no right to buy.

The timing was quite staggering. Britain was in the midst of a crippling recession. Interest rates were rising fast, people were defaulting on their mortgages, and unemployment was reaching a five-year high. Against that backdrop, West Ham fans were now being asked to stump up a massive sum just to then stump another massive sum to buy a season ticket. As ill-timed and ill-conceived business ventures go, this was up there with asking King Herod to invest in baby clothes, or Nelson Mandela to buy shares in handcuffs.

Understandably, the fanbase was furious. There were immediate talks of protests and boycotts. In the space of 24 hours the bright hopes of optimism around the season had descended into gloom.

**DAVE:** *This club was created by the working class, people who had nothing but West Ham, the shirt on their backs and the families they provided for. So when a pompous, middle-class, trained accountant proposed the idea of charging fans just for the privilege of being guaranteed a season ticket, it was always gonna go down like a shit sandwich. I understand the club were trying to raise money, but surely there were other ways to do it? This was another example of how disengaged the owners were from the fans.*

**EX:** *The club has sadly forgotten its roots and history way too many times in the past. On paper, the Bond was a good deal if you were one of the very few people who* had access to that sort of money. But this was just another example of abandoning our working-class, East End roots, by introducing a system that excluded the majority of fans from attending. It was a shocking idea, and poorly executed. The first nail in the coffin of what would quickly become a depressing season.

## Town and Out?

The bubbling unrest on the terraces wasn't helped by a spell of form that saw us lose six of our next eight games.

It was an incredible collapse. A week after a creditable 0-0 with Liverpool in front of the ITV cameras, we put in a battling performance at Old Trafford where we might have won a point if Mike Small hadn't shown the composure of a squirrel crossing the M25.

Then the wheels fell off well and truly. We were smashed by Everton (0-4), Villa (1-3) and, most galling of all, a 3-0 defeat at Notts County where we made Neil Warnock's bunch of bruisers look like the 1970 Brazil team.

Overnight, we'd gone from plucky promoted side hitting above their weight to a heavyweight punchbag for the First Division's finest. By New Year's Day, any positivity for the season ahead had plummeted faster than house prices in Pompeii. We had reverted to the side that looked so inadequate pre-season when Sampdoria strolled round the pitch eating a Solero.

No one summed that up better than Mike Small. The hustling, bustling presence of late autumn had been replaced by a man with the motor skills of a fridge freezer. It was as if, almost overnight, the Midas touch had deserted him completely. The scuffed shots that had been nestling in the corner were now bobbling harmlessly out of play. His first touch was more like a boomerang, and his hold-up play suffered immensely. With each passing game, the reserves of confidence dwindled before our eyes. It was awful to watch.

And then there were the offsides. The constant offsides. They say that desperate men take desperate measures. In Small's case, such was his aching determination to arrest his slump in form that he adopted a starting position ten yards behind the opposition back four, in the hope the linesman wouldn't notice. That's no easy task when you're 6'2" and 15 stone.

In early January we were handed a blessed reprieve from the miserable monotony of our First Division form thanks to a draw with non-League Farnborough in the FA Cup. In my mind, this was a chance to rack up a few goals, build back some much-needed morale and hopefully regain some form for the relegation run-in. I had conveniently forgotten the terrible day in Torquay two years prior. Though it wouldn't take long for that memory to re-emerge.

In two performances that rank amongst some of the worst in West Ham history, we scraped a 1-1 draw then a 1-0 home win in the replay. It was dismal stuff that made Peter Storrie's 500 quid ransom look all the more ridiculous. When your club's not involved, it's easy to slip into clichés about the FA Cup. But when your team, a team of top-flight professional footballers, is being more than matched by a group of part-timers who spend their weekdays working in Woolworths, then the much-hyped 'magic of the cup' is the furthest thing from your mind. Having said that, there were times in that replay with Farnborough when sticking Paul Daniels in our first eleven looked like a decent alternative.

Incredibly, the win did spark an upturn in form. Mike Small's horrendous deflected effort earned us a win at Kenilworth Road, and Mitchell Thomas scored the winner vs Oldham. Two wins, two clean sheets, and we had 16 games left to save a season that had been careering out of control.

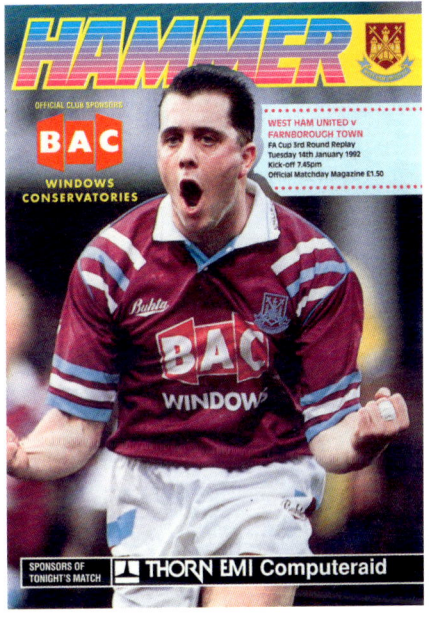

**DAVE:** *The 'us and them' culture at West Ham was at its peak after the announcement of the Bond Scheme, and the subsequent run of results was no coincidence, in my opinion. I think the players could feed off the tension at the time; they must have done. And poor results only added to the doom and gloom. Crawling past Farnborough in the Cup offered little consolation. That said, six points from the following two games saw the arrival of our good friend hope... but it was obvious we needed more than that.*

**EX:** *By now, I was old enough to realise why West Ham fans have a paranoia about drawing lower-league or non-League teams in the FA Cup. As the game in 1990 against Torquay proved, there's something about us that makes us vulnerable to a Cup upset. Even so, the odds were seemingly stacked in our favour here. Even though we were drawn away from home, the game was switched to Upton Park so that Farnborough could get a cut of the bigger gate receipts. Even they didn't really* *care about winning, yet somehow they nearly did. It was a terrible, terrible watch.*

### Waving the Flag

With the club showing signs of much-needed fight, Billy Bonds persuaded the board to dust off the cobwebs from their transfer kitty and bring in an extra body to bolster our survival chances.

There were murmurings of an incoming loanee and, as anyone who has deliberately avoided the bill-payer's permission and spent a small fortune on ClubCall will attest, even the slightest hint of a new signing can provoke a tidal wave of optimism.

For me, there was only one option: it had to be Tony Cottee. TC had endured a bit of a mixed spell at Goodison. He had been in and out of the team – in my eyes a crime that should have seen Howard Kendall banished to the Tower of London – and never plundered the same volume of goals as he had done in Claret and Blue. This season he'd been struggling with injury, but we were at the stage where a half-fit, out-of-form Tony Cottee would hobble happily into the side ahead of Mike Small and Frank McAvennie.

When I read on Ceefax that 'West Ham sign Everton star on loan', it felt like my prayers had been answered. Tony Cottee, the man whose posters had adorned my bedroom wall for so many years, was striding into town to save West Ham United. It was time to get those old Luther Vandross albums back out of the tape deck and dance for joy. TC was back... until he wasn't.

As it happened, the new arrival did indeed come from Everton. And he too had been sidelined by the Everton management. Though this time perhaps for more understandable reasons. Mainly because he wasn't very good.

Welcome to West Ham... Ray Atteveld. The workmanlike utility player was the first Dutchman to appear in Claret and Blue, having played 50+ League games for Everton in a number of different positions, none of them with particular aplomb.

His arrival was a sign of the board's ambition. With the team showing the merest glimmer of hope, a bit of investment could have been just the boost we needed to mount a Great Escape. Instead, here we were with Everton's third-choice right-back riding to our rescue. That's no criticism of Ray Atteveld. But even Ray Atteveld doesn't remember Ray Atteveld's West Ham career (he only played three times and we lost twice). Signing him to save you from relegation was a bit like taking paracetamol for a fractured skull. We might as well have raised the white flag of surrender there and then, saving ourselves the pain of the rest of the season.

As it happened, in the dying moments of a dire 2-0 loss to Everton, with the team playing rubbish and the stench of the Bond Scheme still hanging thick in the east London air, it was the fans who got the flags out. A pitch invasion in protest at the ill-fated investment 'opportunity' saw one punter pick up the corner flag, sit in the middle of the pitch and refuse to be moved on by the authorities, whilst others rushed on to join him. The situation plumbed new depths when Julian Dicks was required to act as a peacemaker, the unlikeliest career change since someone asked Freddy Krueger if he was interested in running a drive-thru circumcision clinic.

Jokes aside, it was the nadir of a season that had finally disappeared down the khazi. The team was crap, and the fans were fed up of being treated like it.

**DAVE:** *To this day, I think this is one of the strangest signings we have ever made, and there have been a LOT of them over the years. During crisis talks at the club, who the f\*\*k tabled Ray Atteveld as a solution?! I know the board were as tight as a crab's arse but, f\*\*k me, Ray Charles would have been a better option. It symbolised a lack of courage, a lack of ambition and a lack of a genuine desire to stay in the top division. No wonder there were protests. What did they expect?!*

**EX:** *I used to rack up some huge sums on ClubCall, the source of regular grief from my parents. I thought we were on to signing a big star from Everton, and ClubCall were brilliant at sensationalising headlines. They must have been minted in the '90s, most of it from people like me, desperate for any kind of good news. The worst bit about it was how long it took to get started. The music went on forever, then the commentator spoke in the slowest voice imaginable. I think I sat through ten minutes, spaffed a fiver and then found out we'd signed Ray Atteveld. All I was left with was a massive phone bill, and another bollocking from my parents. It really wasn't worth it.*

### Goodbye Frankie Mac

Late spring brought good and bad news. After the mass protests and supporter unrest that had undermined the whole season, the board finally relented on the Bond Scheme. So, you could buy a season ticket without being held to ransom for the privilege.

On the negative side, next year's ticket would mean watching second-tier football. The meek surrender of our top-flight status (alongside Luton and Notts County) had been confirmed in April, though we showed some semblance of pride by putting on a mysteriously magnificent performance in beating

Manchester United, a win that would infuriate Alex Ferguson and ultimately cost his side the title to Howard Wilkinson's Leeds.

When Nottingham Forest visited for the final game of the season, we weren't just saying farewell to the First Division, it was also the end of the road for Frank McAvennie at West Ham United. It was desperately sad that a journey which started in 1985 when the blonde-haired, blue-eyed Scot burst on to the scene and took us to the brink of domestic glory, would end in relative ignominy with us marooned at the bottom of the League.

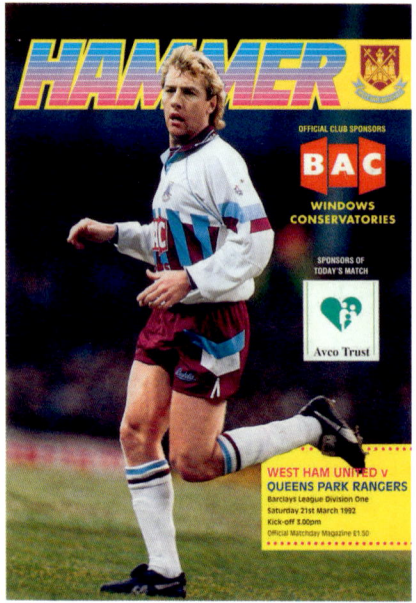

Then again, this was not the Frankie Mac of old, at least not on the pitch. The catastrophic leg break had cost him a yard of pace, and whilst he was still quite the marksman by all accounts in London's nightlife, his day job had suffered terribly.

As a football fan there's no joy in watching your heroes gradually lose their powers. It's an exercise in near-total denial. You cling to the memories of yesteryear, convince yourself that what's old could be new again. But watching Frankie dart around to little effect during this stinker of a season had made for grim viewing. In fairness, his lifestyle hadn't helped prolong his career at the top level. The Scot famously never met a champagne bottle he didn't like. And his subsequent efforts in training were legendary. He might as well have turned up at Chadwell Heath with a deckchair and a pina colada.

Still, if there was anyone who could lift the gloom at Upton Park for one day only, then it was Frankie Mac. Which is exactly what he did. Summoned from the bench, he rolled back the years and scored a second-half treble. We stuffed Forest 3-0 and Frankie was the Man of the Match. I would say it meant he could begin his early evening with a bottle of champers, but to be honest that was probably part and parcel of his daily routine. If Macca wasn't knee deep in a bottle of Moët by the time *Neighbours* started, something was drastically wrong.

Anyhow, the golden boy soaked in Bubbles for one last time, and we ended a season that had fallen flat six months earlier on something of a high. It was going to be an important summer for Billy Bonds. This felt different to the relegation of '89. We were the worst team in the League by a mile. And whilst 22 of the country's best clubs looked forward to the glitz and glamour of the Premier League, which would be launching with a bang in August, we were back to scrapping in the Second Division.

Much-needed riches, courtesy of a huge £304 million deal with Sky TV, were about to pour into the coffers of top-flight treasurers. For West Ham United, fortune was hiding from us all over again.

**DAVE:** It was heartbreaking to see Frank in Claret and Blue for the last time but, f**kin' 'ell, what a way to go! I don't think Billy was actually going to bring him on. Apparently, it was actually Mitchell Thomas who saved the day. He faked an injury so Frank could get on the pitch. The rest is history, and it was an incredible way to say goodbye. God only knows what the bar bill was like at Stringfellows that night!

**EX:** It was a fitting end to Frank's career, and I'm so glad it ended that way. He was a proper folk hero. Admittedly, Forest didn't offer much opposition, most of their players were on the beach already. But it was a great way to draw the curtain on his time at the club.

His departure meant we were going to start the season in the second tier with only one recognised striker. Mike Small's form had come down quicker than the Christmas decorations. I can only think of someone like Michael Ricketts to compare it to. Ricketts stormed to the top of the Premier League scoring charts with Bolton in the early 2000s, got an England call-up, looked completely out of his depth and then his career divebombed after that. West Ham fans know that Mike Small did it first.

**DAVE:** The legend of Mike Small. You never heard him speak. There were no interviews with him in print or on video. It's like he was a phantom striker, a figment of our imagination. Did it really happen? Still, those goals against Spurs and Arsenal were the highlight of the whole season. The arse fell out of it after that.

**Football League First Division - 1991/92**

| Date | Opponent | H/A | Score | Attendance | Scorers |
|---|---|---|---|---|---|
| 17 August | Luton Town | H | 0–0 | 25,079 | |
| 20 August | Sheffield United | A | 1–1 | 21,463 | Small |
| 24 August | Wimbledon | A | 0–2 | 10,081 | |
| 28 August | Aston Villa | H | 3–1 | 23,644 | Small, Rosenior, Brown |
| 31 August | Notts County | H | 0–2 | 20,093 | |
| 4 September | QPR | A | 0–0 | 16,616 | |
| 7 September | Chelsea | H | 1–1 | 18,875 | Small |
| 14 September | Norwich City | A | 1–2 | 15,348 | Small |
| 17 September | Crystal Palace | A | 3–2 | 21,363 | Morley, Thomas, Small |
| 21 September | Manchester City | H | 1–2 | 25,558 | Brown |
| 28 September | Nottingham Forest | A | 2–2 | 25,613 | Small (2) |
| 5 October | Coventry City | H | 0–1 | 21,817 | |
| 19 October | Oldham Athletic | A | 2–2 | 14,365 | Small, McAvennie |
| 26 October | Tottenham Hotspur | H | 2–1 | 23,946 | Thomas, Small |
| 2 November | Arsenal | A | 1–0 | 33,539 | Small |
| 17 November | Liverpool | H | 0–0 | 23,569 | |
| 23 November | Manchester United | A | 1–2 | 47,185 | McAvennie |
| 30 November | Sheffield Wed | H | 1–2 | 24,116 | Breacker |
| 7 December | Everton | A | 0–4 | 21,563 | |
| 21 December | Sheffield United | H | 1–1 | 19,287 | Dicks (p) |
| 26 December | Aston Villa | A | 1–3 | 31,959 | McAvennie |
| 28 December | Notts County | A | 0–3 | 11,163 | |
| 1 January | Leeds United | H | 1–3 | 21,766 | Dicks (p) |
| 11 January | Wimbledon | H | 1–1 | 18,485 | Morley |
| 18 January | Luton Town | A | 1–0 | 11,088 | Small |
| 1 February | Oldham Athletic | H | 1–0 | 19,012 | Thomas |
| 22 February | Sheffield Wed | A | 1–2 | 24,150 | Small |
| 29 February | Everton | H | 0–2 | 20,976 | |
| 3 March | Southampton | A | 0–1 | 14,548 | |
| 11 March | Liverpool | A | 0–1 | 30,821 | |
| 14 March | Arsenal | H | 0–2 | 22,640 | |
| 21 March | QPR | H | 2–2 | 20,401 | Breacker, Small |
| 28 March | Leeds United | A | 0–0 | 31,101 | |
| 1 April | Tottenham Hotspur | A | 0–3 | 31,809 | |
| 4 April | Chelsea | A | 1–2 | 20,684 | C Allen |
| 11 April | Norwich City | H | 4–0 | 16,896 | Bishop, Rush (2), Dicks (p) |
| 14 April | Southampton | H | 0–1 | 18,298 | |
| 18 April | Manchester City | A | 0–2 | 25,601 | |

| | | | | | | |
|---|---|---|---|---|---|---|
| 20 April | Crystal Palace | H | 0–2 | 17,710 | |
| 22 April | Manchester United | H | 1–0 | 24,197 | Brown |
| 25 April | Coventry City | A | 0–1 | 15,398 | |
| 2 May | Nottingham Forest | H | 3–0 | 20,629 | McAvennie (3) |

**FA Cup**

| | | | | | | |
|---|---|---|---|---|---|---|
| 4 January R3 | Farnborough Town | A | 1–1 | 23,449 | Dicks |
| 14 January R3R | Farnborough Town | H | 1–0 | 23,869 | Morley |
| 25 January R4 | Wrexham | H | 2–2 | 24,712 | Morley, Dicks |
| 4 February R4R | Wrexham | A | 1–0 | 17,995 | Foster |
| 15 February R5 | Sunderland | A | 1–1 | 25,475 | Small |
| 26 February R5R | Sunderland | H | 2–3 | 25,830 | M Allen (2) |

**League Cup**

| | | | | | |
|---|---|---|---|---|---|
| 24 Sept R2 1L | Bradford City | A | 1–1 | 7,034 | Small |
| 9 October R2 2L | Bradford City | H | 4–0 | 17,232 | Small, Morley, Keen, Parris |
| 29 October R3 | Sheffield United | A | 2–0 | 11,144 | McAvennie, Small (p) |
| 4 December R4 | Norwich City | A | 1–2 | 16,325 | Small |

| | P | W | D | L | GF | GA | GD | Pts |
|---|---|---|---|---|---|---|---|---|
| 1 Leeds United | 42 | 22 | 16 | 4 | 74 | 37 | +37 | 82 |
| 2 Manchester Utd | 42 | 21 | 15 | 6 | 63 | 33 | +30 | 78 |
| 3 Sheffield Wed | 42 | 21 | 12 | 9 | 62 | 49 | +13 | 75 |
| 4 Arsenal | 42 | 19 | 15 | 8 | 81 | 47 | +34 | 72 |
| 5 Manchester City | 42 | 20 | 10 | 12 | 61 | 48 | +13 | 70 |
| 6 Liverpool | 42 | 16 | 16 | 10 | 47 | 40 | +7 | 64 |
| 7 Aston Villa | 42 | 17 | 9 | 16 | 48 | 44 | +4 | 60 |
| 8 Nottingham For | 42 | 16 | 11 | 15 | 60 | 58 | +2 | 59 |
| 9 Sheffield Utd | 42 | 16 | 9 | 17 | 65 | 63 | +2 | 57 |
| 10 Crystal Palace | 42 | 14 | 15 | 13 | 53 | 61 | -8 | 57 |
| 11 QPR | 42 | 12 | 18 | 12 | 48 | 47 | +1 | 54 |
| 12 Everton | 42 | 13 | 14 | 15 | 52 | 51 | +1 | 53 |
| 13 Wimbledon | 42 | 13 | 14 | 15 | 53 | 53 | 0 | 53 |
| 14 Chelsea | 42 | 13 | 14 | 15 | 50 | 60 | -10 | 53 |
| 15 Tottenham H | 42 | 15 | 7 | 20 | 58 | 63 | -5 | 52 |
| 16 Southampton | 42 | 14 | 10 | 18 | 39 | 55 | -16 | 52 |
| 17 Oldham Ath | 42 | 14 | 9 | 19 | 63 | 67 | -4 | 51 |
| 18 Norwich City | 42 | 11 | 12 | 19 | 47 | 63 | -16 | 45 |
| 19 Coventry City | 42 | 11 | 11 | 20 | 35 | 44 | -9 | 44 |
| 20 Luton Town | 42 | 10 | 12 | 20 | 39 | 71 | -32 | 42 |
| 21 Notts County | 42 | 10 | 10 | 22 | 40 | 62 | -22 | 40 |
| 22 West Ham Utd | 42 | 9 | 11 | 22 | 37 | 59 | -22 | 38 |

ISSUE 13

**Fortune's**
ALWAYS HIDING
THE WEST HAM FANZINE THAT'S NOT VERY CHEAP

**WHAT THE ✱✺@☢**

**IS THIS?**

1992/93
DAGENHAM
MOTORS
Bukta
Bukta
WHUFC
MIZUNO
MIZUNO
Mitre

## The Outsiders

The summer of 1992 was about as miserable a time as ever to be a West Ham United fan. And even the national team didn't offer any distraction. Normally, a tournament summer gives fans a chance to recharge their batteries, forget about the dire performances of their chosen domestic team and watch the world's best footballers strut their stuff.

Unfortunately, Graham Taylor hadn't read the memo. Two years after the highs of Turin – where only the width of a goalpost and Peter Shilton's concrete boots stopped England making the World Cup final – Taylor presided over an absolutely pathetic Euro 92 campaign. The England boss's strategy of getting rid of our good players, picking crap ones and then playing them out of position saw the Three Lions limp out of the competition with no wins, one goal and three utterly abject performances.

These days, people dub Euro 92 as England's 'forgotten tournament'. I can only assume that was a label issued by people who forgot to actually watch it. Anyone who sat through England-Sweden knows that when they close their eyes at night they can still see the horror of David Batty at right-back. It was turgid stuff. And whilst no one can ever justify the appalling abuse Taylor suffered at the hand of Fleet Street – he was infamously labelled a 'turnip' by the poison pen of *Sun* journalists – anyone with the tactical acumen of a Brussel sprout could tell you that subbing off Gary Lineker was a dreadful idea.

Thankfully, no sooner had the sun gone down on England's hopes than the bright lights of the Premier League sparked on the horizon. By late summer, the Rupert Murdoch marketing machine had gone into overdrive thanks to a radio, newspaper and television blitzkrieg championing the rebirth of English football's top flight. No expense was spared. Simple Minds' 'Alive and Kicking' was the official soundtrack to glossy TV adverts featuring Paul Stewart driving a Ferrari, Andy Ritchie answering a mobile phone on a treadmill and, rather curiously, Anders Limpar eating breakfast in bed.

For the first time since that summer of Italia 90, it felt like the whole country was excited about the Beautiful Game. The whole country except us. We'd managed to lose our top-flight status at precisely the most pivotal moment in the recent history of First Division football.

Spirits weren't helped by developments elsewhere in the second tier – specifically at Newcastle, who had made a miraculous escape from relegation the previous season thanks to the arrival of Kevin Keegan. Megabucks chairman Sir John Hall wasted no time in splashing the cash to get the Geordies into the Promised Land of the Premier League. The likes of Paul Bracewell, Barry Venison, John Beresford and the rumoured arrival of Rob Lee from Charlton meant that Keegan's men were immediately installed amongst the betting front-runners for promotion.

Meanwhile, in east London, dust was gathering on our transfer budget like the shampoo bottle in Duncan Goodhew's bathroom. Thankfully, Billy Bonds realised it was time for some new blood. And that summer he made one of the most crucial signings in West Ham history.

**EX:** *Italia 90 was my first World Cup, and it felt magical. Schillaci. Colour. Passion. It cemented my love for football. From that moment on, I loved Gazza (despite his Tottenham affiliations). That whole England team was legendary. And then it all fell apart with Taylor. I think of it like the first relationship you ever have. There's a passionate love affair, a honeymoon period and then it starts to get gloomy, frustrating, before ending in massive disappointment. And that love for the England team wasn't properly rekindled until Euro 96.*

**DAVE:** *I think you can draw parallels between West Ham and England: both go into every competition with genuine optimism and enthusiasm but ultimately experience pessimism and disappointment. I'm surprised the song 'Bubbles' hasn't been adopted by England fans by now! Incredibly, the only difference is that West Ham are more successful than the national side! F\*\*kinell, if that doesn't tell you how bad we are as a nation, nothing will! That tournament also saw the last ever Saint & Greavsie show. On reflection, what a shit summer that was! At least we had West Ham to turn to...*

**EX:** *As for the Premier League, I loved the Sky ads. They made it seem so exciting with all the Americanisms: cheerleaders, fireworks and all that. I used to get really jealous that when they panned through the team badges, and West Ham weren't in it. It was all glitz and glamour. Meanwhile, we were stuck with Barnsley away.*

**DAVE:** *Unlike Ex, I didn't much care for Sky and the Premier League. I was that little bit younger. My football world started and finished with West Ham United. All I cared about was who we were playing Saturday and, in my delusional optimism, how many we were going to win by.*

## Friends Reunited

Harry Redknapp had a highly respectable career at Upton Park, having debuted as a winger back in 1965 and played over 170 games in Claret and Blue before continuing his career in the lower leagues. He finished his playing days at

Bournemouth before jumping into the manager's seat to help the cash-strapped Cherries avoid relegation to the Conference.

Redknapp had developed a reputation as one of the more colourful characters in lower-league football. A popular man-manager with a shrewd eye for a bargain, he built a squad of waifs and strays on the sort of budget that Tiny Tim had for Christmas presents in *Scrooge*. That team was good enough to get Bournemouth into the second tier.

If there was one criticism of Bonzo during his time as boss, it was his transfer dealings. In the main, the stalwarts of the team were still the signings made by Lou Macari during that madcap few months at the helm. Bonds seemed to spend money like it was his own, a deeply honourable trait but one that wasn't necessarily shared by his peers in the murky world of football finance. You can't peruse the transfer market like it's the drill section at B&Q, you have to move fast and make things happen. Deals are famously done in the twilight hours, with clandestine meetings at motorway service stations. Players are traded like horses. It's a cut-throat business where sometimes you have to leave your morals at the door. That wasn't Billy's style.

**HARRY REDKNAPP**
Picks the Cherries' team

Redknapp was an entirely different operator. At Bournemouth he famously negotiated a deal that so infuriated Maidstone United's manager at the time – Barry Fry – that he threatened to send round "two geezers to blow your f**king kneecaps off, Redknapp." We might get the same reaction if we ever asked for a fee for Mike Small.

Bringing Harry Redknapp back to the club as his assistant seemed to be an acknowledgement from Bonds that he needed an extra piece in the jigsaw to get promotion. We were going to have to spend what little money we had wisely – which meant looking for value in the lower leagues. We couldn't afford any more Mitchell Thomas mistakes.

Redknapp got to work instantly, recognising that there was work to be done with the squad. We had deficiencies in some key areas: specifically defence, midfield and attack. One of the first new arrivals was Peter Butler, a gruff Yorkshire terrier from Southend, who would add some extra bite to a midfield that had been too lightweight the previous season.

There was also reinforcement in attack as lively winger Mark Robson arrived from Spurs, where he'd spent the majority of his time out on loan at the likes of Exeter and Plymouth. And Harry added a familiar face by bringing in diminutive wideman Matty Holmes from Bournemouth for a small fee.

They seemed like solid, if unspectacular additions, certainly in comparison to the stars arriving at St James' Park. But maybe that was exactly what we needed.

**EX:** *Harry Redknapp was Billy's mate, and his arrival seemed like a very good move as he'd made a name for himself down at Bournemouth. His signings were just what we needed. To this day, Peter Butler remains incredibly underrated. I hadn't heard of Mark Robson, and my first impression wasn't great. I couldn't get over how skinny he was. The last time I saw legs like that they were sticking out of a nest. I remember turning to my dad and saying, "How can he play football with legs like that?" Pretty well, as it happens. For a free transfer, he quickly turned out to be a real bargain.*

*Meanwhile, Matty Holmes looked like Lee Evans, but he was quick and lively on the ball. The sort of winger fans love to see. It didn't take long to see that all three deals were really good business. And, though Harry hates the term, it was our first insight into what a wheeler-dealer he was.*

**DAVE:** *In the long term, Billy asking Harry to help with West Ham ended up like asking John Terry to help with your marriage counselling! It didn't end well for him – or their friendship, sadly – but in the short-term Harry instantly added value to their partnership with three excellent signings. As fans, we love to see one of our own in the dugout. Now we had two, and this was an exciting time for the club.*

### Slater for... Scotland?

The new arrivals meant that someone needed to go to balance the books. And after a League season where we only won nine games, we were hardly flush with valuable assets.

When Celtic, under the stewardship of Liam Brady, came in with a £1.5 million bid for Stuart Slater, the board couldn't accept the bid fast enough. And, in fairness, the fans agreed. It was incredible to think that 18 months ago Slater had been an England Under-21 international with the world at his feet. Since then, he'd gone 55 games without a goal, and the weight of all that hype and hullabaloo seemed to hang round his neck like a millstone. There was a spark missing from his play. That explosive burst of pace – that had ripped Everton to shreds on that famous night under the lights – had disappeared. And his form suffered terribly. These days he looked like he'd graduated with an Honours Degree from the Mike Small School of Self-Confidence.

Clearly Brady, who had taken Slater under his wing during the youngster's tentative years in the first team, felt that he could help the winger fly to new heights once again. But the fee felt a little generous for a player who once could have commanded twice that sum. Similar to the loss of Frank McAvennie, it felt like the end of an era. He was the last of an exciting production line of home-grown talent. Like Cottee, Dickens and Ince before him, another young talent was leaving for pastures new. Only this time there was no one obvious to replace him. Yet another bond between the team and the terraces had been broken.

**EX:** *It was the end of an era, and my first understanding that your heroes don't stay forever. When Stuart left, I was absolutely gutted. He'd only been here three years. Why was he leaving so early? It felt like a personal betrayal. My blind loyalty to my first Hammers hero wouldn't let me accept that he was crap the season before, and it was the right time to sell him. As a kid, you don't think about that. All I could do was take his poster down off my wall and cherish the memories.*

**DAVE:** *It's heartbreaking when you think about Stuart's demise. His ability, coupled with being an Academy graduate, made him a fans' favourite at West Ham. I guess it just goes to show that you can have all the talent in the world, but if you suffer seriously bad luck with injuries (as Stuart did), then you'll never fulfil your true potential. Whilst I was gutted to see him go, in hindsight it was the right decision because not only had he lost his way at West Ham, he never rediscovered top form elsewhere.*

### Retirement? Not for Me, Clive

Clive Allen had burst on to the scene as a teenage sensation at QPR in the late '70s, but it felt like he had been part and parcel of English football for an eternity. In fact, I'm pretty sure if you look closely at pictures of the famous Christmas Day kickabout of 1914, amongst the barbed wire, the trenches and the tributes to fallen comrades, you'll see Clive Allen scoring a tap-in from two yards out and celebrating like he's just single-handedly conquered the Western Front.

Since those early days at Loftus Road, the Stepney-born striker (and cousin of Martin, as well as 1980 West Ham hero Paul Allen) had become a seasoned operator at the highest level. Throughout the '80s he'd scored goals at QPR,

Crystal Palace, Spurs (where he plundered an astonishing 49 goals in the 1986/87 season) and even enjoyed a little sojourn in the south of France with Bordeaux before returning to Blighty with Manchester City.

Now here he was at Upton Park, having pitched up for a small deadline-day deal from Chelsea at the back end of last season, making a handful of appearances in our relegation run-in. With his 16th pre-season as a professional footballer under his belt, and all those miles on the clock, it didn't feel unreasonable to ask how much gas Allen had left in the tank – particularly after seeing Frank McAvennie's gradual decline.

From the onset it was clear that Clive's mind, if not his legs, retained the sharpness of old. He wasn't going to run the channels, and he had the acceleration of a snail in flip-flops, so there was no point playing the ball over the top; but he had the same laser focus on goalscoring as the Terminator had on Sarah Connor.

He got off to a scoring start at Oakwell in the opening game of the season. A sublime turn sent his marker halfway across the Pennines and Allen finished clinically into the top corner to earn us a welcome three points. After two morale-sapping defeats against Charlton and Newcastle, where a rejuvenated David Kelly scored and produced the sort of performance that was so rarely seen in Claret and Blue, Allen netted a much-needed winner against Watford that would prove to be the catalyst for our season.

When the old maestro scored a screamer and a trademark tap-in during a 5-1 thrashing of Bristol City at Ashton Gate, any doubts about the digits on his passport were dispelled. The goalscoring charts spoke for themselves. The Allen-Morley axis was proving to be a handful for the even the division's most hardened defences. Seven goals in seven games and a three-game winning streak meant that by the end of September we were right back into the promotion mix.

But we were only just getting started.

**DAVE:** *Sometimes in football you need a bit of luck and, as luck would have it, Clive had fallen out with Chelsea boss Ian Porterfield – so he asked his cousin Martin, who was also his neighbour at the time, to have a word with Billy about moving to West Ham. I'm so pleased Billy acted on that because in my opinion Clive is one of the best strikers this country has produced. Despite approaching the end of his career, I was excited to see what he would do in Division One, and he didn't disappoint.*

**EX:** *The interesting thing about Allen is that he was a top player, a former top goalscorer in the country, and he didn't mind dropping down a division to keep* *playing. Players don't do that these days. They'd rather retire (if they can afford it), than reduce themselves to playing at a lower standard. It's sad, really, because it means fans at smaller clubs don't get to see top players in their twilight years.*

## 10/10 in October

Our sensational League form continued into October, and with the top flight enjoying an international break as Graham Taylor's England set their sights on World Cup qualification, ITV made us top billing for a rare Sunday-afternoon slot on domestic telly.

With the eyes of the nation upon us, we turned in another tremendous performance, smashing the Wearsiders for six without reply. At the heart of the result were stellar showings from our widemen Mark Robson and Kevin Keen. The latter looked far more comfortable at this level, unrecognisable from the player who had flitted in and out of games last season. Demanding the ball, beating a man with a drop of a shoulder and providing accurate delivery from out wide, he was a constant source of creativity for Morley and Allen. He opened the scoring against Sunderland with a long-range drive and delivered perhaps his finest individual showing in Claret and Blue in front of a live television audience. It was well-deserved exposure for an unassuming player who could probably walk unnoticed through his own living room.

Robson, meanwhile, was proving to be a very astute acquisition. Given he was a free transfer from Spurs and had done little of note in his career to date, expectations were fairly low on his arrival. Yet he had exploded out of the blocks as a West Ham player. His main weapon was a delightful left peg, the sort of cultured limb that could peel a satsuma. And his link-up play with Julian Dicks was a joy to behold. They were the oddest of couples in many regards. Julian's style of play tiptoed on that fine line between competitive aggression and Grievous Bodily Harm. Whilst the rather lightweight Robson, who looked like he might lose an arm wrestle with Winnie the Pooh, was all cute touches and clever movement. He scored twice against Sunderland and turned provider in a 4-0 drubbing away at Bristol Rovers the following week.

The other summer signing, Peter Butler, put in an imperious performance at the Memorial Ground. He was well accustomed to rolling up his sleeves and getting results at these kind of footballing outposts. The Yorkshireman wasn't a West Ham midfielder in the traditional sense. Not particularly gifted technically, Butler was a spit-and-sawdust sort of footballer who loved nothing more than sticking the boot in – and his whole-hearted approach had made him something of a fan favourite.

Two games. Ten goals without reply. And new stars starting to shine. Harry Redknapp's prowess in the transfer market had already started to prove its worth.

**DAVE:** *To this day, that performance against Sunderland was one of the best I have ever seen from West Ham. We absolutely tore them apart, and the way we passed the ball was a prime example of 'The West Ham Way'. Alvin Martin was given Man of the Match, which was quite an achievement for someone who was looking eligible for a free bus pass at the time! The champagne could have gone to a number of players, though; there was a real sense of togetherness amongst the group, and to follow that with a 4-0 win away from home was a real statement of intent.*

**EX:** *Mark Robson had a phenomenal impact. Those little legs were actually very good and tricky. He was an old-school, classic winger, who would take on the full-back and whip a cross in. I miss wingers like this. In the East Stand, before it was redeveloped, the crowd was much closer to the pitch. You were right on top of the sideline, so much so that in the higher seats it was hard to see the players in the corners. So when wingers like Robson got the ball, everyone stood up to see what he was going to do next. You don't get players who genuinely get bums off seats any more.*

**DAVE:** *Robson was great, but I have to say Peter Butler was superb. There was a touch of the Billy Bonds about him. In his heyday, Bonzo was the bodyguard for Trevor Brooking in midfield. Butler was the same. A proper workhorse. You can't put a price on the energy and enthusiasm he brought to the team. He was the hardest grafter every single week – and the fans loved him for it.*

### New Year, New West Ham, Same Old Julian

In the '90s, some things just went together. Robson and Jerome. PJ and Duncan. Julian Dicks and disciplinary problems.

To describe Julian as 'committed' would be like calling The Incredible Hulk 'temperamental'. His reputation didn't help matters. His nickname – 'The Terminator' – made him an easy target for referees, and sometimes you wondered if it wouldn't save everyone a lot of time and effort if they just booked him in the tunnel beforehand.

Miraculously, he had only accumulated one red card on West Ham duty before the start of the '92/93 season, a record which he managed to quadruple in the space of four gloriously violent months of the new campaign.

An elbow that left Franz Carr's nose looking over his shoulder saw Dicks red-carded at Newcastle, then he left a tattoo of his studs on Steve Bull's thighs at Molineux, before sending Ted McMinn into orbit at the Baseball Ground. Thankfully, we were already 2-0 up and cruising in the latter fixture, thanks to goals from Robson and Morley, but still had to negotiate 60 minutes with ten men, Kevin Keen acting as the unlikely emergency left-back.

The backs-to-the-wall victory in the Midlands was a significant showing of our new-found spirit. Whilst Newcastle were blowing teams away with their balls-to-the-wall attacking football under Kevin Keegan, we were proving to be quite the clinical outfit, though thankfully less reliant on clean sheets than we had been two seasons ago when Ludo Miklosko – and his hands the size of dinner plates – were a foundation of our promotion bid.

This time around, our attacking arsenal was far more potent. Trevor Morley was back to his best, Clive Allen could scent space in the penalty area like Yogi Bear sniffing out a picnic basket, and goals from the likes of Keen and Robson meant we cruised through late winter/early spring with a succession of 2-0 wins.

Ordinarily, that sort of form would have been enough to easily secure the second automatic promotion spot. However, down on the south coast a storm was brewing in the shape of Jim Smith's Portsmouth, whose own promotion bid was showing no signs of faltering. Pompey were powered almost exclusively by striker Guy Whittingham, a former British Army serviceman whose glut of goals had earned him the nickname 'Corporal Punishment' by the Fratton Park faithful.

Whilst Julian Dicks was football's Terminator, Whittingham looked like he was straight off the production line at Skynet HQ. He couldn't be reasoned with or bargained with. He showed no pain, no remorse or fear. And he absolutely would not stop until he had shithoused our dreams of second place. Every Saturday was the same: hurriedly tapping into Ceefax to check the Portsmouth result, followed by the crushing blow of seeing he'd scored another hat-trick and secured another three points for our promotion rivals. His rise to fame was as fast as it was unexpected. The previous season he'd managed eleven goals in the third tier, and now he was the leading scorer in the entire country with 30+ strikes already to his name, showing no signs of abating. Just our luck.

What made Whittingham's form all the more painful was that, should the second- and third-placed teams have identical points tallies, the promotion spot would be decided by goals scored. And with Corporal Punishment's right foot turning into a sub-machine gun every Saturday afternoon, we had to keep our foot on the pressure. We couldn't afford any distractions.

**DAVE:** Julian epitomises the magic and beauty of football at that time. Back when it was genuinely a contact sport. People forget that football is a tribal, territorial sport. The opposition are coming to take points away from you. So, you want players to have to fight for their club, for the badge, for everything it represents. Football used to be a contact sport. I miss those days immensely.

I once asked Julian how he use to deal with pacy wingers. He said, "Back in my day, you could smash the f**kers in the stand." In this day and age he would probably be given a prison sentence! But that's why we loved him so much. Not only could he play but he had passion, intensity and a winning mentality that would resonate with the fans. I only wish he would have smashed Guy Whittingham into the Chicken Run, that might have stopped him scoring over 40 goals that season!

**EX:** If a player was sent off now three times in four games, there'd be uproar on social media. You'd be labelled a disgrace and plastered all over the back pages. But back then it added to his legacy as a hard man. There's a classic image of Julian Dicks taking out two Wolves players and Billy Bonds – himself one of the toughest footballers to ever play the game – running down the touchline to restrain him. Nobody messed with Julian.

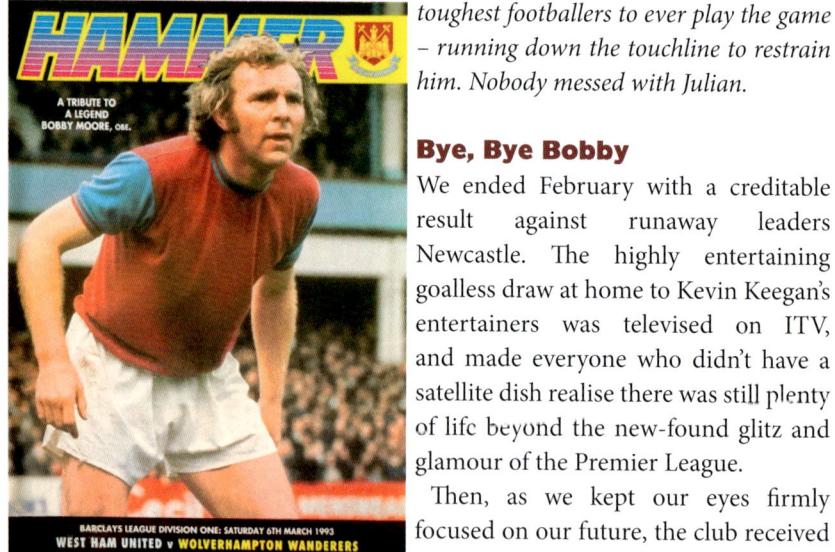

### Bye, Bye Bobby

We ended February with a creditable result against runaway leaders Newcastle. The highly entertaining goalless draw at home to Kevin Keegan's entertainers was televised on ITV, and made everyone who didn't have a satellite dish realise there was still plenty of life beyond the new-found glitz and glamour of the Premier League.

Then, as we kept our eyes firmly focused on our future, the club received some devastating news about a titan of our past: on February 24th, Bobby Moore passed away due to liver and bowel cancer.

Bobby's ill health had been well publicised, and he had been pictured in the commentary box for Capital Gold a week earlier looking desperately unwell – yet carrying out his duties with his customary dignity.

It was typical of a man who was beloved not just for his storied abilities on the field, but for the values he represented. There have been thousands of genuinely great footballers, and there will be thousands more. Few, however, will command the same respect that the world held for Bobby Moore. It speaks volumes that the most revered image of England's legendary captain isn't the one of his finest hour – hoisted on his team-mates' shoulders and holding the Jules Rimet Trophy in 1966. In some ways, this was too indulgent for a notoriously humble man. Instead, when many think of Bobby Moore, they think of that game in Mexico four years later: a titanic battle with Pele – the greatest player the world had ever seen – and the heartfelt embrace in the moments after the final whistle. It represents everything the England and West Ham number six stood for: courage, dignity, respect – values that had since disappeared from English football under a stampede of hooliganism in the '70s and '80s.

His passing sent a shockwave through the fanbase. And the next home game against Wolves became a fond farewell to a man whose shadow loomed large over this part of east London. Thousands of scarves, shirts and wreaths had adorned the gates to the Boleyn Ground since the news had broken.

When the whistle blew on matchday, Wolves were the unfortunate visitors, swept away on a tidal wave of emotion from the terraces as goals from Dicks, Morley and Holmes sealed a 3-1 win that still felt somewhat hollow at the final whistle.

**DAVE:** *When Bobby passed away it was powerful. It affected the whole world, not just West Ham fans. It's incredible to think that a boy from Barking could go on to become one of the most iconic figures in sporting history and, let's not forget, not only did he achieve so much in football, he also did a lot for the image of the East End. He was an incredible man, and I'll never understand why West Ham didn't use him to some capacity after his retirement? He would have been the greatest ambassador a club could wish for, and we completely wasted that opportunity. Unbelievable.*

**EX:** *When my dad came and told me Bobby Moore had died, it was the first time I remember seeing his emotions. He was normally a very stoic guy, but this had really choked him up. He took me to the stadium and we walked round. I can still remember all the wreaths and scarves. I've got an order of service from Bobby's funeral and the Wolves programme, too. Hopefully, I'll pass them down to my kids. They're a part of West Ham history.*

## Speedie Picks Up the Promotion Pace

The one truism of any promotion trail is that at some point you're going to hit a bump in the road. Brian Clough used to say that players are like racehorses, not carthorses (though anyone who saw Ray Atteveld might disagree) and you need to treat them as such.

As a team starts to flag near the finish line of a promotion season, it's common for managers to seek out fresh legs. Free up some of the workload from your hardworking thoroughbreds. Bring in a little bit of energy, a little bit of positivity to a tired dressing room. Or in the case of David Speedie, bring in a little bit of bastard.

Throughout his career, the Scottish striker had acquired a reputation as one of the most horrible opponents in English football. By all accounts, playing against David Speedie was about as enjoyable as having a nest of wasps take up temporary accommodation in your arsehole. Despite being only 5'6" in stature, he was a giant personality. And frankly, a giant pain in the backside.

Speedie was well known at Upton Park, having played here many times for Chelsea, where he formed a fine partnership with Kerry Dixon. Whilst Big Kerry would use his athletic frame to unsettle his opponents, Speedie relied almost exclusively on his mouth. A world-class gobshite, he spent every second of every minute delivering verbals to players, officials and the crowd. He was the sort of player loved by his own fans, and instantly hated elsewhere in the Football League. And he was by no means a favourite of the Chicken Run.

In fairness, he was a half-decent player in his time. A Scotland international (he allegedly called Graeme Souness a "muppet" on his international debut), he'd been on the brink of the Scotland 1986 World Cup squad (before telling Alex Ferguson to "stick it" when asked to go on the standby list) and had a record of scoring high-quality, if not a high quantity, of goals. However, his most recent spells at Southampton, Birmingham and West Brom had delivered a meagre return of just four in 28 League games. So his arrival at West Ham was hardly greeted with fanfare. Still, Billy Bonds had crossed paths with him enough to know that his knack of scoring important goals in important games could be very handy during a tense run-in. And with Clive Allen's injury potentially ruling him out for the entire season, he gave us much-needed options up front.

The early signs weren't good. Though his industry wasn't in doubt, Speedie looked rustier than Robert Maxwell's wristwatch in front of goal. When he missed an absolute sitter in a 2-2 draw with Millwall, there were murmurs of discontent from the terraces. After five goalless appearances, which included two chastening defeats at the hands of Oxford and Southend, the dissent grew louder.

The pressure was on when Leicester came to Upton Park in front of the ITV cameras. It was exactly the sort of occasion Speedie had cherished over the years and, finally, he delivered. Two instinctive finishes eased the tension as we coasted to a 3-0 win. He netted again on a nervy afternoon to help us to a 2-1 win over Bristol Rovers, and played well in a crucial victory at Swindon – where Clive Allen made a scoring reappearance from the subs' bench – that set up a final day for the ages at Upton Park.

**EX:** *I remember my dad saying, "We haven't signed that horrible bastard from Chelsea, have we?" I was surprised because I always just thought of him as a really good player. I didn't know anything about David Speedie's reputation. I knew he scored a lot of goals for Chelsea and Coventry. I remember watching his Liverpool debut and scoring vs United live on telly. Then he went to Blackburn and helped them get promotion. He seemed like a great signing.*

**DAVE:** *Signing David Speedie on loan was a smart move from Billy, for his work rate alone that deal made sense at that stage of the season. He had a bit of a slow start but actually left West Ham with a goal ratio of one in three. So I will always be thankful for his time with us. He can be overlooked probably because of the duration of his time here. In fact, part of me wonders if he'd even have signed for us in this day and age. Social media would probably have erupted, as these days it's a metric for club officials to gauge the reaction of the fanbase. And there wasn't a lot of love for David Speedie in the East End.*

**EX:** *It's an interesting point. There were loads of fans who had the same reaction as my dad, but no way to express it. So, you just had to get on with it and hope he was decent. More recently, we've had El-Hadj Diouf and Ben Thatcher linked with us under Sam Allardyce, but the reaction from fans on social media was so bad the club didn't do the deals. I don't think we missed out on much there, to be honest. David Speedie, however, deserves a mention in the history books.*

## Home Invasion

There have been many words written about Upton Park's demise in recent times. It may not hold quite the same gravitas of the epic win over Manchester United on the Boleyn's swansong in 2016, but that afternoon on May 8th, 1993 was up there among the greatest days on Green Street.

The ground was packed to the proverbial rafters. Bathed in sunshine, it reeked of Heineken, sweat and Silk Cut. In between the nervous inhalations of nicotine, and occasional bursts of 'Bubbles', you could hear the buzz of transistor radios as punters waited anxiously for news from Portsmouth.

A win alone wouldn't be enough. We had a one goal advantage over our rivals, so not only did we have to secure three points, but also we had to ensure we weren't outscored by Pompey.

The odds weren't in our favour. Our opponents – John Beck's arch-shithouses Cambridge United – needed a result to preserve their second-tier status. Meanwhile Pompey, who hadn't lost a home game since we beat them back in September, hosted mid-table Grimsby. The Mariners had nothing to play for and were probably already booking their sunbeds. They were likely to provide the feeblest of opposition.

The first half was a terrible spectacle, not helped by the state of the surface. Baked in sunshine, there were large clusters of dry mud across vast expenses of the pitch. It looked like someone had steamrollered a giant Sara Lee gateaux across the centre circle. The best tactic was to loft the ball wide and then get it in the mixer, which played into the hands of Cambridge's bruising centre-halves.

Thankfully, there was inexplicably good news from Portsmouth where Grimsby, playing with the reckless abandon of men looking forward to their first cocktail on the Costa del Sol, had taken a shock lead.

Having regrouped at half-time, and with news from Pompey putting a pep in our step, we scored two minutes into the second half when Speedie did what he'd done his whole career – and scored a big goal on a big occasion. After a spot of head tennis in the box following a corner, the Scot turned and volleyed in a sweet strike from a difficult angle.

It settled the nerves and briefly gave us a two-goal advantage. However, news filtered through of an equaliser at Fratton Park, and the tension rose again. With minutes on the clock, and knowing one more goal would secure the game and promotion, Billy Bonds sent on Clive Allen to do what he did best. With seconds remaining, and thousands of fans camped on the sidelines ready to invade the pitch at the final whistle, Julian Dicks charged into the penalty area and squared the ball across the six-yard box where Allen had the easiest of tap-ins.

Game over.

Even a late Portsmouth winner didn't matter. We'd pipped them to the post by the barest of margins. The crowd, in their thousands, were on the pitch. Cambridge were down. And West Ham United were back where we belonged.

**EX:** *I remember so much about that game: the nerves on the drive to the ground. Listening to Capital Gold. The tension was awful. And we really made hard work of it. When the final whistle went, it was magical. Well, almost. My dad stopped me AGAIN from going on the pitch. I could have easily made it down to the bottom tier and joined in the celebrations. But Dad stopped me. To this day, I wish I could have been part of it. Pitch invasions were so much more common in the '90s, and this one was iconic in West Ham's history.*

**DAVE:** *Whatever happened to pitch invasions? Ex is right – they were everywhere in the '90s. I know people talk about Health & Safety, but come on. Football is a passionate game. A last-minute winner, a goal against your biggest rivals, sometimes you lose yourself in the emotion. Stopping people getting on the pitch, even just for a few seconds, is another example of football taking the magic away from a working-class sport.*

*When I think about special moments, moments that give me goosebumps, this game against Cambridge is definitely up there. The sheer euphoria of Clive Allen casually passing that ball into an empty net and the pure carnage that followed is something of absolute beauty. There was a lot of pressure on us that day and, apart from the groundsman, nobody went missing. What a feeling, to be part of the Premier League!*

**Football League First Division - 1992/93**

| 16 August | Barnsley | A | 1–0 | 6,798 | C Allen |
|---|---|---|---|---|---|
| 22 August | Charlton Athletic | H | 0–1 | 17,054 | |
| 29 August | Newcastle United | A | 0–2 | 29,855 | |
| 5 September | Watford | H | 2–1 | 11,921 | C Allen |
| 12 September | Peterborough U | A | 3–1 | 10,657 | C Allen, Keen, Morley |
| 15 September | Bristol City | A | 5–1 | 14,130 | C Allen (2), Robson, Morley (2) |
| 20 September | Derby County | H | 1–1 | 11,493 | Morley |
| 27 September | Portsmouth | A | 1–0 | 12,388 | C Allen |
| 4 October | Wolverhampton W | A | 0–0 | 14,391 | |
| 11 October | Sunderland | H | 6–0 | 10,326 | C Allen, Robson (2), Keen, Martin, Morley |
| 17 October | Bristol Rovers | A | 4–0 | 6,187 | C Allen, Dicks, Keen, Morley |
| 24 October | Swindon Town | H | 0–1 | 17,842 | |
| 31 October | Cambridge United | A | 1–2 | 7,214 | Morley |
| 3 November | Grimsby Town | A | 1–1 | 9,119 | Morley |
| 7 November | Notts County | H | 2–0 | 12,345 | C Allen, Morley |
| 15 November | Millwall | A | 1–2 | 12,445 | Robson |
| 21 November | Oxford United | H | 5–3 | 11,842 | Breacker, C Allen, Dicks (2), Morley |
| 28 November | Birmingham City | H | 3–1 | 15,004 | C Allen (2), Morley |
| 4 December | Tranmere Rovers | A | 2–5 | 11,782 | C Allen, Morley |
| 12 December | Southend United | H | 2–0 | 15,739 | C Allen, Morley |
| 20 December | Brentford | A | 0–0 | 11,912 | |
| 26 December | Charlton Athletic | A | 1–1 | 8,337 | Dicks |
| 28 December | Luton Town | H | 2–2 | 18,786 | Breacker, Dicks |
| 10 January | Derby County | A | 2–0 | 13,737 | Robson, Morley |
| 16 January | Portsmouth | H | 2–0 | 18,127 | Foster, Morley |
| 27 January | Bristol City | H | 2–0 | 12,118 | Robson, Morley |
| 30 January | Leicester City | A | 2–1 | 18,838 | Gale, Robson |
| 6 February | Barnsley | H | 1–1 | 14,101 | Jones |
| 9 February | Peterborough U | H | 2–1 | 12,537 | Butler, Jones |
| 13 February | Watford | A | 2–1 | 13,115 | Robson, Keen |
| 21 February | Newcastle United | H | 0–0 | 24,159 | |
| 27 February | Sunderland | A | 0–0 | 19,068 | |
| 6 March | Wolverhampton W | H | 3–1 | 24,679 | Dicks, Morley, Holmes |
| 9 March | Grimsby Town | H | 2–1 | 13,170 | Dicks (2) |
| 13 March | Notts County | A | 0–1 | 10,272 | |

| | | | | | |
|---|---|---|---|---|---|
| 20 March | Tranmere Rovers | H | 2–0 | 16,369 | Dicks (2) |
| 23 March | Oxford United | A | 0–1 | 9,506 | |
| 28 March | Millwall | H | 2–2 | 15,723 | Keen, Morley |
| 3 April | Birmingham City | A | 2–1 | 19,053 | Bishop, Brown |
| 7 April | Southend United | A | 0–1 | 12,813 | |
| 11 April | Leicester City | H | 3–0 | 13,951 | Keen, Speedie (2) |
| 13 April | Luton Town | A | 0–2 | 10,959 | |
| 17 April | Brentford | H | 4–0 | 16,522 | Butler, Keen, Morley, M Allen |
| 24 April | Bristol Rovers | H | 2–1 | 16,682 | Dicks, Speedie |
| 2 May | Swindon Town | A | 3–1 | 17,004 | Morley, C Allen, Brown |
| 8 May | Cambridge United | H | 2–0 | 27,399 | Speedie, C Allen |

### FA Cup

| | | | | | |
|---|---|---|---|---|---|
| 2 January R3 | WBA | A | 2–0 | 25,896 | C Allen, Robson |
| 24 January R4 | Barnsley | A | 1–4 | 13,716 | Morley |

### League Cup

| | | | | | |
|---|---|---|---|---|---|
| 23 Sept R2 1L | Crewe Alexandra | H | 0–0 | 6,981 | |
| 7 October R2 2 | Crewe Alexandra | A | 0–2 | 5,427 | |

| | P | W | D | L | GF | GA | GD | Pts |
|---|---|---|---|---|---|---|---|---|
| 1 Newcastle Utd | 46 | 29 | 9 | 8 | 92 | 38 | +54 | 96 |
| 2 West Ham Utd | 46 | 26 | 10 | 10 | 81 | 41 | +40 | 88 |
| 3 Portsmouth | 46 | 26 | 10 | 10 | 80 | 46 | +34 | 88 |
| 4 Tranmere Rovers | 46 | 23 | 10 | 13 | 72 | 56 | +16 | 79 |
| 5 Swindon Town | 46 | 21 | 13 | 12 | 74 | 59 | +15 | 76 |
| 6 Leicester City | 46 | 22 | 10 | 14 | 71 | 64 | +7 | 76 |
| 7 Millwall | 46 | 18 | 16 | 12 | 65 | 53 | +12 | 70 |
| 8 Derby County | 46 | 19 | 9 | 18 | 68 | 57 | +11 | 66 |
| 9 Grimsby Town | 46 | 19 | 7 | 20 | 58 | 57 | +1 | 64 |
| 10 Peterborough U | 46 | 16 | 14 | 16 | 55 | 63 | –8 | 62 |
| 11 Wolves | 46 | 16 | 13 | 17 | 57 | 56 | +1 | 61 |
| 12 Charlton Ath | 46 | 16 | 13 | 17 | 49 | 46 | +3 | 61 |
| 13 Barnsley | 46 | 17 | 9 | 20 | 56 | 60 | –4 | 60 |
| 14 Oxford Utd | 46 | 14 | 14 | 18 | 53 | 56 | –3 | 56 |
| 15 Bristol City | 40 | 14 | 14 | 18 | 49 | 67 | –18 | 56 |
| 16 Watford | 46 | 14 | 13 | 19 | 57 | 71 | –14 | 55 |
| 17 Notts County | 46 | 12 | 16 | 18 | 55 | 70 | –15 | 52 |
| 18 Southend Utd | 46 | 13 | 13 | 20 | 54 | 64 | –10 | 52 |
| 19 Birmingham C | 46 | 13 | 12 | 21 | 50 | 72 | –22 | 51 |
| 20 Luton Town | 46 | 10 | 21 | 15 | 48 | 62 | –14 | 51 |
| 21 Sunderland | 46 | 13 | 11 | 22 | 50 | 64 | –14 | 50 |
| 22 Brentford | 46 | 13 | 10 | 23 | 52 | 71 | –19 | 49 |
| 23 Cambridge Utd | 46 | 11 | 16 | 19 | 48 | 69 | –21 | 49 |
| 24 Bristol Rovers | 46 | 10 | 11 | 25 | 55 | 87 | –32 | 41 |

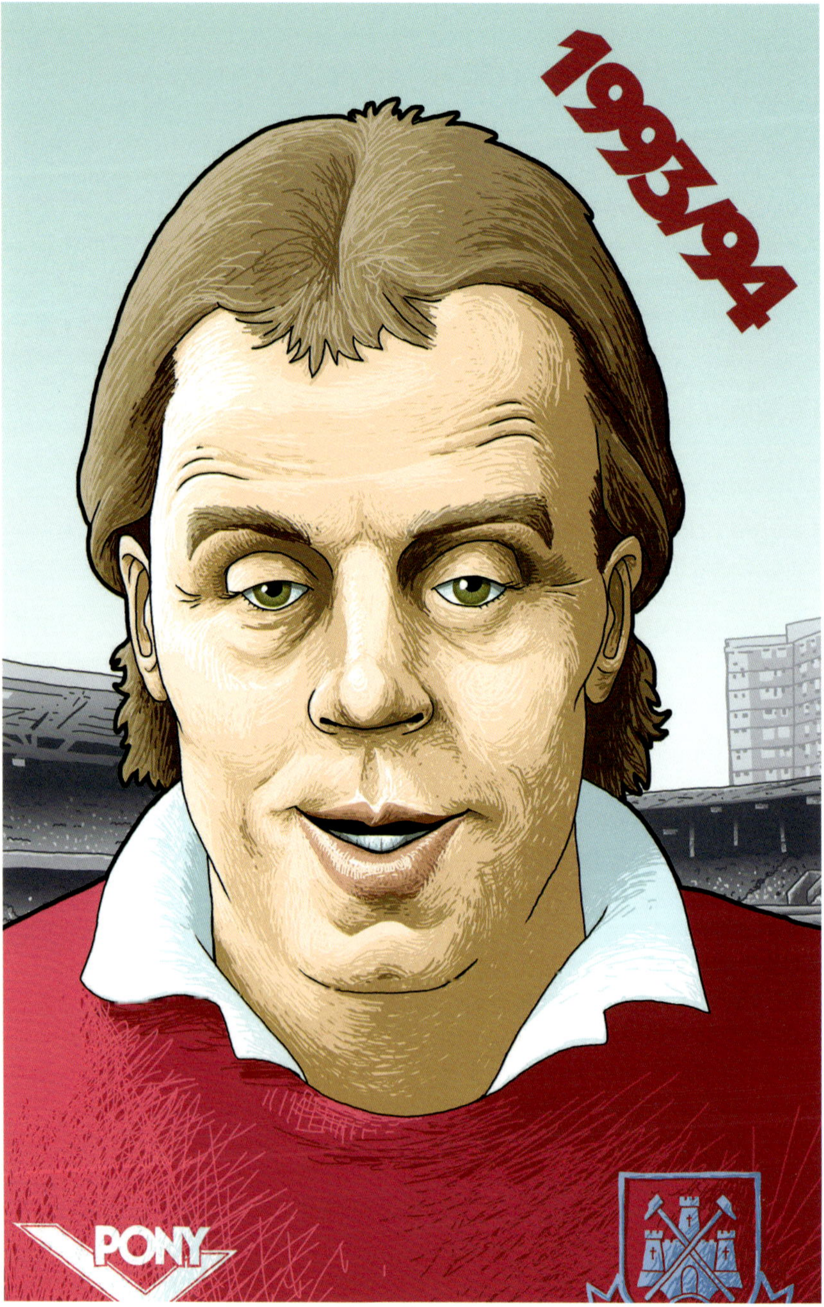
1993/94
PONY

## Be Lucky

That summer was party time in east London as West Ham set sail for the razzle-dazzle of the renamed FA Carling Premiership. After the disastrous transfer strategy of two years prior we hoped that the manager and the board had learned their lessons. We needed to spend more – and spend it wisely – if we were going to stay afloat. Extravagant spending was hardly in the West Ham DNA. Our board tried to save money by using both sides of the toilet paper. So, once again, Harry Redknapp's nous in the market was going to be crucial.

The assistant manager made a trademark move by going back to Bournemouth to recruit a familiar face in Keith Rowland, the Northern Irish left-back signing for a very reasonable £110,000 fee and offering some cover for Julian Dicks during his inevitable suspensions. Further defensive reinforcement came in the shape of Simon Webster, an impressive centre-half from Charlton who cost £500,000 and was considered the heir apparent to Alvin Martin.

We desperately needed cover in that position. Whilst reigning Hammer of the Year Steve Potts was our Mr Reliable, his defensive partners weren't so consistent. Tony Gale and Alvin were in their twilight years as professionals, and Colin Foster had missed almost the entirety of the previous season. The Big Fella had the acceleration of a double-decker bus before the injury, so it was hard to imagine how ten months on the treatment table would have improved his mobility.

Whilst both of the above seemed like sensible business, there were some shocks further forward. Kevin Keen and Mark Robson, two of the promotion season's star performers, were both on their way out of Upton Park. Keen was on his way to Wolves for what seemed like a cut-price £600,000 fee, and three games into the season Mark Robson joined Charlton for a rather paltry £125,000, given he had such a spectacular debut season in Claret and Blue.

Their combined fees would raise the funds required for our biggest outlay: Dale Gordon. 'Disco Dale', whose Soul Glo hair and moustache combination looked like he walked straight off the set of Miami Vice, had tormented West Ham full-backs for years while playing for Norwich. He'd since done two solid years at Rangers and was ready to come back to sunny England. But the £750,000 transfer fee seemed a little hefty, given our overall budget.

Spending the bulk of our money on a winger seemed like a bizarre strategy. The flanks had been our strongest area in the previous campaign. The goals from Keen and Robson had been crucial to our promotion bid. Meanwhile, up front, our resources were looking a little... sparse. Trevor Morley deserved another crack at this level, but Clive Allen's three-month absence at the end of the previous campaign seemed to have taken its toll. In pre-season he looked like he'd lose a bleep test with Miss Marple. Meanwhile, Stevie Jones was surely way too raw a prospect to be a regular starter. It all felt like something of a gamble.

And it didn't take long to realise that our luck was well and truly out. Simon Webster was given a traditional West Ham United welcome by Julian Dicks in training, breaking his leg with a firm but fair tackle that just went horribly wrong. The word coming out of Chadwell Heath was that it was very serious indeed. The question was not just whether we'd see Webster in Claret and Blue this season, rather whether we'd see him at all.

Things didn't improve when the season proper started in August. A home fixture to Wimbledon was a tricky start to life at the top level, but by no means an insurmountable one. Yet somehow our starting eleven made the master shithouses look like Melchester Rovers.

We conceded two awful, awful goals – including one where John Fashanu, 6'2" centre-forward and host of ITV Saturday-night telly sensation *Gladiators* – made himself invisible to our entire back four. For the second goal, Ludek Miklosko tried the sort of amateurish punch you would routinely see outside kebab shops in Romford at 2am. Only Ludo couldn't use the excuse that he was ten pints deep and clasping a doner with chilli sauce in his other hand.

Things didn't improve in a 1-0 loss to Leeds, where our deficiencies up front meant that the Premiership was treated to the sight of Big Colin Foster roped into duty as an emergency striker – much to the derision of the terraces – partnering Morley up front. And despite Clive Allen showing glimpses of the old magic in a 2-0 win over Sheffield Wednesday, we got stuffed 4-0 at home to QPR then conceded three at Old Trafford. We had a golden chance to pick up a win at home to Premiership whipping boys Swindon, who had conceded SEVENTEEN goals in their first six fixtures, but laboured to a 0-0 draw.

Five points from seven League games, a star signing ruled out for the season and Big Colin Foster playing as centre-forward. You didn't need the shrewd investigative instincts of Hercule Poirot to sense that our survival chances were already circling the khazi.

Something drastic had to change. And had to change quickly.

**EX:** *The sale of Robson and Keen was a real shock. The Robson fee seemed pitifully low. I couldn't understand it. They were two stars of our promotion campaign and then we flog them both for one winger – Dale Gordon, the Stepover King – which didn't seem like great business. Although Dale does hold the pub quiz answer of being our first-ever Premier League scorer by netting at Coventry. Sadly, it wasn't long before injury ruled him out for the season, like Simon Webster. Just our luck.*

**DAVE:** *As expected, the bookies had us as favourites to go down, and I could hardly blame them. I was mildly excited by Disco Dale's arrival, but at the expense of Kevin Keen and then Mark Robson? I wasn't convinced. Joining Keith Rowland from Bournemouth was Paul Mitchell and, let's be honest, Phil Mitchell would have been more useful! Then of course there was the tragic case of Simon Webster, who ironically became a physio at West Ham years later. That was half a million quid down the khazi. It wasn't looking good, and after a predictably poor start to the season, I started to feel that our time in the top division would be short-lived.*

## Triple Whammy

Under pressure to restructure the team and turn around a poor start to the season, Harry Redknapp went into overdrive. Realistically, there was only one man in the squad who could command any kind of price tag. He was our captain. He was our best player. And he was also a gigantic pain in the arse.

Julian Dicks was nothing if not consistent. He was as uncontrollable off the field as he was on it. A notoriously bad trainer, whose idea of cardio was jogging to the vending machine for Coke and a Mars Bar, his frequent arguments with the management team had become part and parcel of life at Chadwell Heath. And, as brilliant a player as he was, Bonds and Redknapp had grown tired of the daily grind. The awful incident with Simon Webster had affected Dicks badly, no stranger to serious injuries himself. Maybe a change of scenery was needed for all involved. The problem was finding someone to pay a decent wedge for a man whose knees were fast running out of cartilage, had an appalling disciplinary record and a temper that made the Incredible Hulk look like Bambi.

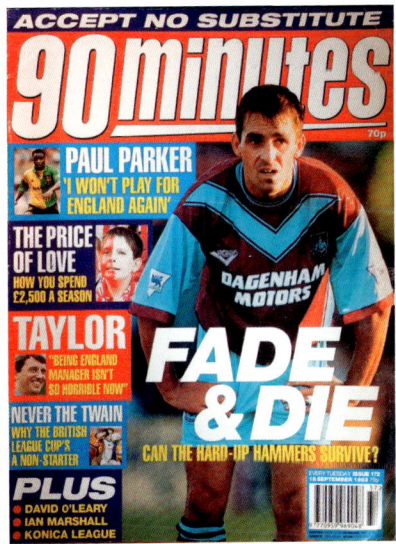

Then along came Graeme Souness. The fiery Liverpool boss looked at Julian and saw a man he wanted to build his new-look dressing room around. On a purely football basis, it seemed a logical move. At his best, Julian was one of the best full-backs in the country. However, given Dicks' track record with previous managers and Souness's recent heart attack, it was perhaps not the best news for the Scotsman's cardiologist.

Then again, this was the man who years later would accept a random phone call from "George Weah's cousin" and allow Ali Dia, a man with the close control of Godzilla, to play 53 minutes of Premier League football. So perhaps we shouldn't have been surprised.

A key part of the deal was that it had to involve player exchange plus cash. David Burrows, a tough-tackling left-back, would slot into the void Julian left behind. 'Bugsy' was the sort of serviceable pro I'd admired from a distance. Much like Tim Breacker, he seemed reliable and consistent at this level, traits that usually meant he would never play for West Ham United.

Skilful midfielder Mike Marsh would join him on the train down to London Euston. I'd seen Marsh play frequently the previous season, though rarely in the same position – which was by no means an exception at Anfield. Graeme Souness's impact at Liverpool had been to sell all the good players, replace them with crap ones, then invariably play them in the wrong position. He seemed to pick the Liverpool starting eleven using a dartboard. *Double top... that's Michael Thomas. Treble 16... and he'll play left midfield. Bullseye... replacing England international and former Player of the Year John Barnes.*

Marsh, a local lad from Kirby, suffered more than most. He seemed a tidy little footballer every time I watched him. But when you're playing right-back one week, centre midfield the next, then sitting on the bench collecting splinters on your bum cheeks, it's hard to build up any kind of identity.

The extra money included in the deal helped bring in some much-needed resource up front. There would be no more Colin Foster. If we were going to have a big lump, we might as well have one that knew what they were doing. Enter a familiar face in the shape of veteran striker Lee Chapman.

The target man had been one of the country's most prolific strikers during the late '80s and early '90s. Indeed, I'd circled his name in my 1988 *Shoot! Annual* as a player I would like to see partner Tony Cottee in the absence of Frank McAvennie. That annual partnered me everywhere: the school playground, the dreaded Saturday-morning shopping trips to Sainsbury's, or car journeys to see friends and family. All occasions were utilised for potential scouting activity, where I weighed out the pros and cons of the likes of Mick Harford, Kerry Dixon, Mark Hateley and Les Ferdinand wearing Claret and Blue.

It was only later in life that I realised the futility of this wonderfully naïve exercise. Given West Ham's meagre budget and prospects, me circling such stellar names was the equivalent of Adrian Mole underlining Samantha Fox's name on Page 3 as a future romantic conquest. At least the hormone-fuelled teenager would get some pleasure out of the exercise. That newspaper probably looked like a painter's radio within minutes. Whereas I would spend weeks pondering signings and scenarios that were utterly implausible from the outset.

Ultimately, Chapman made a move across the Pennines, and it was his sensational form that took Leeds United to First Division champions in 1991/92. He was unstoppable that year, notching 16 goals as the Elland Road outfit pipped Alex Ferguson's men to the title.

But two years can be a long time in football. And the Lee Chapman West Ham signed from Portsmouth for £250,000 in September 1993 was not quite the Lee Chapman of old. After 15 seasons as a pro, time had caught up with him (mind you, most things did) and his body was creaking towards the finish line of a highly respectable career.

Thankfully, Big Lee hadn't been signed to run. He was here to make a nuisance of himself and get his head on anything that came into the mixer. To his credit he, alongside Burrows and Marsh, made an immediate impact.

**EX:** *I was absolutely shocked by this deal. It's strange to look back and remember what it was like when transfers like this could happen out of the blue. There was no social media, no 24-hour sports channels. I just didn't see it coming. After all, Julian was more than just our club captain – he was a West Ham icon. Thankfully, after Stuart Slater's departure, I was a bit more resilient about seeing my heroes go elsewhere. But it still hurt.*

**DAVE:** *I was absolutely devastated when we sold Julian. Devastated. Not only had we lost our top man, but we'd swapped him for two players that I didn't really know? Then when Lee Chapman was signed, it added little consolation because I thought he was too old to play in the Premier League, especially as he initially rejected us to go and play for Portsmouth in the division below. I remember when the three of them were interviewed at Chadwell Heath. Lee and David looked like schoolteachers that had taken little Mike to the headmaster's office for a bollocking! I honestly thought that bit of business was going to take us down.*

**EX:** *I wasn't as down on the deal as Dave was. David Burrows was an established Liverpool player – so he had some pedigree. Also, I took comfort from our decent record on swap deals. The exchange we did with Man City (Mark Ward for Ian Bishop and Trevor Morley) had been great business. Lee Chapman may have been past his best, but he was still a proven goalscorer and a title winner. It was a cleverly constructed deal. Julian had probably gotten too big for us anyway. He would have moved on eventually. Now we had a chance to reset the team, and our season.*

## Happy Chappy

After our shocking start to the season, expectations for the trip to Ewood Park would typically have been lower than a snake's belly. However, the influx of new signings had given the club some much-needed optimism, and all three went into the starting line-up for the game at Blackburn.

What happened next should really be part of West Ham folklore. Given the abundance of awful, awful players we've had during our chequered history in the transfer market, a day when no less than THREE new signings all made their debuts – and all made significant contributions to a West Ham win – should be a milestone celebrated by Hammers fans across the globe.

Blackburn had 14 points from seven games, and in Shearer, Newell, Wilcox and Ripley possessed one of the most potent forward lines in the division. The previous week they'd won at Anfield, so were perfectly within their rights to expect to steamroll us and continue their title aspirations. It took 33 minutes for Lee Chapman to make his mark, seizing on a mistake by Henning Berg to put us in front. That goal spurred the hosts into life and it was only the brilliance of Ludo that kept them at bay, before we scored with the ultimate sucker punch in the second half. Keith Rowland put in cross with his right foot, which most of us thought had been made redundant judging by his performances so far, and Trevor Morley stooped to send a diving header into the net. The away end exploded at the final whistle, whilst in the dugout Billy Bonds and Harry Redknapp congratulated each other on a job well done.

Meanwhile, Julian Dicks' debut for Liverpool hadn't gone according to plan. His new club had been trounced 2-0 in the Merseyside derby, where two former Hammers – Mark Ward and Tony Cottee – scored the crucial goals. It's a funny old game sometimes.

Four days after the elation at Ewood Park, Chapman notched twice in a 5-1 thrashing of Chesterfield in the League Cup. In the space of a week, our season had turned a crucial corner.

**DAVE:** *The result at Ewood is typical of how ridiculously unpredictable West Ham are. The one team that'll always kill an accumulator, and no doubt we murdered a few that day. It was a massive win, and psychologically that would have been so important, especially for the new signings. I remember that game for Chappy's overly neurotic finish into an empty net from two yards out! He was then unplayable against Chesterfield and chants of "There's only one Lee Chapman" started to make me think I was wrong about him. With Bugsy scoring a peach of a free-kick in the same game, I was feeling dangerously optimistic about the season ahead.*

*EX:* It was a great start, to get a win at Blackburn. They were one of the Premier League's glamour sides, propped up by Jack Walker's millions. They were the team you wanted to be on Championship Manager as they started the game with loads of money. The fact that we outplayed them and our new strike partnership gelled instantly was the perfect way to get fans to accept the deal. Obviously, some were worried, anxious or just plain angry about losing Julian. But when you look back in history at some of the most significant West Ham transfers, this was one of them.

## Hammers Riding High

The new-look West Ham United were on a roll, and the three new faces were at the heart of our reversal of fortune. Burrows was proving a more than adequate replacement for Julian, immediately endearing himself to the Chicken Run with some crunching tackles.

Meanwhile, Marsh was proving something of a revelation in midfield. A quick, incisive passer of the ball, he was building a nice partnership with Ian Bishop that gave us more quality in possession than we'd had before.

Up front, Chapman's physical presence had given us a totally different dimension. The veteran striker scored on successive *Monday Night Football* outings as we stuck three past Manchester City at home (where Burrows scored a thumping free-kick right out of the Julian Dicks playbook), then went to The Dell and won 2-0 in our most accomplished away performance of the season. Trevor Morley was also on the scoresheet that night, and he seemed to be enjoying playing alongside his experienced strike partner. Chapman was happy to do more of the donkey work, winning flick-ons and holding the ball up, whereas the indefatigable Morley could hustle and bustle the opposition back four looking for openings. It wasn't the quickest Premiership front line, but it was effective.

If there was one game that summed up Chapman's contribution it was an away fixture at Wimbledon. Traditionally, we looked forward to a trip to Selhurst Park with the same sort of relish Rapunzel had for visiting her hairdresser. The Big Fella was brilliant. He bullied the Dons' defence, scoring one bullet header and adding a second with a clinical finish to seal a 2-1 win. It was an incredible turnaround from that dreadful first game. We were a completely different team, a comfortable mid-table side that wasn't looking nervously over our shoulders.

Chapman had scored seven in 14 games for his new club which, considering he was on the brink of collecting his pension, was quite the achievement. He was defying Old Father Time, a risky strategy in a football context. Sooner or later, Nature's going to decide you've had your fun – then kick you square in the knackers. And that's exactly what happened.

**EX:** *For the first time since I had been going to Upton Park, we were a consistent top-tier side. It was refreshing to be able to turn on Sky and see West Ham in mid table, instead of stuck in the bottom three. It meant I could join in with football conversations at school without people taking the piss out of our results. We were officially a decent Premier League team. Players like Tim Breacker and Steve Potts were solid at the back. Ian Bishop, Martin Allen and Mike Marsh were a nice mix in midfield. And up front, Lee Chapman and Trevor Morley were looking like a really decent partnership. It was such a good time to be a fan.*

**DAVE:** *This was a really good period for West Ham, and I was especially pleased with the win against Wimbledon because when they beat us on the opening day at Upton Park, their chairman Sam Hammam defaced our changing room with some graffiti after the game. I have since fantasised that Terry Brown scribbled 'Sam Hammam is a bellend' in response at Selhurst Park, but given the fact that the stadium was owned by Crystal Palace, that might have been counter-productive!*

*It was a definitely a period that belonged to Lee Chapman. A goal ratio of one in every two was England form. There was no stopping the old boy... or was there?*

### Fall from Grace

We only won two out of our next ten League games, including a 5-0 walloping at Hillsborough that has become forever known in the blue half of Sheffield as 'The Waddle Game'. The former England winger had the game of his dreams, a game that probably still gives David Burrows nightmares to this very day. Waddle tormented us from the first minute, turning Bugsy inside and out like a reversible cagoule. He created countless opportunities, and we folded in the face of one of the finest individual performances in Premier League history. What made it all the more extraordinary was that Waddle had just turned 33.

In contrast, starved of any kind of meaningful service, Lee Chapman had a wretched outing. And that was the problem, his value to the team was entirely dependent on everybody else. He could barely break into a trot, so if the ball didn't come directly to his feet or his head, then he was a liability. it was essentially like playing with a lamppost up front. And the problem with lampposts is that they stick out on the horizon. So when results started to dip, some disgruntled punters picked out the biggest target in front of them.

From being up to the giddy heights of ninth place after beating Coventry in early December, we slid down to 14th in February, which would have been cause for celebration at the start of the season. There were some chastening defeats, including a 3-1 loss to Spurs at home where we were bossed by Micky Hazard, and the same scoreline at Villa where Dalian Atkinson ran us ragged.

Meanwhile, Chapman's form worsened, though he was by no means alone in that regard. On a chaotic *Monday Night Football* at Upton Park, Ludek Miklosko put in the worst performance on camera since Dick Van Dyke's British accent in *Chitty Chitty Bang Bang*. We salvaged a 3-3 draw only thanks to an equaliser from sub Trevor Morley, who'd been dropped for his own poor form, and Chapman was booed as he trudged off the pitch after another fruitless night's work.

Even when Chapman did score, it didn't offer much reprieve. After 118 dire minutes of an FA Cup fourth-round replay at home to Notts County, when he'd received some very loud and obvious catcalls from the crowd, he nodded in a late winner. Afterwards he said that the booing "doesn't help me or the team. It doesn't do the team any good if they're singling one person out."

Luckily for Chapman, late February meant the visit of Manchester United – and the crowd had another target in mind.

**FX:** *This was an amazing fall from grace. Chapman went from scoring every week to nothing at all. I remember the fans getting on his back because he didn't run and work hard – essential ingredients to appease the Chicken Run – which he simply wasn't capable of. His legs had gone. The abuse he got was so bad that I remember* Shoot! *had a poster of West Ham fans abusing Chapman. You'd often see images of fans abusing the opposition, but to have one of supporters giving their own player stick was something else. He must have dreaded playing for us by the end.*

**DAVE:** *'The Waddle Game' was an absolute pisstake. Sometimes I go out the front and have a kick about with my seven-year-old neighbours and, before you know it, I get carried away and go 14-0 up in five minutes! We were like seven-year-olds against Chris that day. He was good but, f\*\*k me, we were awful. That game was in December and, apart from a win against Everton, we didn't win a Premier League game until April. It was a horrendous run of form and, when the chips are down, the very least the fans want to see is 110% effort from the players. But being 73 at the time, Chappy couldn't give us that energy – so he became the whipping boy.*

### Ince's Warm Welcome

It had been four-and-a-half years since Paul Ince posed in a Manchester United shirt. A decision up there with Gerry Francis's loyalty to his perma-mullet as one of the worst in football history. Now Ince was finally making his return to what was once his spiritual home – and Upton Park was ready.

It had been a testing start to the day for my dad and me. After waiting an hour on hold to the ticket hotline weeks before, then forking out 52 quid for two seats in the West Stand, our tickets for the game never materialised. It was sometimes the way with the old ticket office. Calling them up was like opening a bag of Revels. You might get Manchester United at home, you might get Norwich away, or you might get stubs for the matinee showing of *Ace Ventura*.

Anyway, after being issued with replacements – literally two scraps of paper with 'OFFICIAL TICKETS' scrawled hastily across them in biro – we'd found our way to our spot just before kick-off, had an argument with a couple who had the same seats as us (the office had kindly made amends for not posting our tickets by sending them to someone else instead) then somehow found two spare places to watch the game.

The ground was a bearpit. All corners greeted Ince's every touch with a cacophony of boos and booming cries of "JUDAS." That seemed a little harsh. Judas Escariot was a lot of things, but at least he wasn't f\*\*king stupid enough to bowl up to the Last Supper dressed as a Roman centurion.

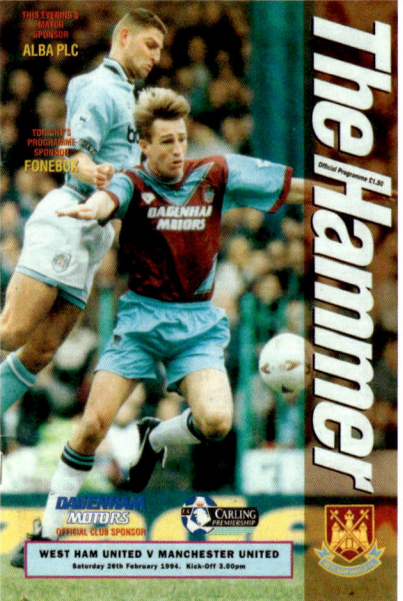

United needed to silence the crowd early, and when Mark Hughes put them in front after fine work from a young Roy Keane, the hostility cooled a little. The travelling fans were in full voice and, in the row behind me, a fan focused his ire on a familiar target.

"Chapman! Chaaaaap-maaaaaan! How about running for once, Chapman!"

Even though we were holding our own in the game, still it continued.

"Chapman! Oi, Chapman you useless bastard! Do something will ya?"

Midway through the second half, the ball went wide to Matty Holmes. His cross was overhit but Chapman harried the United defence enough for a split-second mistake. For the first time in a while, his luck was in. The ball dropped on to his left peg and he lifted it over Schmeichel.

"That's more like it, Chapman! Why can't you do that every week?"

Suddenly the Big Fella had a new lease of life. Chasing down a backpass, he forced the Danish keeper into a hurried clearance which went to Holmes again.

Another cross found Morley this time, and we were suddenly 2-1 up.

As the clock ticked down and the volume rose, the Upton Park masses were set to celebrate the sweetest of comeback victories. There were only seconds remaining. And that was enough for us to throw away three welcome points in the most West Ham way ever.

Ludo couldn't get enough purchase on Denis Irwin's low cross into the box, diverting it into the path of Ince to bundle home the equaliser. He'd had the last laugh in the most dramatic of circumstances. You couldn't begrudge him his frantic celebration in front of the away end. He'd taken more stick than King Herod at Mothercare's Christmas party. Most players would have crumbled under that sort of abuse, but Ince stood tall. In a big moment, the lad who had blossomed under John Lyall's tutelage proved that he was every bit the player his beloved mentor hoped he would be. Even the most vocal of his detractors couldn't disagree with that.

Wearing that shirt was still a f\*\*king stupid idea, mind.

**DAVE:** *I have never seen hatred like what we saw that day at Upton Park. It was ferocious, a proper hostile atmosphere. You'd think Rolf Harris had been invited to paint at one of the local schools! Looking back, it was over the top, really. In fairness, he wasn't just disrespectful to West Ham when he left, but he had this air of arrogance about him that was very antagonistic, calling himself 'The Guv'nor', and I think that played a part in the reception.*

**EX:** *The abuse where I was sat was absolutely horrific. Our seats were around lots of old men of a certain generation. There was a guy throwing banana skins and making weird noises. I remember asking my dad, "What is that all about?" and then being shocked by the answer. It made no sense. We had black players in our team – how would they feel, seeing stuff like that?*

*I remember hearing that Fergie had deliberately not played Ince in previous fixtures between the two clubs because he was wary of the hostility. That shows his man-management skills. Still, I think this was far worse than even he could have imagined. Nonetheless, there are certain games as a West Ham fan where you feel the script has been written. Ince scoring in the last minute was bound to happen in the pre-determined story of this football club.*

## Cup Chaos at Kenilworth Road

The morale-boosting performance against United didn't give us the bounce we might have hoped for. A dire draw at Swindon and then three successive defeats meant we were sliding down the table alarmingly.

The FA Cup offered a welcome distraction. We'd followed up the laboured win over Notts County with a nervy win at non-League Kidderminster; the much-maligned Lee Chapman again scoring the only goal in a game where plenty of pundits were predicting an upset.

It left us with a generous quarter-final tie at home to First Division Luton. The Hatters were enduring a miserable season in the second tier, and given we seemed to have just about overcome our innate ability to make lower-league opposition look like the 1966 World Cup winners, there was some buzz building that this might be our year.

Evidently, no one had told the players. The team failed to sparkle under the bright lights of the Sky TV cameras. A 0-0 draw meant a replay at Kenilworth Road, again live on the telly. And as kick-off approached, I was overcome by a deep sense of foreboding.

By this time, Luton Town ranked alongside Oldham as the two sides that stirred most hatred in my otherwise placid heart. Fast approaching my 16th birthday, I had moved on from the naïvety of my youth. The *Shoot!* annuals were packed away in the loft. I had migrated from *Match* magazine to *90 Minutes* in search of more learned football literature. However, some scars lingered from my tender years. The Valentine's Day Massacre at Boundary Park still hurts to this very day, and it was another League Cup semi-final that ignited my dislike of Luton. In 1988/89, John Lyall's final season, there was very little to savour. Poor David Kelly's feet were like feather dusters, Alan Devonshire's knees were as structurally sound as a packet of Quavers, and Allen McKnight had the ashen-faced look of a man who'd just received a dinner invitation from Hannibal Lecter.

We had slid meekly towards relegation, but in the Littlewoods Cup we looked a different team altogether, sailing through to the semis with a series of impressive wins, including a famous 4-1 thrashing of champions Liverpool where Paul Ince scored twice. The run culminated in a semi-final draw with the Hatters, or as I preferred to call them: "The Cheats."

I was referring, of course, to the plastic pitch at Kenilworth Road which, like Oldham, in my eyes had unfairly improved Luton's league position for many years. In the late '80s, I'd seen enough highlights on *Saint & Greavsie* to know that the football played on plastic was not the same as the football played elsewhere. Week after week, the best players in the land would look like clowns as they stumbled around like deckhands on the *Titanic*, trying desperately to retain their balance while chaos unfolded around them. Our players were capable enough of doing this on grass, they didn't need the added incentive of an artificial surface.

Anyway, that particular League Cup semi-final was an unmitigated disaster. We got stuffed, live on telly, 3-0 in the home leg, lost 2-0 away, and I was the butt of many a joke in the school corridors as my knock-off West Ham PE bag took a kicking in-between classes.

Now with the plastic pitch long gone and Luton returned to their rightful position of relegation fodder in the First Division (though I secretly hoped they'd plummet all the way to the Beazer Homes League), the FA Cup draw felt like the chance for revenge. After all, we were a different team these days. The only surviving members of our eleven from that day were Alvin Martin and Steve Potts. And whilst Alvin's advancing years meant he had the flexibility of Robocop, 'Pottsy' was our most consistent and reliable performer.

At least he had been. Until one awful moment under the lights when the Ghost of the Plastic Pitch came back to haunt us.

The scores were locked at 2-2 in a game that we're legally obliged to call 'highly entertaining for the neutral', but a real colon-cleanser if you support either side. We'd taken the lead through Martin Allen; livewire Luton striker Scott Oakes scored twice to put the home side ahead, before a smart finish from Ian Bishop restored parity. We were in the ascendancy and pushing for a winner when Lady Luck, who we hadn't seen since pre-season when she all but ended Simon Webster's football career, reared her ugly head again.

A panicked Luton clearance sent the ball steepling high into the Bedfordshire skyline. It was the sort of vertical ball that no one wants to control. As it slowly re-entered Earth's atmosphere, precisely three things went wrong that would doom our FA Cup dreams for another season.

Firstly, Steve Potts – the ever-reliable Steve Potts – made his first mistake of the decade. As the Mitre Delta hurtled back to *terra firma*, it was Potts who had the unenviable task of bringing it to a halt. As he did so, the ball squirmed under his studs and away from his immediate vicinity.

Secondly, what none of us realised when Luton finally did rip up their plastic monstrosity was that they would replace it with patches of soil presumably airlifted from Arthur Fowler's allotment. The exact area of the pitch where Potts was located looked like Monty Don had been digging around with his shovel planting his tulip bulbs. Predicting the path of the ball was almost impossible. Unfortunately for us, it fell beautifully into the path of the onrushing Oakes.

Thirdly, as the Luton forward latched onto the ball on the halfway line and raced towards goal, the only covering defender was Alvin, who at this stage of his career would have struggled to keep pace with Oakes unless he thumbed a lift off Nigel Mansell.

Oakes ran through, scored his hat-trick goal and we were out of the Cup again at the hands of lower-league opposition.

F**king Luton.

**DAVE:** *When I think of the most heart-wrenching games I have seen as a West Ham fan, this is definitely right up there. For a quarter-final, Luton was a decent draw for us, and I think some of us were even looking forward to Wembley. Despite wasting the opportunity at home, I was still confident we would get the job done in the replay. Then it happened. The moment that probably still haunts Pottsy to this day. Who better for that ball to fall to than 'Mr Reliable'? The irony.*

**EX:** *If you haven't been to Luton before, it's a surreal experience as an away fan. You walk underneath someone's bedroom and along a raised path along the back of the away stand, you can actually peer into people's houses. It's absolutely surreal. Then the stadium, and I use that term loosely, itself is utterly bizarre. One side is all corporate boxes. It's one of my most hated grounds. So losing there absolutely crushed me. If we'd won, we would have gone on to play Chelsea in the semi-final, which would have been a great occasion.*

**DAVE:** *As if that night wasn't embarrassing enough, the hat-trick hero for Luton was actually more famous for the fact that his dad was in the band Showaddywaddy. What a nightmare.*

**EX:** *All the newspaper headlines next day were about Scott Oakes and Showaddywaddy. It was comical. It was crap. It was so typical West Ham.*

### The Resurrection

Eight points from ten games since the turn of the year had sent us into freefall. With the FA Cup down the khazi, and relegation now a possibility, two games over the Easter weekend – against Ipswich and Spurs – were critical to our chances of resurrecting our season.

Billy Bonds decided to make changes. Clive Allen took his walking stick and made his way to Millwall. Meanwhile, Mitchell Thomas made his loan move to Luton permanent.

In the first eleven, Billy decided it was time to end the pain and suffering of Lee Chapman. The goal against United hadn't quite rejuvenated his career as we might have hoped. In fact, it was to be his last in Claret and Blue. Much like Allen, Old Father Time had tapped him on the shoulder and said "Enough's enough, lad. You've done your bit. Put your feet up."

In his place came Matthew Rush. I'd read about the youngster frequently in *Hammers News* and matchday programmes, where he was touted as something of a prospect. The youngster made an instant impact, hitting a 30-yard volley at home to Ipswich as we got a much-needed 2-1 win. In previous years, this would have been enough to convince me we had the future of English football playing in Claret and Blue. However, I was still bruised by the memory of Mike Small, who flew through the first half of that infamous '91/92 season like Superman, and then spent the second half looking like he was playing in wellies made of Kryptonite.

With three points in our pockets, and a little breathing space from the basement battle, we travelled to White Hart Lane for what would become unquestionably the greatest moment of the season. We hadn't won in this part of north London for eleven long years. And in that time we'd taken some proper hidings – the most recent a 3-0 thrashing where Gary Lineker scored a hat-trick. Two years on and a lot had changed.

Mainly, we were no longer cannon fodder for the rest of the League. The rebuild under Billy and Harry had turned us from a perennial yo-yo club into a side that could at least hold its own in the top flight.

Meanwhile, Spurs had lost the mighty Lineker and replaced him with Ronny Rosenthal, which was the football equivalent of trading in your Ferrari for Thomas the Tank Engine. The former Liverpool striker hadn't lived down that absolutely criminal open-goal miss at Villa Park in the inaugural Premier League season. Some things stain your reputation forever, no matter how hard you try. For instance, I'm sure if you asked Sweeney Todd to this day, he'd still tell you he could give you one hell of a short back and sides.

Anyway, when the whistle blew at Spurs on that sunny Easter Monday afternoon, few could have imagined what would follow. Namely that West Ham United would rise again after an inglorious eleven-year absence and haunt our most storied rivals. Those packed in the away end smelt an upset when Steve Jones scored possibly The Most Steve Jones Goal Ever. 'The Billericay Bombshell' was never the most gifted technically, but always had a good eye for goal. Running on to a through ball from Ian Bishop, Jones took a terrible first touch that sent him halfway to Seven Sisters, before uncorking a 20-yard curler into the bottom corner. From then on, we were all over them.

For fans of a certain vintage, the 4-0 away win at Stamford Bridge was the peak of John Lyall's Boys of '86. Similarly, whenever people think of Billy Bonds, they'll always remember the day we went to White Hart Lane and gave Tottenham

Hotspur an object lesson in the art of association football.

Trevor Morley put us 2-0 up from the spot, and despite sub Teddy Sheringham giving Spurs a lifeline, Morley slotted in beautifully to restore our deserved two-goal cushion. By this time, the home crowd had started to drift towards the exits, anxious to escape the embarrassment unfolding before their eyes. Yet worse was still to come. Ian Bishop, who had been effortlessly stroking passes all over the pitch like he was enjoying a Cuban cigar and a cognac, had one more moment of mastery up his sleeve. His flighted through ball found Matt Holmes in space on the left flank and the winger flashed a cross into the six-yard box where Mike Marsh, the understated and underrated Mike Marsh, volleyed home a sensational fourth.

After that result, the rest of the season should really have become an afterthought. We were no longer troubled by relegation and on our way to a highly creditable 13th position. The players would have been forgiven for putting on their flip-flops and telling tall tales of that win over Spurs alongside a few *cervezas*. Yet, incredibly, there was more to come.

Our last League visit to Arsenal had been Mike Small's finest hour under the lights at Highbury before the gloom of the Bond Scheme set in. This time the ground baked in end-of-season sunshine and, after 78 snoozy minutes, Morley pounced on a poor Andy Linighan backpass to put us ahead. In the dying moments, Martin Allen put the home side out of sight with a 25-yard thunderbastard that ripped past Alan Miller.

Those games would glow in our hearts for the duration of the summer – a summer where England were absent from USA 94, a summer where names like Romario, Baggio and Bebeto were the talk of world football. But for me, it was a summer where I closed my eyes on balmy nights and saw Mike Marsh and Martin Allen lording it over our London rivals.

West Ham United were a legitimate Premier League team. Billy and Harry had proved to be the perfect partnership. There was so much to look forward to.

**DAVE:** *Some goals don't get spoken about as much as they should do and that* *absolute beauty from Matthew Rush against Ipswich is one of them. What a screamer! It was a goal that also contributed to a much-needed win, but understandably it's the game at Shite Hart Lane shortly after that brings an even bigger smile to my face. I was so pleased for Jonesy that day because he's a big West Ham fan and he will take that goal to the grave with him. It's made him a club legend. I certainly didn't expect us to go and score another three. It was euphoria. One of the best awayday wins in recent history.*

**EX:** *I remember listening to Capital Gold with Jonathan Pearce screaming his way through our 4-1 win at White Hart Lane. It felt absolutely glorious going into the school the next day, sticking it to my mates who were Tottenham fans. I didn't think it could get any better than that.*

**DAVE:** *It's amazing to think that we then went to Arsenal in the same month and got a win there as well. This was an unbelievable result, and one that really belongs to Mad Dog. The goal, the diving celebration and those limbs in the away end when that ball smashed into the top corner. F\*\*king beautiful. It brought closure to what was a really memorable season for me.*

**EX:** *I went to the game at Highbury with my mate and his dad who were massive Gooners, but had to in the home end. I sat on my hands when Allen scored. Mad Dog has since told us that his family members were in that corner of the stadium where he dived into the crowd. What a moment that must have been. I just remember walking out of the stadium and feeling smug in the car with my mate and his dad, trying not to rub their faces in it. What a goal. What a game. What a season.*

## FA Premier League - 1993/94

| | | | | | |
|---|---|---|---|---|---|
| 14 August | Wimbledon | H | 0–2 | 20,369 | |
| 17 August | Leeds United | A | 0–1 | 34,588 | |
| 21 August | Coventry City | A | 1–1 | 12,864 | Gordon |
| 25 August | Sheffield Wed | H | 2–0 | 19,441 | C Allen (2) |
| 28 August | QPR | H | 0–4 | 18,084 | |
| 1 September | Manchester United | A | 0–3 | 44,613 | |
| 11 September | Swindon Town | H | 0–0 | 15,777 | |
| 18 September | Blackburn Rovers | A | 2–0 | 14,437 | Morley, Chapman |
| 25 September | Newcastle United | A | 0–2 | 34,179 | |
| 2 October | Chelsea | H | 1–0 | 18,917 | Morley |
| 16 October | Aston Villa | H | 0–0 | 20,416 | |
| 23 October | Norwich City | A | 0–0 | 20,175 | |
| 1 November | Manchester City | H | 3–1 | 16,605 | Holmes, Chapman, Burrows |
| 6 November | Liverpool | A | 0–2 | 42,254 | |
| 20 November | Oldham Athletic | H | 2–0 | 17,211 | Martin, Morley |
| 24 November | Arsenal | H | 0–0 | 20,279 | |
| 29 November | Southampton | A | 2–0 | 13,258 | Chapman, Morley |
| 4 December | Wimbledon | A | 2–1 | 10,903 | Chapman (2) |
| 8 December | Leeds United | H | 0–1 | 20,468 | |
| 11 December | Coventry City | H | 3–2 | 17,243 | Butler, Morley (p), Breacker |
| 18 December | Sheffield Wed | A | 0–5 | 26,350 | |
| 27 December | Ipswich Town | A | 1–1 | 21,024 | Chapman |
| 28 December | Tottenham Hotspur | H | 1–3 | 20,787 | Holmes |
| 1 January | Everton | A | 1–0 | 19,602 | Breacker |
| 3 January | Sheffield United | H | 0–0 | 20,365 | |
| 15 January | Aston Villa | A | 1–3 | 28,869 | M Allen |
| 24 January | Norwich City | H | 3–3 | 20,738 | Morley, Sutton (og), Chapman |
| 12 February | Manchester City | A | 0–0 | 29,118 | |
| 26 February | Manchester United | H | 2–2 | 28,832 | Chapman, Morley |
| 5 March | Swindon Town | A | 1–1 | 15,929 | Morley |
| 19 March | Newcastle United | H | 2–4 | 23,132 | Breacker, Martin |
| 26 March | Chelsea | A | 0–2 | 19,545 | |
| 28 March | Sheffield United | A | 2–3 | 13,646 | Holmes, Bishop |
| 2 April | Ipswich Town | H | 2–1 | 18,307 | Morley, Rush |
| 4 April | Tottenham Hotspur | A | 4–1 | 31,502 | Morley (2, 1 p), Jones, Marsh |

| | | | | | |
|---|---|---|---|---|---|
| 9 April | Everton | H | 0–1 | 20,243 | |
| 16 April | Oldham Athletic | A | 2–1 | 11,669 | M Allen, Morley |
| 23 April | Liverpool | H | 1–2 | 26,106 | M Allen |
| 27 April | Blackburn Rovers | H | 1–2 | 22,186 | M Allen |
| 30 April | Arsenal | A | 2–0 | 33,700 | Morley, M Allen |
| 3 May | QPR | A | 0–0 | 10,850 | |
| 7 May | Southampton | H | 3–3 | 26,952 | Williamson, Monkou (og), M Allen |

## FA Cup

| | | | | | |
|---|---|---|---|---|---|
| 8 January R3 | Watford | H | 2–1 | 19,802 | M Allen, Marsh |
| 29 January R4 | Notts County | A | 1–1 | 14,952 | Jones |
| 9 February R4R | Notts County | H | 1–0 | 23,373 | Chapman |
| 19 February R5 | Kidderminster | H | 1–0 | 8,000 | Chapman |
| 14 March QF | Luton Town | H | 0–0 | 27,331 | |
| 23 March QFR | Luton Town | A | 2–3 | 13,166 | M Allen, Bishop |

## League Cup

| | | | | | |
|---|---|---|---|---|---|
| 22 Sept R2 1L | Chesterfield | H | 5–1 | 12,823 | Chapman (2), Morley (2, 1 p), Burrows |
| 5 October R2 2L | Chesterfield | A | 2–0 | 4,890 | Boere, M Allen |
| 27 October R3 | Nottingham Forest | A | 1–2 | 17,857 | Morley |

| | P | W | D | L | GF | GA | GD | Pts |
|---|---|---|---|---|---|---|---|---|
| 1 Manchester Utd | 42 | 27 | 11 | 4 | 80 | 38 | +42 | 92 |
| 2 Blackburn Rov | 42 | 25 | 9 | 8 | 63 | 36 | +27 | 84 |
| 3 Newcastle Utd | 42 | 23 | 8 | 11 | 82 | 41 | +41 | 77 |
| 4 Arsenal | 42 | 18 | 17 | 7 | 53 | 28 | +25 | 71 |
| 5 Leeds United | 42 | 18 | 16 | 8 | 65 | 39 | +26 | 70 |
| 6 Wimbledon | 42 | 18 | 11 | 13 | 56 | 53 | +3 | 65 |
| 7 Sheffield Wed | 42 | 16 | 16 | 10 | 76 | 54 | +22 | 64 |
| 8 Liverpool | 42 | 17 | 9 | 16 | 59 | 55 | +4 | 60 |
| 9 QPR | 42 | 16 | 12 | 14 | 62 | 61 | +1 | 60 |
| 10 Aston Villa | 42 | 15 | 12 | 15 | 46 | 50 | –4 | 57 |
| 11 Coventry City | 42 | 14 | 14 | 14 | 43 | 45 | –2 | 56 |
| 12 Norwich City | 42 | 12 | 17 | 13 | 65 | 61 | +4 | 53 |
| 13 West Ham Utd | 42 | 13 | 13 | 16 | 47 | 58 | –11 | 52 |
| 14 Chelsea | 42 | 13 | 12 | 17 | 49 | 53 | –4 | 51 |
| 15 Tottenham H | 42 | 11 | 12 | 19 | 54 | 59 | –5 | 45 |
| 16 Manchester C | 42 | 9 | 18 | 15 | 38 | 49 | –11 | 45 |
| 17 Everton | 42 | 12 | 8 | 22 | 42 | 63 | –21 | 44 |
| 18 Southampton | 42 | 12 | 7 | 23 | 49 | 66 | –17 | 43 |
| 19 Ipswich Town | 42 | 9 | 16 | 17 | 35 | 58 | –23 | 43 |
| 20 Sheffield Utd | 42 | 8 | 18 | 16 | 42 | 60 | –18 | 42 |
| 21 Oldham Ath | 42 | 9 | 13 | 20 | 42 | 68 | –26 | 40 |
| 22 Swindon Town | 42 | 5 | 15 | 22 | 47 | 100 | –53 | 30 |

1994/95

## The Only Way Isn't Essex: Joey Goes Home

After staying up comfortably the prior season, West Ham fans were able to enjoy a stress-free summer without worrying about the club's fortunes. And whilst England's awful spell under Graham Taylor meant they were absent from the World Cup, there was plenty of action Stateside to keep football fans happy. The competition started and ended with a missed penalty: Diana Ross screwed a shot wide in the opening ceremony and Roberto Baggio sent a shootout spot-kick into orbit during the final. Mind you, he wasn't playing a medley of his greatest hits at the time.

Much like Italia 90 four years prior, domestic fans were treated to a plethora of global talents on screen. Romario and Bebeto's goals brought the gold back to Brazil. Daniel Amokachi and Sunday Oliseh helped Nigeria's Super Eagles soar to new heights, and Romania won the hearts of the world with their unexpected march to the quarter-finals. The latter were spearheaded by three exciting attacking talents. Gheorghe Hagi had a left peg that could peel a satsuma, Ilie Dumitrescu was a vibrant attacking force on either flank, and Florin Raducioiu was Eastern Europe's most clinical finisher since Hannibal Lecter.

Unlike Italia 90, the stars we saw on screen then made sensational appearances on home soil. Slowly but surely, the Premier League was becoming a desirable destination for football's finest. Amokachi was on his way to Everton. Arsenal bolstered their midfield with the recruitment of Swedish dynamo Stefan Schwarz. Only for Tottenham to shock the world by announcing the signing of Jurgen Klinsmann, a World Cup winner and goalscorer supreme with the likes of Inter and latterly AS Monaco. His arrival was swiftly followed by Dumitrescu, with fellow countryman Gica Popescu reportedly on his way too, as Ossie Ardiles brought some balls-to-the-wall attacking flair to White Hart Lane.

It was hard not to look across London at our rivals' new hero and not go green with envy. Whilst Alan Sugar was wining and dining Europe's finest on his yacht in the south of France, we were conducting clandestine deals with Oxford's Joey Beauchamp in a service station on the M25.

In fairness, the winger was seen as one of the second tier's most exciting talents, as evidenced by a £1 million fee. Our transfer business had been pretty solid in recent seasons, dusting the cobwebs off the chairman's cheque book and making every penny count. There was every reason to think we may have unearthed another lower-league gem in the mould of Robson, Butler and Holmes. Hence, whilst he may not have been a household name, Beauchamp's arrival was greeted with a reasonable degree of optimism by the West Ham faithful.

That optimism lasted approximately 24 hours. West Ham's new winger arrived at Chadwell Heath on a sunny day in July, introduced himself to the car park attendant, shook hands with the receptionist, and then duly marched into Billy Bonds' office to ask for a transfer.

Beauchamp's revelation was that he hadn't realised the driving distance between Oxford and Essex. Missing his friends and family – after one solitary day of travel – he saw his future elsewhere. So long as elsewhere was within 30 minutes of his f**king front door.

The look on Billy Bonds' face must have been priceless. This was a man who had bled Claret and Blue for 27 years. He'd played with the Holy Trinity of Moore, Hurst and Peters. He'd warm up for combat on those Saturday-afternoon battlefields of the '70s by block tackling the dressing room wall. He had fought and scrapped for every inch of success he'd had in his career. And now here he was, faced with a young man who'd been given the opportunity of a lifetime, sacking it off after 24 hours.

In fairness, it probably said more about how players were treated back in those days than it did Beauchamp. He was a youngster who loved his local club, being around friends and family, and now he faced the prospect of leaving them behind. In this day and age, player liaison officers would do everything to ensure the youngster made a comfortable transition into his new life and location. Back then, there was no one to help. Joey's induction into life in east London was a VHS of the *EastEnders Christmas Special*, a plate of pie and mash and a battered *A to Z*.

Pre-season had once again got off to a terrible start. Incredibly, things were about to get far, far worse.

**EX:** *I was really excited about signing Beauchamp. £1 million was a big fee for us. I remember reading an article in* Shoot! *magazine that spotlighted up-and-coming lower-league players. Beauchamp was right at the top of the list. It seemed like Harry Redknapp had worked his magic again, unearthing another diamond in the rough. Beauchamp was highly rated and would surely be an improvement on our last high-profile winger Dale Gordon, who cost a load of money, scored one goal, and was never seen again. Unbelievably, this deal was actually worse.*

**DAVE:** *The story of Joey Beauchamp was a baffling one. When he joined West Ham, he signed the contract at Heathrow Airport, which in his words "is only 45 minutes from Oxford, I didn't know just how much further on West Ham would be from there." How could he not have known? Pick up a map, ask someone, do a dummy run. This isn't a day trip to Colchester Zoo, mate! However, in later years* *we came to learn that like most stories, there are two sides. Joey didn't want to leave Oxford, but they needed the money to avoid liquidation. He was also a family man that loved his local area and only ever wanted to play for the club he supports. When I think about it, on a human level, I admire that and was pleased that, after a spell at Swindon, he returned to Oxford and became a legend there.*

**EX:** *Dave's right that, when you look back, it took a lot of character for a young man to make that decision so quickly. It must have been so difficult. He was on the brink of achieving something people dream of, earning more money than he would ever have imagined. It's a shame that player care back in those days was so neglected. Maybe he could still have been a top-tier player. When you look at footage of him, he would have been the sort of player West Ham fans would have loved. Ultimately, he went back and home and became an Oxford icon. The deal was still a disaster for West Ham. But within a few weeks, we had even bigger problems.*

## Bonds Bombshell

Harry Redknapp's impact during his relatively short spell as assistant hadn't gone unnoticed outside of east London. He'd proved himself the perfect sidekick to Billy Bonds, and together the two old friends had established us in the Promised Land of the Premier League.

Now another one of his old clubs wanted to bring Redknapp back home. Bournemouth were ready to offer him the position of manager. The lure of a manager's job, alongside the fact that he still lived by the seaside, was enough for him to tender his resignation to the board. It was an entirely reasonable decision – and one that, though disappointed, West Ham fans would have understood.

What happened next is, to this day, still somewhat shrouded in mystery. Only those who were part of a frenetic 48 hours of activity will know the true story. Redknapp made his decision known on the team's traditional tour of Scotland. And it sent the board into a frenzy. Evidently, there was genuine concern how the team would fare without Harry's influence. His knowledge of the transfer market had been crucial to the club's success, and tactically he seemed to have taken us to another level. But they couldn't offer him the manager's position he craved without making a significant change. A change that would have catastrophic consequences for Billy and Harry's friendship.

The offer was made to Billy Bonds for him to "move upstairs" into a Director of Football role and let Harry take over first-team duties. It was, understandably, a hammer blow to Bonds' pride, who decided to tender his resignation and end over two decades of history with Upton Park.

The reaction was seismic. I remember reading the headlines on Ceefax and being utterly baffled. For the first time in my life supporting West Ham United, we weren't fighting relegation. We were a respectable top-tier side. And that was all down to Billy and Harry. For two years I'd seen them smiling in programmes, fanzines and VHS reviews. Two best mates together, living the West Ham dream. And now it was over.

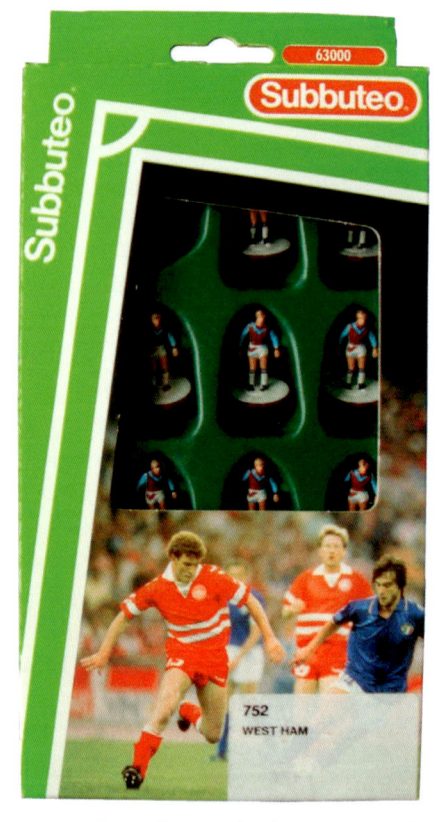

I'd fallen out with friends in years gone by. There had been many a game of Subbuteo where a player had been decapitated in a fit of rage, or a joystick launched at the wall after a controversial game of Sensible Soccer. Normally things were resolved over a Capri-Sun and Curly Wurly.

And indeed, as the smoke cleared from the firestorm of publicity, there was talk of reconciliation. That Billy and Harry had no hard feelings. There were going to be pictures taken at Chadwell Heath, a handshake and best wishes for the future.

But there were no pictures. There was no reconciliation. There was no more friendship. Billy Bonds was gone.

Redknapp barely had time to rue the loss of his old pal or enjoy the perks of his new role. The new season was approaching fast on the horizon. His best friend was gone, he had no assistant manager and his star signing was homesick. Just another pre-season at West Ham United Football Club.

**EX:** *People falling out is such a difficult thing to process when you're young. Your world is so small and uncomplicated that whenever you fall out with your friends, it's only a matter of time before you patch things up. Deep down, I hoped this would always happen with Billy and Harry, and it's such a shame that it never did.*

**DAVE:** *To this day, what happened between Billy and Harry remains a bit of a* taboo subject. Even former players who played under them typically refuse to pass comment. It was obviously awkward and confusing for everyone. Whilst I felt really sorry for Billy, I suppose it was inevitable that Harry's ambition was going to match his managerial potential. The board had a very difficult decision to make. And I'm not sure there was a solution that suited everyone. It's a sad situation that broke a friendship, a friendship that hasn't been mended to this day.

**EX:** As a fan, I felt like I was in an impossible situation, too. It was like choosing between my favourite uncles. Harry was the jovial, happy one. Whilst Billy was the more stoic and reliable one. I didn't know what to think. All I knew was that it seemed an awful way for such a devoted servant of the club to depart.

Billy expected every player would want to sign. Harry was a bit more switched on. He did the majority of the deals. Meanwhile, Billy couldn't understand people who didn't have the same love of West Ham, the same dedication and professionalism as he did.

## A Legend Returns

The chaos and confusion contributed to a predictably poor start to the season proper. We had one point and no goals from our opening three games, where we looked utterly toothless. Twelve months on from the triple swoop for Marsh, Chapman and Burrows, it was time for Harry to dive into the transfer market again and save our season.

Some precious funds had been freed up by the sale of Joey Beauchamp to Swindon Town, a more acceptable driving distance from his Oxfordshire home, for a player-plus-cash fee that saw defender Adrian Whitbread become a Hammer. Whitbread had one immediately familiar face in the dressing room as John Moncur had arrived from the County Ground in the summer. The ball-playing midfielder had settled in nicely alongside Ian Bishop at the heart of centre midfield, a rare bright light in our dismal start to the new campaign.

But it was up front where we really needed reinforcements. It had been six months since Lee Chapman last scored a goal, and with each passing day he was becoming more immobile. He had all the athleticism of a giraffe in wellies.

We needed an injection of youth, and it arrived in the form of attacking midfielder Don Hutchison, a £1.5 million signing from Liverpool. Much like Mike Marsh, the tall midfielder had been thrust into the Reds' first team under Graeme Souness who saw something of a kindred spirit in the young midfielder: Scottish, outspoken, with an unadulterated love of sticking the boot in.

After Souness's departure and a falling out with new boss Roy Evans, it was time for a change of scenery. At the time, Hutchison was flatmates with Jamie Redknapp, who apparently passed him the phone and said, "Talk to Dad, he wants you at West Ham." It was a remarkably efficient way of doing a deal, and might explain why our transfer business with Liverpool was so straightforward during the decade.

"Hello son, I'm after a central midfielder who's strong in the tackle and with a decent eye for goal."

"Funny you should say that, Dad. I live with a fella called Don Hutchison."

<Fast forward to 2000>

"Hello son, me again. Listen, I'm looking for a hot-headed right-back and a non-scoring centre-forward, preferably both overpriced and underperforming."

"Not sure about that, Dad. But I'll ask Rigobert Song and Titi Camara if they know anyone."

The £1.5 million fee for Hutchison stretched the budget, but Redknapp's judgment – once again – was proved correct almost immediately. The new signing scored on his debut, the only positive in a 3-1 defeat to Newcastle. He was also booked in that game, and so began a trend that would mark his time in Claret and Blue.

Whilst 'Hutch' had endeared himself to the fanbase with his first goal, it was clear that he wasn't the out-and-out goalscorer we needed. And it was hard to see where we might get one. We were 21st in the table after four defeats in five.

We needed someone who wasn't motivated by money (because we didn't have any) or our status as relegation certainties. We needed someone who would play for the badge, who would burst with pride every time he pulled on the shirt.

And seven days later, we got him. Most of you reading this won't remember where you were and what you were doing on the afternoon of Wednesday 7th September, 1994. I can still see it in my mind's eye. I was in my bedroom, on my knees, with fists pumped in celebration and roaring at the top of my voice, like I had just scored a last-minute winner in the FA Cup final.

The reason for my outburst of raw emotion was flickering on the screen in front of me. A lone Ceefax page, paused for what seemed like an eternity. The headline beaming out like a beacon across the Gotham City skyline.

WEST HAM RE-SIGN COTTEE

We had asked for a hero. And we'd got one. It had been six long years since I'd glumly taken down the myriad of posters of TC that adorned my bedroom walls. Their replacements had been pale imitations of the great man: David Kelly falling over whilst hitting a powder-puff shot straight into a keeper's arms, Mike Small trying to control the ball like it was coated in molten lava. Now I could put right what once went wrong. Tony Cottee was back.

The deal with Everton, where Cottee had lost his position to Nigerian Daniel Amokachi, another Premier League newcomer who'd arrived on the back of a successful USA 94, meant we had to say farewell to David Burrows as Redknapp exploited football's swap-shop. Whilst it was sad to see 'Bugsy' go, the dearth of striking options at our disposal meant it was the right decision.

TC went from returning hero to red-carded zero when he was sent off on his first start in an otherwise encouraging 0-0 draw at Anfield. The emotion of the occasion had clearly caught up with the mild-mannered forward. That was the only possible explanation for embedding his studs into poor Rob Jones' shins like he'd just caught the full-back in bed with his wife.

His home debut, however, was all the more romantic. In a performance full of one-touch football, we belied our basement status, running rings around Ron Atkinson's Villa. Marsh hit the post, whilst Mark Bosnich twice made point-blank saves to deny Cottee the dream debut goal. With three minutes remaining, the romantic return was finally sealed when TC scrambled home Breacker's cross to give us three vital points.

It felt like a turning point in the season. We won two out of our next three games, including a 2-1 victory at Stamford Bridge where Johnny Moncur notched his first for the club. Harry Redknapp's Midas touch in the transfer market had struck gold once again.

And he had his eyes on bringing one more treasure back to Upton Park.

**DAVE:** *Ah, the return of Tony Cottee. What a thing of beauty. I remember feeling so relieved because he was well established and would guarantee us goals, as opposed to a punt on an unknown striker, or a journeyman in the twilight of their career, which was often the case when we bought forwards. It was TC. He was still in his 20s. He was one of our own, a club legend and a proper fox in the box. Even when he was sent off at Anfield for decapitating Rob Jones, I remember thinking, "TC's up for this." I was SO pleased to see him back.*

**EX:** Before it was officially announced, I was obsessed with TC's return. I was constantly on ClubCall checking to make sure it was happening. There was such a sense of relief when it was confirmed.

I always had a bizarre affiliation with TC. My Auntie Gillian taught him in secondary school in Romford. One time where he didn't do his homework, she said, "Tony – you'll never get a job unless you try harder." He said he didn't need a job because he was going to be a footballer. When Auntie Gillian asked, "Well, how many boys actually make it?", he responded, "I don't know, but I'll definitely be one of the ones that does." And he was right.

**DAVE:** Hutch was a quality signing too, by the way. He was a good lad, with plenty of character and self-belief, which you probably needed in that West Ham dressing room. As a player, he was naturally a cross-country runner, so his work rate was second to none. That fitness level, along with his love for a tackle and eye for a goal, meant he was always going to be liked at Upton Park.

### "I'll Be Back"

With David Burrows gone, and Keith Rowland our only viable option at left-back, Harry went into the market looking for a bargain. Once again, he found one on Merseyside. And once again, it was a familiar face, though admittedly with an unfamiliar waistline.

Don Hutchison wasn't the only player to fall foul of the new regime at Anfield. New boss Roy Evans was bringing back the legendary work ethic of the Boot Room, which meant there was no place for Julian Dicks. His 12-month spell had been underwhelming, not helped by the fact that he was now significantly overweight. The Liverpool backroom staff were appalled by his lack of application in training and were only too delighted to grant his request for a move. When word reached Harry of his availability, he was quick to act.

Any concerns about re-signing a player that had been such a pain in the arse (from a management perspective) first time around were offset by the ludicrously low fee that Liverpool were demanding. They might as well have sent him back to Euston Station in gift wrap. It was worth the risk. The Terminator was back. Bigger and badder than ever.

Julian made his return – to a raucous reception – at home to Southampton. Though he was noticeably heavier, there were plenty of familiarities about his play. His left peg looked every bit as cultured as any in the division, and aerially he was a more commanding presence than Burrows at the back. Despite his extra poundage, he was still able to maraud forward, too – even if he did have the initial acceleration of a grand piano.

Typically, the returning hero marked the occasion by receiving a booking for a characteristic full-blooded challenge on Paul Allen that nearly sent him home without his ankles. Goals from Martin Allen and the impressive Matthew Rush, whose energy on the wing was adding a new dimension to the side, earned a comfortable win. In the next home game Dicks scored the winner from the penalty spot against bottom side Leicester. Normal service had been resumed.

**EX:** *I thought my excitement had peaked with TC, but it did with The Terminator. He was already a West Ham legend in my eyes, and one of the best left-backs in the whole country. I remember when they showed the pictures of him signing, he wore this distinctive oversized peach jumper that looked so unflattering, especially as he had been bombed out of Liverpool for being overweight. Not that I was bothered. All I cared about was that Julian was back. I got my old 'Dicks 3' T-shirt out from the loft, dusted off the cobwebs and was ready for his return. The fashion was so big and baggy back in those days that the T-shirt probably still fits me now. It's certainly a better fit than Julian's peach jumper.*

**DAVE:** *The euphoria of TC's return could only be eclipsed by one man for me: The Terminator. When it became official, that was it – I shaved my head, got 'Dicks' on the back of my shirt, and bought a hamster called Julian (he was a nasty f\*\*ker as well). The chairman said that Harry must have been "off his rocker" to sign him back because of the weight he was carrying, but as far as I'm concerned he could have been 30 stone, his presence and his aura was electrifying. I remember that winning penalty against Leicester; it was classic Julian.*

*I also remember that game for Don Hutchison getting sent off after 33 minutes! Don, still in his infancy at West Ham, was told by Martin Allen that if he "kicks the shit out of Mark Draper, the fans would love him." So that's what he did. On reflection, I don't think Don would have thanked Martin for that piece of advice. Harry Redknapp certainly didn't! He looked like he'd swallowed a wasp on the touchline.*

### Little and Large

The win over the Foxes was followed by three frustrating defeats. We were a competitive side against anyone in the division, but we just couldn't score.

Harry Redknapp had worked his genius again by persuading Ipswich to part with £70,000 in November for the limited services of Lee Chapman. It was an astonishing piece of business, and thankfully Harry did the decent thing and hid the receipts. By January, the Big Fella was on loan at Southend.

Meanwhile Trevor Morley, top scorer the previous campaign and firm fan favourite, was woefully out of sorts. As always, there was plenty of effort and endeavour, but unfortunately no goals to go with it. He hadn't scored for nine long months. His time in the top division was coming to an end, too.

Without an effective strike partner, Tony Cottee had struggled to find his scoring boots. The goal against Villa on his home debut was his only successful effort on target since his homecoming. Though one in eight League games was hardly Steve Potts territory, it wasn't quite the return we were hoping for.

The frontline needed inspiration, and it came from an unlikely source. There had been more sightings of the Loch Ness Monster than there had been of Jeroen Boere in a West Ham shirt. The 6'3" Dutchman had arrived from the magnificently-named Go Ahead Eagles for £250,000 the previous season but had featured little for the first team. In an effort to adapt to English football, he'd gone on loan to Portsmouth and West Brom, yielding zero goals in ten appearances. Ordinarily, this might have been the catalyst for an ignominious return home rather than a promotion to the first team.

However, Boere had two things in his favour. He was massive. And we were desperate.

The big Dutchman started at Loftus Road, where we found ourselves 2-0 down thanks to our central defence leaving Les Ferdinand with the sort of room in the six-yard box that made you wonder if he had a body odour issue, and then Trevor Sinclair scoring a dazzling solo effort to double their lead. With the seconds ticking down, Boere got on the end of a Cottee cross to halve the deficit. Though it proved only a consolation, there was enough promise to suggest the little-and-large duo might form a useful partnership.

That suspicion was confirmed after a visit to Leeds a week later. Traditionally, we had the same sort of success rate in Yorkshire as a door-to-door croissant salesman. And when we were two down inside 25 minutes, it looked like another trip north would end in defeat. On the stroke of half-time, Boere met a Keith Rowland cross with a brilliant bullet header before nodding in an equaliser late in the second half to earn us a point.

Cottee was looking much more sprightly with a target man alongside him, and he exploded back into life by notching a hat-trick in a 3-0 thumping of Manchester City at Upton Park. Boere's influence on the side had exceeded Harry's wildest dreams, and when we ended 1994 with an impressive 3-1 win over Nottingham Forest (Cottee notching his fifth in four games), we approached the New Year in the relative comfort of 16th position.

**DAVE:** *I don't think Jeroen was signed for his goals. He was signed for Tony Cottee's goals, because TC has always been at his best with a big, strong partner next to him. A younger Lee Chapman would have been perfect but that ship had sailed, so when Boere was signed, whilst physically he was impressive, I can't say I was overly excited. That said, he brought the best out in Tony during that period, and they actually formed a decent partnership. Another 'triffic' bit of business from Harry Redknapp.*

**EX:** *It was odd for him to suddenly appear in the first team. He'd been at the club for a while, never really played, never even considered him as an option. To be honest, he seemed like a bit of a waste of money. I was shocked when I saw him play. He was pretty good technically and so effective in the air. Like Dave said, he formed a classic combination with Cottee. Jeroen did the muscle work and won the headers, whilst Tony could feed off his knockdowns and find space in the penalty area.*

### A Grim Start for Rieper

It wasn't just Boere who was introducing himself to West Ham fans. The game at Elland Road had also featured a first glimpse of Danish international Marc Rieper, who'd signed on loan from Brondby.

His arrival, like that of Boere, showed Harry Redknapp's willingness to look further afield in search of a bargain. Whilst his success at West Ham so far had been based on unearthing gems from the lower leagues, he realised that English football was changing rapidly. It wasn't just the bigger teams with the bigger budgets that were bringing in exotic names. Nottingham Forest had signed Bryan Roy, Sheffield Wednesday had Dan Petrescu, and Leeds had brought in Lucas Radebe.

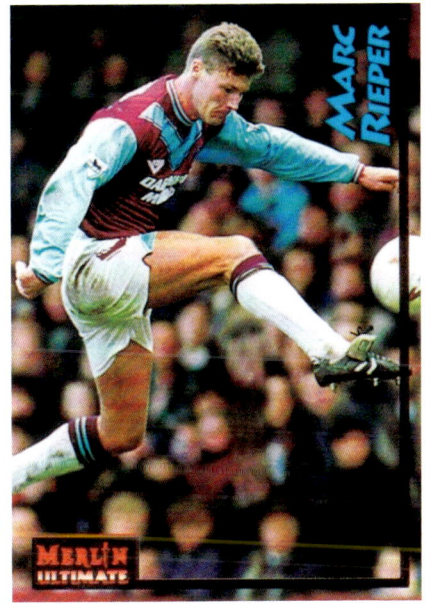

The transfer market was becoming a global business. And if you were prepared to shop around, you could pick up plenty of value for money on foreign shores.

Tall and broad-shouldered, Rieper looked like the sort of no-nonsense defender we'd been craving for years, who could step into the shoes of Alvin Martin. He might as well have been wearing flippers if his debut at Leeds was anything to go by. He was all over the place alongside his new central defensive partner – a shell-shocked Steve Potts – who looked like he was trying to teach a fridge freezer to tango. Both were at fault for the shocking start to the Leeds game, and Rieper was quickly relegated to the role of substitute.

His first eight appearances for the club yielded one win, two draws, five defeats and not a single clean sheet. A return to the starting line-up against Chelsea showed serious signs of improvement, only for the Blues' diminutive striker Mark Stein – who was roughly the size of Rieper's big toe – to go and snatch a late winner.

**EX:** *Everyone called him 'Grim Rieper' because he was so poor to start with. But once he found his feet, he was a massive player for us (in every sense). It gives credibility to the notion that players take time to settle in the Premier League, particularly when they arrive from overseas. Before the Blackburn game it was announced he was signing permanently, and the crowd gave him a great reaction. He was classy, read the game well, calm, composed and good in the air. Rieper was a complete defender.*

**DAVE:** *Marc Rieper's poor start at West Ham certainly wasn't a sign of things to come! What a player he turned out to be. I loved him. Physically, it was funny seeing him next to Stevie Potts. He looked like he had taken his son to the park for a kickabout!*

*In terms of overseas signings, I remember being even more excited by Dieter Eckstein, who signed a few months later, but I don't think he ever kicked a ball for us?! Signing players from abroad seemed like a bit of a gamble, but Marc was definitely one that paid off (eventually).*

### SuperDon Saves The Day

The slump in form coincided with the absence – initially through suspension, followed by injury – of Don Hutchison. The early-season arrival of the Scottish midfielder may have come out of the blue, but there was no doubting his importance to the team – or the terraces.

Hutch was the type of player fans love: fully committed, always in the centre of the action and with a knack of scoring crucial goals. He was also incredibly versatile, equally at home in central midfield or making a nuisance of himself up front. Tomas Soucek probably had a picture of him on his bedroom wall.

Residing in 20th position and up to our arseholes in the relegation dogfight, we needed strong characters, and we needed goals if we were going to avoid the drop. Hutchison's return to the side brought both.

After six defeats in seven games, a fixture at Highbury in early March was about as welcome as a box of Krispy Kremes at a WeightWatchers convention. But Don scored the winner in a classic smash-and-grab performance to get us back on track. He notched again in a draw against fellow strugglers Southampton, and then another in a 2-0 win at Villa Park, where John Moncur made one of his infrequent appearances on the scoresheet. Once more, SuperDon was proving himself a big player for the big occasion.

And there was none bigger than a late April visit of title contenders Blackburn in front of the Sky TV cameras. All the talk before the game was about Kenny Dalglish's quest to bring a first Premier League trophy back to Ewood Park. Busloads of Rovers fans were on their way down the M6 from Lancashire to see their side take another step towards Dreamland. And in the VIP area, Sky's Nick Collins spoke to an unlikely 'superfan' who had made the trip all the way from San Antonio, Texas.

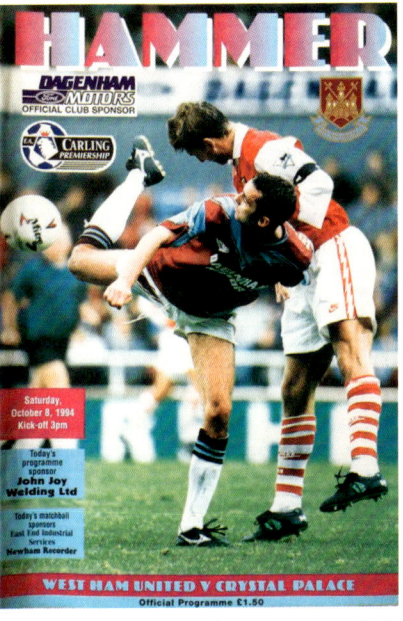

WWF superstar Shawn Michaels, aka 'The Heartbreak Kid', appeared in the tunnel for an interview with intrepid Sky reporter Collins to discuss his love of "the Blackburn Rovers." In his distinct Texan drawl, the wrestler described how a "distant relative" had links to Blackburn, thus sparking his newfound allegiance – which sounds remarkably similar to the level of scrutiny applied to Andy Townsend's Irish bloodlines.

Michaels typically spent his weekends battling the likes of The Undertaker, so even he must have been impressed by Marc Rieper's performance that day. The dominant Dane was magnificent, giving 30-goal star striker Alan Shearer a battering all afternoon. With Rovers effectively shut down at one end, Rieper duly made a nuisance of himself at the other, by drilling home a header to put us in front. The points were secured when a brilliant Bishop pass found Rush whose

113

rapid breakaway allowed Moncur a shot at goal. Flowers denied him, but there was Hutchison to sweep home the decisive goal.

A penultimate home game of the season pitted Hutch against his former club Liverpool, and the equation was simple: a win would keep us in the top flight. Hutchison was made for moments like this. Two goals and a Man of the Match performance secured our survival, an achievement that seemed almost impossible back in January. His form during the run-in had been sensational: seven goals in 12 games from midfield marked him out as one of the most dangerous players in the division, a division where West Ham would once again be residing next season.

**DAVE:** *It's so typical of West Ham to be on the bones of our arse then somehow, against the odds, manage to get wins against Arsenal, Blackburn and Liverpool. The Liverpool game in particular was special, though. The atmosphere, the nervous tension, Harry twitching like a rabbit's nose. The adrenaline in the stadium was incredible, as was Don Hutchison.*

*It's interesting with Don because he said that when he played, if he started a game well then in his head he would go on to play like a top-class attacking midfielder. But if he started badly, he would go on to play like an erratic defensive midfielder. He certainly started well against Liverpool. It was a superb performance, and there was a massive sigh of relief from the fans at full-time.*

**EX:** *In some ways, Don was the classic maverick player. When he was playing well, he was a godsend. For a tall player, he was deceptively skilful. He had an excellent touch, used space intelligently and could always produce a clever little flick to create something out of nothing.*

*When he wasn't playing so well, he could sometimes seem like a luxury. You wanted him to keep it simple and just work a bit harder. I think part of the problem was it was always difficult to work out his best position. He could play as a number ten, he could play in centre midfield. So he was often moved around the pitch. When he was played further forward, he was capable of sniffing out a crucial goal – and his form during this run-in was brilliant.*

### Ludo Wins the League

With safety assured, there was just one assignment incomplete for the season: deny Manchester United the title. The scars of Paul Ince's last-gasp leveller the previous campaign had never really healed, and though West Ham had no particular affinity for Blackburn (though Tony Gale had played his part in their

League push since signing on a free transfer in the summer), we had a healthy dislike of seeing the Reds lift the trophy.

A last-day title decider was the sort of televisual spectacular that Sky had dreamed of when they started ploughing money into English football. So far, their return on investment had delivered plenty of glitz and glamour – the influx of overseas stars was making it must-see viewing compared to the doldrums of the '80s – but it hadn't served up any serious drama at the top end of the League; Manchester United had lifted the silverware the first two seasons, winning both titles comfortably in the end.

Blackburn began the day two points ahead, but with a vastly inferior goal difference, with a daunting trip to Anfield in the offing. If United won and Rovers didn't, then it meant the championship was heading for Old Trafford for the third year in succession. The smart money was on the latter.

There were some mitigating circumstances, however. Liverpool fans would rather paint their houses blue than see United win the League again, and the fact that it was their former hero Kenny Dalglish in charge at Blackburn meant there was added motivation to cheer the away side.

It must have placed the Liverpool players in an awkward position. If United went ahead down in east London, then the Anfield crowd would actually want them to lose, whilst professional pride meant that the players had to make a contest of it.

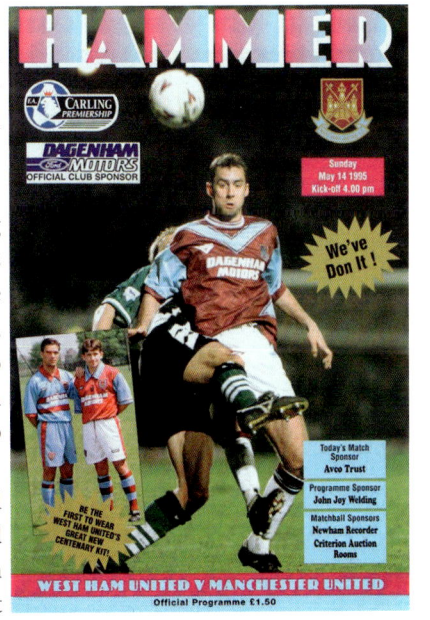

There were no such issues at Upton Park, where the atmosphere demanded that our lot get stuck in. Paul Ince was predictably booed from the outset, though with noticeably less fervour than before, for his past indiscretions. Roy Keane was being barracked too, presumably for being Roy Keane.

The noise levels increased with every crunching tackle as our players refused to sit back and let United settle. When Michael Hughes, whose lovely left peg had been a key part of our late-season revival, volleyed home from a Matt Holmes cross, Upton Park erupted. The upset was on.

Alan Shearer then scored at Anfield to put Rovers in the driving seat at the interval. Whatever Alex Ferguson said at half-time worked wonders. There's been a lot of talk about the Scot's infamous 'hairdryer' treatment over the years. Unless we were there in person, we'll never know quite what it entailed. But whatever orifice the United gaffer buried that piping hot appliance in, it worked wonders. United's players emerged with a real pep in their step.

The second half was one of the most one-sided affairs in Upton Park history. We were camped in our 18-yard box from the restart, unable to escape. Brian McClair headed the visitors level early on, and it seemed only a matter of time before United got the second. We had seen this before.

Word came down from the North that Liverpool had equalised, a goal that the Kop celebrated with the zeal of a crocodile that's found out he's won a free subscription to *Reader's Digest*. The title was slipping from Blackburn's grasp and, despite our heroic efforts, seemed destined for Manchester.

Except it wasn't. Because two things happened that day that no one could have predicted.

Firstly, Brian McClair and Andy Cole would perform like strikers you might get free with a Happy Meal. Secondly, Ludo Miklosko produced one of the defining individual performances of the era. Time after glorious time, he denied United from point-blank range. Two one-on-one stops from Cole were, given the gravity of the situation, absolutely world-class goalkeeping.

The game finished level. And despite Blackburn doing their best to bottle it – by conceding a last-gasp winner to Jamie Redknapp, United's failure to get three points meant the League title was heading to the blue and white part of Lancashire. People will point to Jack Walker's millions, Kenny Dalglish's management genius or Alan Shearer's glut of goals. But those who were at Upton Park, or watching the telly that day in May 1995, know the real truth: Ludo Miklosko had single-handedly won Blackburn the League.

**DAVE:** *What a special day this was! I sometimes wonder how we would have done* if we'd needed to win that game. The fact that there was no pressure on us definitely worked to our advantage and, let's not forget, this wasn't against a mid-table side looking forward to their holidays, this was against Man United looking forward to lifting the title.

The desire from our players that day was second to none, and in terms of Ludo's performance... I challenge anyone to show me a better individual display from a keeper in Premier League history. He was absolutely incredible.

**EX:** What a day. Considering there was nothing in it for West Ham, the atmosphere and tension was huge. People assumed we were just going to roll over, that we were on the beach already. I'm sure there were a few United fans who really fancied their chances. But Ludo just turned into Superman. His saves were unbelievable.

The best part for me was going into school next day and goading the Man United fans in my class. I distinctly remember it was really sunny, and when we played football at lunchtime I actually volunteered to go in goal, just so I could throw myself around and scream "LUDOOOO" and wind up the glory-hunting United fans in school.

**DAVE:** When the final whistle blew, it was as if we had won the title ourselves! John Moncur had been tormenting Roy Keane for the entire 90 minutes and, at the end, Roy said to John, "I'll see you in the tunnel, I'm gonna f**king do you." John replied, "I won't be in the tunnel, I'll be out here celebrating with the fans!" Roy was FUMING, apparently!

The cherry on the cake is that Tony Gale had the entire Blackburn squad singing 'Bubbles' in the dressing room at Anfield. Beautiful.

## FA Premier League - 1994/95

| Date | Opponent | H/A | Score | Attendance | Scorers |
|---|---|---|---|---|---|
| 20 August | Leeds United | H | 0–0 | 18,610 | |
| 24 August | Manchester City | A | 0–3 | 19,150 | |
| 27 August | Norwich City | A | 0–1 | 19,110 | |
| 31 August | Newcastle United | H | 1–3 | 17,375 | Hutchison (p) |
| 10 September | Liverpool | A | 0–0 | 30,907 | |
| 17 September | Aston Villa | H | 1–0 | 18,326 | Cottee |
| 25 September | Arsenal | H | 0–2 | 18,495 | |
| 2 October | Chelsea | A | 2–1 | 18,696 | Allen, Moncur |
| 8 October | Crystal Palace | H | 1–0 | 16,959 | Hutchison |
| 15 October | Manchester United | A | 0–1 | 43,795 | |
| 22 October | Southampton | H | 2–0 | 18,853 | Rush, Allen |
| 29 October | Tottenham Hotspur | A | 1–3 | 26,271 | Rush |
| 1 November | Everton | A | 0–1 | 28,353 | |
| 5 November | Leicester City | H | 1–0 | 18,780 | Dicks (p) |
| 19 November | Sheffield Wed | A | 0–1 | 25,300 | |
| 26 November | Coventry City | H | 0–1 | 17,251 | |
| 4 December | QPR | A | 1–2 | 12,780 | Boere |
| 10 December | Leeds United | A | 2–2 | 28,987 | Boere (2) |
| 17 December | Manchester City | H | 3–0 | 17,286 | Cottee (3) |
| 26 December | Ipswich Town | H | 1–1 | 20,562 | Cottee |
| 28 December | Wimbledon | A | 0–1 | 11,212 | |
| 31 December | Nottingham Forest | H | 3–1 | 20,664 | Holmes, Hughes, Cottee |
| 2 January | Blackburn Rovers | A | 2–4 | 25,503 | Cottee, Dicks |
| 14 January | Tottenham Hotspur | H | 1–2 | 24,578 | Boere |
| 23 January | Sheffield Wed | H | 0–2 | 14,554 | |
| 4 February | Leicester City | A | 2–1 | 20,375 | Cottee, Dicks (p) |
| 13 February | Everton | H | 2–2 | 21,081 | Cottee (2) |
| 18 February | Coventry City | A | 0–2 | 17,563 | |
| 25 February | Chelsea | H | 1–2 | 21,500 | Hutchison |
| 5 March | Arsenal | A | 1–0 | 36,295 | Hutchison |
| 8 March | Newcastle United | A | 0–2 | 34,595 | |
| 11 March | Norwich City | H | 2–2 | 21,464 | Cottee (2) |
| 15 March | Southampton | A | 1–1 | 15,178 | Hutchison |
| 18 March | Aston Villa | A | 2–0 | 28,682 | Moncur, Hutchison |
| 8 April | Nottingham Forest | A | 1–1 | 28,361 | Dicks |
| 13 April | Wimbledon | H | 3–0 | 21,804 | Boere, Dicks (p), Cottee |
| 17 April | Ipswich Town | A | 1–1 | 18,882 | Boere |
| 30 April | Blackburn Rovers | H | 2–0 | 24,202 | Hutchison, Rieper |
| 3 May | QPR | H | 0–0 | 22,923 | |

| | | | | | |
|---|---|---|---|---|---|
| 6 May | Crystal Palace | A | 0–1 | 18,224 | |
| 10 May | Liverpool | H | 3–0 | 22,446 | Hutchison (2), Holmes |
| 14 May | Manchester United | H | 1–1 | 24,783 | Hughes |

## FA Cup

| | | | | | |
|---|---|---|---|---|---|
| 7 January R3 | Wycombe Wand | A | 2–0 | 9,007 | Brown, Cottee |
| 28 January R4 | QPR | A | 0–1 | 17,694 | |

## League Cup

| | | | | | |
|---|---|---|---|---|---|
| 20 Sept R2 1L | Walsall | A | 1–2 | 5,994 | Ntamark (og) |
| 5 October R2 2L | Walsall | H | 2–0 | 13,553 | Hutchison, Moncur |
| 26 October R3 | Chelsea | H | 1–0 | 18,815 | Hutchison |
| 30 November R4 | Bolton Wanderers | H | 1–3 | 18,190 | Cottee |

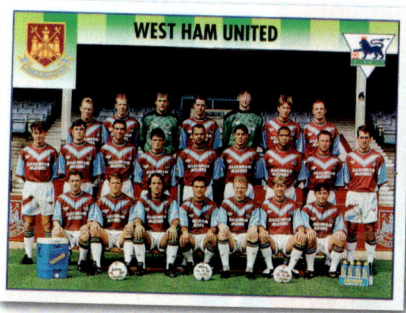

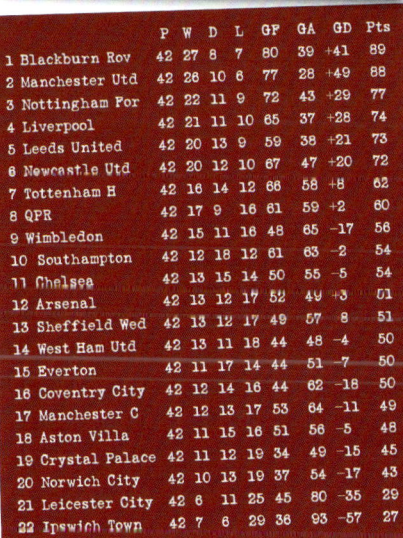

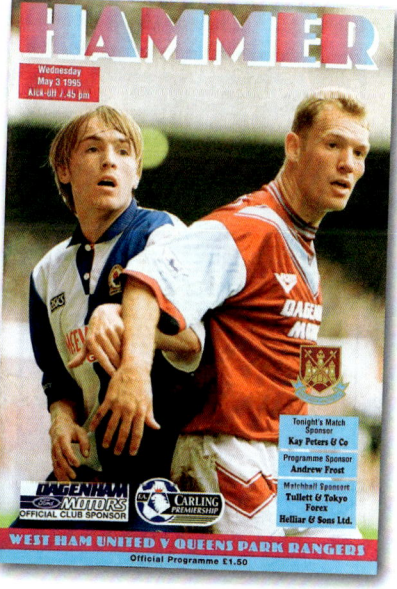

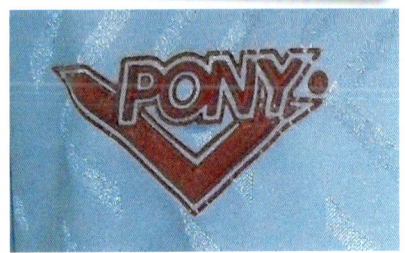

| | P | W | D | L | GF | GA | GD | Pts |
|---|---|---|---|---|---|---|---|---|
| 1 Blackburn Rov | 42 | 27 | 8 | 7 | 80 | 39 | +41 | 89 |
| 2 Manchester Utd | 42 | 26 | 10 | 6 | 77 | 28 | +49 | 88 |
| 3 Nottingham For | 42 | 22 | 11 | 9 | 72 | 43 | +29 | 77 |
| 4 Liverpool | 42 | 21 | 11 | 10 | 65 | 37 | +28 | 74 |
| 5 Leeds United | 42 | 20 | 13 | 9 | 59 | 38 | +21 | 73 |
| 6 Newcastle Utd | 42 | 20 | 12 | 10 | 67 | 47 | +20 | 72 |
| 7 Tottenham H | 42 | 16 | 14 | 12 | 66 | 58 | +8 | 62 |
| 8 QPR | 42 | 17 | 9 | 16 | 61 | 59 | +2 | 60 |
| 9 Wimbledon | 42 | 15 | 11 | 16 | 48 | 65 | −17 | 56 |
| 10 Southampton | 42 | 12 | 18 | 12 | 61 | 63 | −2 | 54 |
| 11 Chelsea | 42 | 13 | 15 | 14 | 50 | 55 | −5 | 54 |
| 12 Arsenal | 42 | 13 | 12 | 17 | 52 | 49 | +3 | 51 |
| 13 Sheffield Wed | 42 | 13 | 12 | 17 | 49 | 57 | −8 | 51 |
| 14 West Ham Utd | 42 | 13 | 11 | 18 | 44 | 48 | −4 | 50 |
| 15 Everton | 42 | 11 | 17 | 14 | 44 | 51 | −7 | 50 |
| 16 Coventry City | 42 | 12 | 14 | 16 | 44 | 62 | −18 | 50 |
| 17 Manchester C | 42 | 12 | 13 | 17 | 53 | 64 | −11 | 49 |
| 18 Aston Villa | 42 | 11 | 15 | 16 | 51 | 56 | −5 | 48 |
| 19 Crystal Palace | 42 | 11 | 12 | 19 | 34 | 49 | −15 | 45 |
| 20 Norwich City | 42 | 10 | 13 | 19 | 37 | 54 | −17 | 43 |
| 21 Leicester City | 42 | 6 | 11 | 25 | 45 | 80 | −35 | 29 |
| 22 Ipswich Town | 42 | 7 | 6 | 29 | 36 | 93 | −57 | 27 |

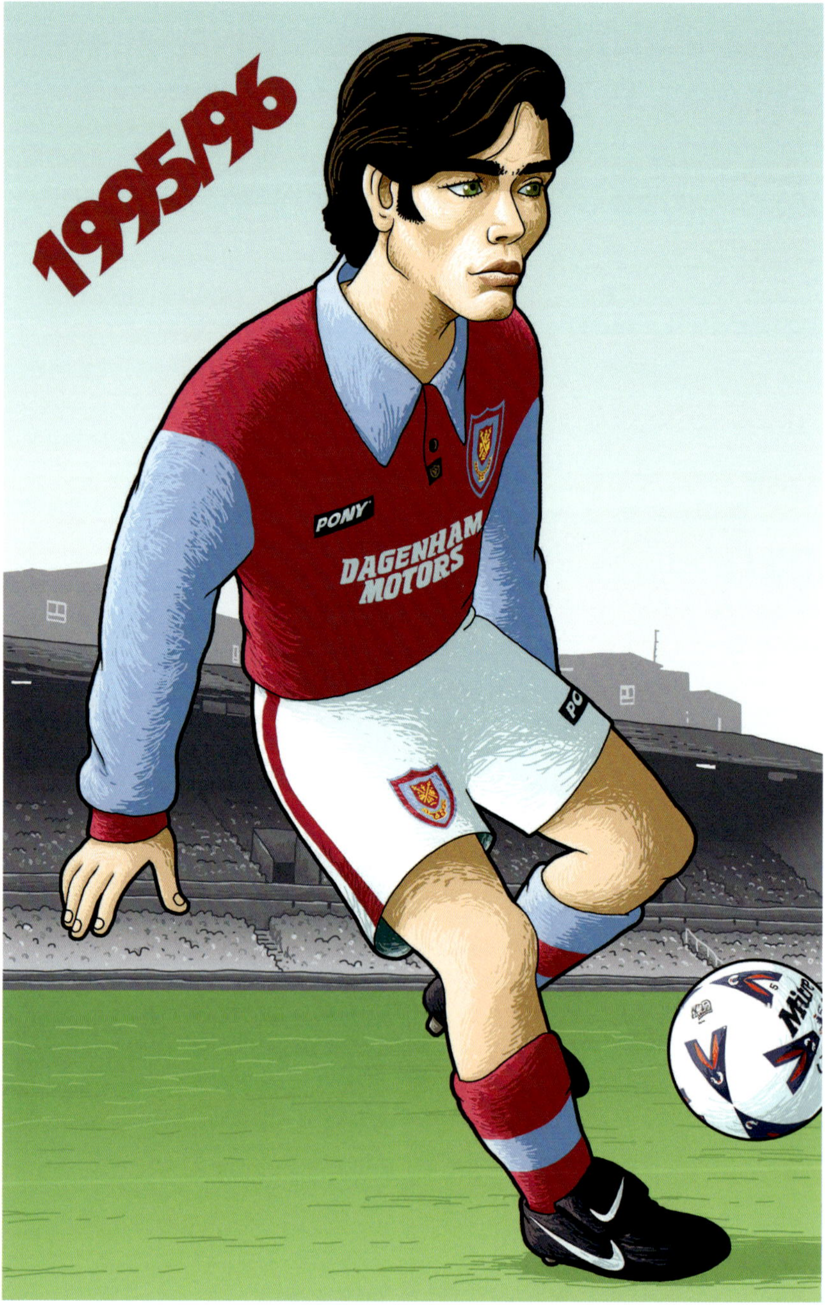
1995/96
PONY
DAGENHAM MOTORS

## All Quiet on the West Ham Front

Pre-season is normally a time for fans, players and managers alike – refreshed from the summer break – to look forward to the new campaign with the hope that sunny times lie ahead for our respective sides.

However, in previous years the pre-season had brought nothing but misery to West Ham United. Whether it was the Paul Ince saga, Simon Webster's awful injury or Billy Bonds' distasteful departure, July and August had rarely brought good tidings.

So it was quite a relief for the summer to pass without incident at Upton Park. The club seemed remarkably settled as it prepared for its third straight season of top-tier football. Finally, we seemed to have ditched the dreaded tag of being a 'yo-yo' club.

Once again the Premier League was proving itself as the place to be for the world's best footballers. After Tottenham opened the doorway last season with the signing of Jurgen Klinsmann (who had mercifully f\*\*ked off to Bayern after a sensational season at Spurs much to the chagrin of Alan Sugar), it was Arsenal who took centre stage with two superstar signings from Serie A: Dennis Bergkamp from Inter for £7.5 million, and England international David Platt was back in Blighty after spells at Bari, Juve and Sampdoria.

However, it was another Dutch arrival from Italy who stole the headlines. Ruud Gullit, one of the best players on the planet in the late '80s and early '90s, made the remarkable decision to join Chelsea. It meant that the man who famously shared a pitch with Rijkaard and Van Basten would now count Erland Johnsen and Paul Furlong amongst his new team-mates.

Buoyed by his successful overseas buys last season, and still scarred by Joey Beauchamp's domestic disaster, Harry Redknapp decided to once again wade into European waters for his marquee signing of pre-season. Striker Marco Boogers arrived from Sparta Rotterdam for £800,000 to fill the gap left by Trevor Morley's departure to Reading.

The Dutchman wasn't the only new face. Australian midfielder Robbie Slater joined the club as part of a swap deal that saw Matty Holmes join champions Blackburn. He was joined by a fellow Antipodean in the shape of Stan 'Skippy' Lazaridis, who had impressed during a friendly on the Hammers' post-season trip Down Under.

Compared to the big names arriving for big money elsewhere, none of the trio really set the pulse racing.

But we realised that we were shopping in a different market to the rest of the division's big spenders. Once again, we had to put our faith in Harry's eye for a bargain. Michael Hughes, Marc Rieper and Jeroen Boere had played key parts in our survival. Maybe Marco Boogers would make himself a West Ham legend?

We'd soon find out.

**EX:** *Stan Lazaridis is another example of West Ham's unique recruitment strategy. He was a player no one had ever heard of, playing for a team no one had ever heard of, who was Man of the Match against us in a post-season booze-up Down Under. The players were drunk for about 30 days straight. I think the cast of* Neighbours *could have probably nicked a draw against us. Thankfully, on this occasion it turned out to be a great bit of business. When the players did finally sober up, they all realised that Stan was a quality player.*

**DAVE:** *By now, I had trust in Harry's eye for a player. For that reason, any signing through the door was met with some degree of excitement. However, signing Robbie Slater at the expense of Matty Holmes didn't sound like a great deal to me, as I thought Matty was a very tidy player. And I'd never heard of Marco Boogers. So, the excitement was also diluted by the superstars being signed elsewhere. In comparison, our business was underwhelming; but at least we were enjoying a drama-free pre-season for once. There were no controversial managerial changes, no career-ending injuries, and no marquee signings disappearing before they'd kicked a ball for us. In that respect, we had a lot to be grateful for.*

### Boogers' Video Nasty

Harry Redknapp's knowledge of the lower leagues was built on a network of contacts from his days as Bournemouth manager. However, with no European scouting network to speak of (Frank Lampard Snr's summer holidays in Benidorm didn't count), he had to resort to more unusual means in his hunt for a strike partner for Tony Cottee.

In the early '90s, when the internet was still in its infancy and YouTube was merely a glint in the eye of the information superhighway, tape trading was an essential part of popular culture. At my school it was a battered copy of *Under Siege*, which featured *Baywatch* beauty Erika Eleniak bursting topless out of a birthday cake.

Similarly, in the summer of 1996, Harry Redknapp had relied on VHS footage in his search for an impressive front pair. In retrospect, it seems a highly dangerous strategy. If Sandra had taped that night's *Bullseye*, the Hammers could have started the season with Jim Bowen up front.

Nonetheless, he was impressed enough by what grainy footage he saw of Marco

Boogers to make him our new centre-forward. Sadly, it soon became clear that the Dutchman wasn't quite the imposing target man that the tapes had suggested. He looked like he'd spent pre-season on hunger strike, and his efforts in training made Jabba The Hutt look like Linford Christie.

What's more, the West Ham medical – presumably undertaken using the very latest in Fisher-Price technology – had failed to spot a chronic knee injury. We didn't know it yet, but there was no way Boogers was going to cope with the hurly-burly of Premier League football.

He made his debut as a substitute against Leeds on the opening day of the season, where he was comfortably eclipsed by the efforts of Tony Yeboah, Leeds' new signing from Hamburg, who scored two tremendous goals to take the points back to Yorkshire. First impressions weren't great, and there were already some murmurs from the stands.

Struggling for form and fitness, Boogers was keen to make amends at Old Trafford the following week. Once again, he started on the bench, before being summoned by Redknapp in the 72nd minute with us trailing 2-1 after a battling performance.

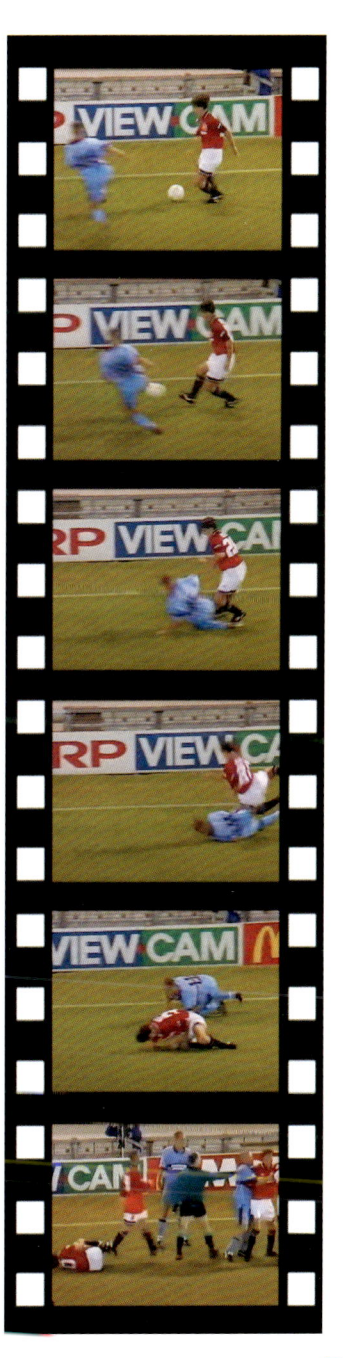

His command of English wasn't particularly good, and clearly something got lost in translation as Harry Redknapp gave him his tactical instructions. The striker immediately launched into a wild two-footed tackle on Gary Neville that left England's resident right-back desperately checking his ankles were still intact with the frenzied panic of a man who's lost his car keys. Boogers was red-carded for his exertions, and could probably count himself lucky he wasn't spending Christmas in Broadmoor.

That was his only memorable contribution in Claret and Blue, though another misunderstanding would taint his reputation in English football. After being signed off with stress, he was then granted compassionate leave to return to his native Holland for the birth of his first child.

He wouldn't be allowed to go quietly. A miscommunication between West Ham's ClubCall reporter, who said the family had travelled 'by car again,' and a tabloid journalist spawned this infamous headline.

BARMY BOOGERS GONE TO LIVE IN A CARAVAN!

Now the merest of fact-checking would have uncovered that, i) Boogers was neither deemed medically unstable, nor ii) seeking solace from his problems in the simplistic luxury of a recreational vehicle. However, the British press have never been ones to let the truth get in the way of a good story.

Whatever version of events you believed, one fact was undisputable: once again West Ham were in desperate need of a striker.

**EX:** *Marco Boogers joins the long list of infamous West Ham signings that ended in complete and utter disaster. I was massively excited when we signed him, because by that stage I was convinced that every overseas player coming to the Premier League was going to be a star. I soon learnt otherwise. These days, I can forgive the tackle, but what really bugs me is that Marco Boogers didn't speak English. How is that even possible? Anyone that's ever had the pleasure of meeting Dutch people on holidays, at festivals, or even school trips, knows that they speak absolutely perfect English. Yet somehow, we found the only one on the planet who didn't – and he struggled to settle immediately.*

**DAVE:** *Robbie Slater told us that "if Marco Boogers would have made that tackle in today's game, he would have gone to jail!" and it's hard to disagree. It was an absolute atrocity. The most memorable thing for me isn't the actual contact, or Gary Neville rolling around on the floor afterwards. I can still picture Julian's reaction, rushing to Marco's defence as if everyone was going over the top for what he probably deemed as a decent challenge! Absolute carnage, and carnage that was later manipulated by the press.*

**EX:** *I completely fell for the caravan story. Mainly because it seemed like precisely the sort of thing that would happen to us. What other club would have a star signing run off to live in a caravan? It sounded like classic West Ham. The fact it was so blatantly untrue shows you how powerful the papers were back then, when* *you didn't have the internet or alternative sources as means of verification.*

**DAVE:** I agree. When you look at those headlines, it's shocking that they were allowed to print stuff like this. It's like Trevor Brooking popping down the Barking Road for a bottle of Coca-Cola and the next morning the headlines read 'Brooking caught buying coke in east London.' It sabotaged Marco's reputation, really. However, to this day he is regarded as one of the worst signings in our history, and it's hard to argue with that.

### Back in Business: Harry's Swap Shop

No one could ever accuse Harry Redknapp of acting slowly. In a similar predicament last season, he'd turfed out David Burrows and brought in Tony Cottee and Julian Dicks. Somewhat surprisingly, Redknapp had decided that Jeroen Boere's future lay elsewhere, and he moved to Crystal Palace for £375,000 – leaving us woefully short (in every sense) up front with only Tony Cottee to count on for goals. And having failed with his big foreign gamble, he erred on the side of caution with a replacement for Boogers. It was time to bring in someone tried and tested to lift our fortunes.

West Ham fans' last sighting of Iain Dowie in club colours had been in that final-day farce in 1991 when we celebrated the title win on the pitch at Upton Park, only for a last-minute Oldham equaliser elsewhere to rip the silverware from our grasp. Nonetheless, despite having a face that that might give Freddy Krueger sleepless nights, Dowie was still held in reasonably high regard on the Upton Park terraces. His four goals in that run-in had helped us secure promotion.

The Northern Irishman had since spent four years at Southampton before a short spell at Palace ended in relegation. So, whilst Boere was on his way to Croydon, Dowie was headed back to Chadwell Heath to sign on the dotted line.

It wasn't a signing to get particularly excited about. Kids weren't roaming the playgrounds of east London pretending to be Iain Dowie – unless it was Halloween. And parents didn't want their kids growing up to be like the big striker, not if they had any hope of grandchildren. Ultimately, Dowie was a man who put in shift and did the ugly things well. You could say the same about our local binmen. But whilst Boogers might have been rubbish, at least Dowie had some kind of Premier League pedigree.

Maybe it was good to stick with what you know.

**EX:** *I was shocked that we sold Jeroen Boere. He'd played a crucial role in our good end to the previous season, and the price seemed very low. But we knew what we* were getting with Dowie – he was big and strong, and very good in the air. He didn't have an abundance of quality, but would always put a shift in.

**DAVE:** I was genuinely pleased to see Iain Dowie come back. It felt like a shrewd move by Redknapp because Tony Cottee always played better in a front two. He thrived on his partner doing the donkey work, that's why his relationship with McAvennie blossomed in '86. By his own admission, Tony wanted to concentrate on scoring goals and could never understand why strikers were expected to carry out any defensive duties. Iain was the opposite, what he lacked in goals he made up for in work rate. On paper they seemed like a decent partnership.

### Julian Stamps Out Gullit's Class

Dowie made his debut for his second spell on a *Monday Night Football* at home to Chelsea, testing the goalkeeper early on in a bright start under the lights. But from then on, there was only one star of the show.

The mystery of Ruud Gullit's arrival at Chelsea had still yet to be explained. Whether it was Glenn Hoddle's powers of persuasion, or the significant sums of money Ken Bates had deposited in his bank account, the Dutchman had already started to prove his worth. He duly took centre stage in front of the Sky cameras, pinging crossfield passes galore and dictating the game like an ageing quarter-back. He might as well have been playing in his pipe and slippers. It was humiliating. We couldn't get near him and nor could his team-mates. At times he seemed to be playing eleven different positions concurrently. In fairness, if your only option is to pass the ball to Scott Minto, you've probably got every right to just do it your f\*\*king self.

The Blues raced into a 2-0 lead, and ordinarily Gullit's sensational showing would have been the topic of the half-time conversation, until Julian Dicks intervened in his own inimitable style to steal the headlines.

Chelsea's diminutive striker John Spencer and Dicks had been having their own private off-the-ball battle after the lively Scot left one on Julian in the early exchanges – possibly the most unwise decision since JFK told his driver to keep the roof down. As the half drew to a close, the two clashed again. With Spencer sprawled on the floor, Julian planted the studs from his trailing leg right into the Chelsea striker's skull leaving the forward with the sort of gaping wound that looked like he'd been playing headers and volleys with a machete.

Even Johnnie Cochran couldn't defend this. It was the most blatant of red card offences, yet somehow the referee let Julian escape with just a yellow, which spared us the immediate ordeal of another suspension. Spencer, whose hastily applied bandage made him look like the distant cousin of Tutankhamun, had the last laugh by netting the killer goal in the second half.

The 3-1 defeat, followed by a 1-0 loss at Highbury, left us with two points from six games. For the third Premier League season in succession, we'd started like we were in quicksand. We needed to get moving fast – before we started sinking into a dreaded relegation battle.

**EX:** *We've had the pleasure of doing numerous events and podcasts with Julian. He's a totally different character off the pitch. He's quiet, thoughtful and very mild mannered. He still denies that he meant to do it. When you watch the replays, it's a little hard to believe. But he maintains it's the truth.*

**DAVE:** *Ex is right. And whilst that's unbelievable to a lot of people, it's not in Dicksy's character to shy away from the truth. With a wry smile, he reflects on certain tackles that have sent wingers halfway into the Chicken Run, often with an undercurrent of pride and sadistic pleasure. So for him to say that stamping on John was accidental that night, I do actually believe him. What's funny is that it was actually Spencer's 25th birthday that day, too. He probably went home with a stitch for every year!*

**EX:** *I was an AC Milan fan in the '90s, when everyone had an Italian team because of Channel 4. I have Italian roots in my family. And I loved that Dutch side that won the 1988 Euros with Gullit, Rijkaard and Van Basten. I never dreamed I'd actually see any of them play in person. Gullit was like a Rolls-Royce of a player, spraying passes all over the place. When people ask me about the best performance I've seen from an opposition player, I still say that one. Gullit was a class above everyone else.*

## Lucky Seven

Unsurprisingly, Julian's indiscretion dominated the discussion around West Ham United in the following days. And rather than lie low, our skipper conceded a penalty (which Ian Wright missed), and then got sent off for two shocking tackles in a defeat at Highbury, where our numbers were so low that veteran keeper Les Sealey was forced to come on from the subs' bench and play the final ten minutes up front, much to the amusement of old adversary Tony Adams.

To compound Julian's misery, ten days after the incident with Spencer, the FA – having dithered like a man perusing the drills in B&Q – duly announced their intention to charge Dicks 'with conduct likely to bring the game into disrepute.'

It was familiar territory. The red card against Arsenal was Julian's ninth as a full-time professional, and he'd also clocked up a mightily impressive 52 bookings. He had racked up so many disciplinary fines that Sir Bert Millichip and Graham Kelly could have bought themselves a holiday home in Tenerife.

With another ban brewing, Dicks had a chance to make amends in the home game with Everton. A game which gave us our first win at the seventh time of asking, and also showed why The Terminator was such a terrace hero in east London. With six minutes gone, Iain Dowie was manhandled in the area and the referee pointed to the spot. Dicks wasted no time in hammering the penalty past an outstretched Neville Southall. After Vinny Samways had equalised, an awful Earl Barrett challenge on Lazaridis was penalised and we had another chance from 12 yards. Same taker. Same corner. Same result. Two penalties and a precious first three points of the season.

Looking back, these are the moments that made Julian so special. He'd had an absolutely rotten couple of weeks. He was playing crap, his face had been plastered all over the back pages, he'd been the subject of radio phone-ins, and he'd been labelled a 'disgrace' by pundits relishing their opportunity to stick the metaphorical boot in. It would have been easy to shirk responsibility. And there have been many players over the years who would have crumbled under that sort of pressure.

Instead, Julian fronted up and put in a match-winning performance when the team needed it most. That's what made him a legend.

The win against Everton proved to be the catalyst our season needed. We earned a creditable point down at Southampton, and then Julian scored again from the spot as we stuffed Bristol Rovers 3-0 in the League Cup.

That game also saw the return of Michael Hughes on loan from Strasbourg. The Northern Irishman's direct running and cultured left peg had been crucial during the latter half of the previous season, and he showed his quality again by creating Tony Cottee's winner on an absolute stinker of a *Monday Night Football* at Selhurst Park, when you wouldn't have blamed viewers of Wimbledon vs West

Ham for turning over and watching *Coronation Street* instead.

Alongside Hughes, our other new signings were starting to find their feet in Claret and Blue. Robbie Slater was providing the most impressive Australian performances since Kylie Minogue's surprise cameo in *The Vicar of Dibley*, and Iain Dowie ended his goal drought with a bullet header at home to Blackburn (where only a last-minute Shearer strike denied us all three points), before notching again in a 1-0 win at Hillsborough the following week.

A haul of eleven points from five games meant Harry's side were marching towards mid table, but the boss wasn't done yet. Further additions to our growing 'League of Nations' (as the newspapers were dubbing us) came in the shape of John Harkes on loan from Derby. The American international made his first start in a sensational 3-0 spanking of Bolton at Burnden Park, where young Danny Williamson stole the show with a sublime solo effort in the last minute.

By the time we beat QPR in late November, where Tony Cottee morphed into Diego Maradona to score the winner, we were tenth in the League and high on confidence. The squad now included players from Czechoslovakia, Denmark, Holland, Australia and Northern Ireland, but somehow Harry Redknapp had moulded us into a harmonious unit that NATO would be proud of.

Little did we know that there would be further additions from far afield in the New Year. Including some of the most infamous signings in West Ham history.

**DAVE:** *Julian has often been questioned on his penalty technique, and his answer has always been the same: "No technique. Head down. F\*\*king smash it." That game against Everton summed him up as a person and as a leader. Balls of steel and a resilience that inspired the players and the fans.*

**EX:** *If you looked at Julian Dicks' disciplinary record, and if he worked at your business, you'd be very concerned and disappointed at how he let you down so regularly. But because he epitomised that typical East End mentality – he don't take any shit, he would always fight back – that made him a folk hero. Of course, it helped that he was a technically brilliant player, too. Sadly, the media narrative was that he was a thug who got sent off all the time. That reputation probably stopped him getting an international cap.*

**DAVE:** *We had some real quality in that squad, and one that I had high hopes for was Danny Williamson. That goal against Bolton is ANOTHER one that doesn't get talked about enough. Collectively, it felt like things were starting to fall into place.*

**EX:** *Michael Hughes was an excellent permanent addition to the squad, having proved himself during his loan spells. He had that little bit of extra technical quality. Robbie Slater was a decent player, too. He was more of a workhorse than Hughes, but he was still a decent signing.*

*And I really believe that, if not for injuries, Danny Williamson could have been an England international. That goal summed up his quality. The strange thing about Burnden Park was that there was a supermarket behind the goal at one end. I hope no one had a restricted view of that finish, because it was one of the best in West Ham's top-flight history.*

### When Harry Met Dani

The New Year saw the departure of Don Hutchison to Sheffield United. With Dowie and Cottee forming an effective partnership up front, and Bishop and Moncur fixtures in central midfield, the Scot had gradually been isolated from first-team action. The emergence of Williamson, a confident and clever midfielder from the youth ranks, limited his chances further.

Harry decided to use the funds to bring in reinforcements on the flanks. Eyebrows were raised when he made a move for Tottenham's expensive outcast Ilie Dumitrescu. The Romanian winger had been shunted out to Sevilla on loan after a poor start to his Premier League career. The fact that Spurs were so eager to agree a deal should have raised alarm bells. It's a bit like Skeletor buying He-Man a birthday cake.

It would be a while before Dumitrescu's work permit would be granted, which meant another new arrival stole all the headlines.

"My missus fancies him. Even I don't know whether to play him or f\*\*k him," said Harry Redknapp in reference to the latest addition to his multinational squad.

He was welcoming Daniel Da Cruz Carvalho, a Portuguese forward who had been the undisputed star of the 1995 FIFA World Youth Championship, and had caught the eye in a senior friendly against England a few months later.

Now one of the most talked-about talents in football was on his way to the Premier League. And it wasn't just his gifted left peg that had made Sandra Redknapp's heart flutter.

You see, Dani was a dreamboat. Hair like Johnny Depp and big, puppy-dog eyes that could melt the heart of both man and beast. At 19 years of age, he was fulfilling every teenage boy's fantasy: he was both a male model and a top-class international footballer. His arrival on loan from Sporting Lisbon was seen as a real coup for a club of our size, as according to the papers he was already a target for some of Europe's heavy hitters.

After West Ham fans got a glimpse of his gorgeous visage in a substitute appearance during the win over Nottingham Forest, Dani made his first start under the bright lights of the Sky cameras on the trip to Tottenham. It must have been quite the culture shock. One of the sexiest men alive had gone from sharing a catwalk with supermodels to sharing a dressing room with Iain Dowie. It was like a Premier League production of *Beauty and the Beast*.

The deeply desirable Dani wasn't the only new face on show. Since the dizzy heights of the win over QPR, we'd endured another Christmas where our form went down the khazi, meaning Harry had to plug the gaps elsewhere.

**EX:** The Sun *headline when Dani arrived said: 'LOCK UP YOUR DAUGHTERS'. All the attention was on Dani's looks. Even now, 25-plus years later, I don't recall that on any other player. There must have been other good-looking players before and since, but none got the attention he did.*

**DAVE:** *To this day, Dani is probably the best-looking geezer I have ever seen in my life. Imagine being a 19-year-old male model, playing for West Ham in the '90s? F\*\*k me, he must have absolutely cleaned up on a night out.*

*I just have this vision of Iain Dowie meeting him for the first time and thinking: "Oh for f\*\*k's sake." By all accounts, we were lucky to have Dani as well, because he could play and was known as a hot prospect on the European market.*

**EX:** *Scoring at Spurs on his full debut should have made him an instant hero for me. But unfortunately I was overcome by teenage jealousy. The girl I fancied in Year Ten talked about him constantly, and how she was going to marry him – much to my annoyance.*

## Super Slav

When I read on Ceefax on a winter's day in January 1996 that West Ham had signed a new centre-back, a surge of relief ran through me. It was no secret that our defence needed reinforcements. We'd lost five of our last six games and our back four – which seemed to hand out clear-cut chances like Christmas cards during the festive season – had conceded a whopping 16 goals in the process.

The new signing was named as Slaven Bilic, a Croatian international from Bundesliga side Karlsruhe. I would probably have been more excited for his arrival, were it not for three pressing issues: i) I knew nothing about Slaven Bilic, ii) I knew nothing about the Bundesliga, and iii) I knew nothing about Karlsruhe.

Starved of the internet (the information superhighway was still a twinkle in the eye of Tim Berners-Lee) my primary sources of football trivia were *Shoot!* magazine (where I was more likely to found out about Peter Ndlovu's favourite quiz show than any serious discussion about German football), *Rothman's Football Yearbook* (which focused solely on English football) and Sensible Soccer. The latter had a wide database, but was particularly unhelpful when it came to identifying new faces. All the players were reduced to amorphous 8-bit blobs with no remarkable features, which in Iain Dowie's case was a considerable improvement.

Bilic was described in the press as a 'tough, uncompromising East European' which sounded like the villains on *Die Hard*. So, it was quite the shock when I saw him for the first time on a *Monday Night Football* in February at White Hart Lane. Hair like an indie rocker, earrings and leather jacket – it looked like we'd accidentally signed the lead guitarist from Metallica rather than an international centre-half. For a brief moment, I wondered whether the Curse of Marco Boogers had struck again. What if Harry had unwittingly put the wrong video in the machine again – and instead of watching Karlsruhe vs Mönchengladbach, he was actually watching the free VHS Sandra got with her subscription to *Kerrang!* magazine?

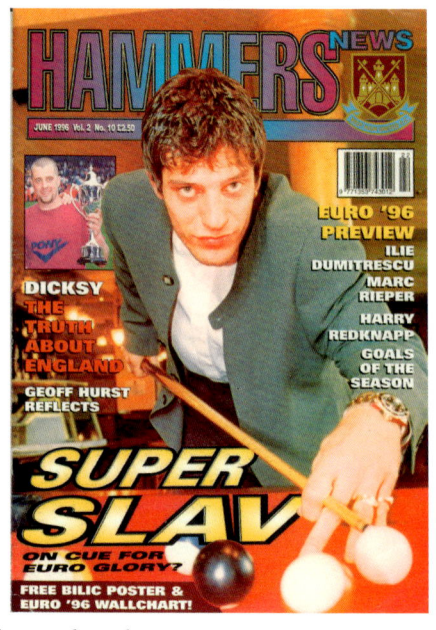

Throwing Bilic into the hurly-burly of a London derby for his debut felt like quite the test of his abilities. With no Stoke in England's top flight, a 'wet Monday night in Edmonton' was a suitable proving ground for the latest fancy foreign signing to hop across the English Channel. And prove himself he did.

We took an early lead when Dani nodded in from a corner. And, in the early going, the youngster caught the eye by linking up nicely with his unlikely striker partner Iain Dowie. Whilst the Big Fella ran hard and jumped high in absolutely appalling conditions, it was the young Portuguese who brought some calm to the chaos of a full-blooded London derby. His first touch was so good you'd swear he'd dipped his boots in Pritt-Stick, and a wiggle of the hips would frequently leave his marker for dead, eliciting swoons from the packed away end.

Dani ran out of steam and was substituted in the second half as Spurs laid siege to our goal. His match-winning goal was enough for him to be voted Man of the Match by the Sky Sports viewers, but the rock at the heart of that rearguard performance was Bilic. The Croatian was absolutely incredible, standing firm as he was battered by the elements and a Tottenham side who threw everything at us. Time after time, he headed away a dangerous cross or put his body on the line to block shots at goal. His heroic display made him an instant fan favourite.

**EX:** *I didn't realise at the time how significant an eventful this was for the future of West Ham United. Like everyone else, I knew nothing about Slaven Bilic except for what I read in the papers. I remember reading he was highly intelligent, he had a law degree and he spoke several languages. Part of me wondered if he'd done any research into West Ham – did he understand the ridiculous club he was joining? As soon as he got on the pitch, his class began to show. I loved him. Looking back, he was the first of the next generation of centre-backs. They were shifting from being headers and tacklers. Now instead of just hoofing the ball clear, they could dribble, pass and build attacks from the back.*

**DAVE:** *These days, we can become an 'expert' on a player we have never heard of by watching a five-minute compilation on YouTube. I miss the days of only having a name to go by on Ceefax or ClubCall. It's the excitement of the unknown – and Bilic was the perfect example. My god, what a signing he proved to be. And if there's one way of endearing yourself to the West Ham fans, it's by playing a big part in a win against Tottenham.*

*You can see why him and Julian became close friends. They were cut from the same cloth. Hard, uncompromising players with good quality and a winning mentality. I loved watching Bilic play. His partnership with Marc Rieper remains one of the best centre-half pairings I have ever seen at West Ham.*

## Dreamboat Dani Drifts Away

The win at Spurs was followed by successive League victories against Chelsea and Newcastle. The signings of Dani, Dumitrescu and Bilic had lifted the mood at Upton Park. Their arrivals – even though Bilic was the only regular starter – heralded a welcome run of form which saw us lose only four times in the latter part of the season.

Bilic was the undoubted star of the new trio. We soon realised that, much like Rieper the year prior, Harry had found another foreign treasure. Aside from his positioning, his anticipation and his strength, what stood out was Slav's leadership and composure – both with and without the ball. He brought calm where too often there had been outbreaks of calamity. In addition, he would frequently stride purposefully out of defence like a modern-day Bobby Moore and launch our attacks from the back.

Unfortunately, the early impressions of Dumitrescu weren't quite so stellar. The Romanian had some eye-catching tricks, but then again so did Tommy Cooper. Worryingly, Dumi seemed like he'd gone to the David Kelly School of Strength & Conditioning. Somehow, every time the ball came his way, he ended up on the deck. In fairness, Kelly had since gone on to forge a very respectable career in the second tier, whereas Dumitrescu was showing the same weaknesses that made him surplus to requirements at Tottenham.

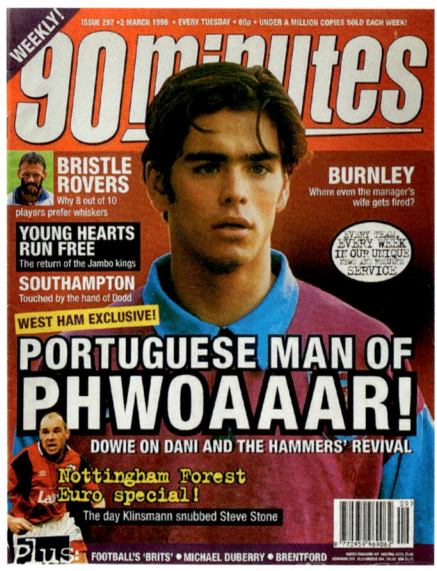

In hindsight, when Ruel Fox – a man roughly the size of my neighbour's hamster – is considered more adept at coping with the physicality of English football, that's a sure sign something's not quite right.

Meanwhile, Dani was having his own issues around being permanently horizontal, though they were entirely of his own making. His superstar looks meant he'd become a darling of the paparazzi. He was linked romantically with a host of pop stars, TV hosts and glamour models. And rather than try to look after a 19-year-old living away from his family for the first time, his agent sought to keep him busy by whisking him off to high-profile London nightspots. This included a bizarre appearance on the red carpet for the West End premiere of *Twelve Monkeys* alongside Bruce Willis and Brad Pitt. Iain Dowie's invite must have got lost in the post.

They say being a top-class sportsman is all about sacrifice. And as Dani adapted to his new status as London's number one swordsman, he realised he would have to forego some aspects of his lifestyle. The first thing to get scrubbed off the list was training. Getting to Chadwell Heath for a 10.30 start was a real pain in the arse, especially when he'd been on the dancefloor until the early hours.

Plus, there was the effect that actually playing professional football was having on his energy levels. Despite his relatively poor command of English, his love of the universal language had become legendary. Keeping up with that sort of schedule wasn't conducive with playing 90 minutes of football.

Redknapp soon lost patience. Robbie Slater wasn't out until all hours cavorting with lads' mag cover girls, although admittedly that probably wasn't by choice. Dani found himself quickly benched and reduced to the role of impact substitute, a role he seemed entirely happy with. After all, he was living the dream of every hormone-fuelled teenage boy. Football was just getting in the way.

He made fleeting appearances, including a goalscoring cameo in a 4-2 win against Manchester City, when his lovely left peg produced one last act of wizardry; but his time at West Ham was over almost as soon as it started. He made only nine appearances in Claret and Blue.

**DAVE:** *I remember thinking, surely no one can be that perfect? Dani can't be a Premier League footballer, with a modelling career, ploughing through pop stars at just 19 years of age? At 19, I was still playing Football Manager in my pants, lusting over the pages of* FHM*! Unfortunately for him, he was the victim of his own success, and a management team that wanted to exploit that. Too much was expected from him. He should've just focused on his main passion in life and committed to it because, ultimately, by having everything, he was running the risk of having nothing. It's a shame it didn't work out for him at West Ham. That broke a few girls' hearts, for sure.*

**EX:** *Typically, there was something too good to be true about Dani signing for West Ham. Dave mentions his main passion in life. To be honest, I think it was nightclubs. He loved the attention. He loved the ladies. He didn't feel that way about football. By the end, he turned up to training hung over, if he even turned up at all. The excellent goal he scored against City showed there was a real talent in there somewhere. But he wasn't motivated enough to make the most of it.*

## Dowie Proves the Doubters Wrong

To the untrained eye, there wasn't much to admire about Iain Dowie. In the most tribal of sports, he was one of those are players that could unite the football universe. No matter what your club or crest, all agreed that you'd rather not see him in your starting eleven.

There were the cheap barbs about his appearance (as you've seen in this book already). You know the stuff: that he was so ugly he had to trick or treat over the phone. But the real disdain for Dowie wasn't his appearance, it was his exploits –

or lack of them – on the pitch. His one-in-four goalscoring ratio hardly had Alan Shearer running for cover.

Hence the reason why his return to Upton Park at the start of the '95/96 season was initially greeted with about as much enthusiasm as the taxman knocking at your front door. Whilst the rest of the League were signing superstars from overseas, we'd gone for Mr Spit and Sawdust. Eight months later, and even the most stubborn of fans would be forced to admit that the target man had eclipsed all expectations.

Before the final home game of the season, Dowie was announced as runner-up in the Hammer of the Year awards to Julian Dicks. What the Big Man lacked in elegance, he made up for in sheer effort – a trait that was much appreciated by the Upton Park faithful. He had hustled and harried centre-halves across the land. And there were bursts of quality, too. He didn't just put his head in where it hurt (even if his features suggested otherwise) – his intelligent link play had brought the best out of Tony Cottee, who finished the season as top scorer with 12 goals.

The goal return still provoked doubts (eight in 33 games), however his overall contribution to the team was clear to see. The late-season wins against Manchester City (where Dowie notched twice) and Bolton (Cottee scoring the winner) meant we finished the season in tenth position, our highest placing since returning to the Premier League.

Considering the awful start, the caravan chaos and our crap Christmas form, it was a terrific result. Despite the constant hokey-cokey of players in and out, we had the makings of a settled side. The question was whether we could kick on – and how would we do it?

Over the course of the season, the Premier League had attracted more exotic names, though often with erratic results. Tomas Brolin had joined Leeds from Parma packing so much extra luggage around his waistline, you wondered if he'd taken up a hobby as a sumo wrestler. Towering target man Andrea Silenzi had joined Forest from Torino and looked about as physically impressive as a feather duster.

Of course, there were successes, too. The delightfully diminutive Juninho had become a star at Middlesbrough, whilst North East neighbours Newcastle had taken Tino Asprilla to their hearts, despite the Toon's capitulation in the title race (blowing a 12-point lead over Manchester United).

Though Harry was starting to enjoy bargain hunting in international markets, the results were similarly erratic. For every Bilic, there was a Boogers. The signing of Dowie proved that there was still plenty of value to be found domestically. But would Harry be tempted to take a gamble on foreign currency again?

Later that summer, we got our answer.

**DAVE:** *West Ham fans have only ever asked for 100% commitment from players. We want players who respect that badge on their chest and give everything they have for the club that we love. That's why Iain Dowie was runner up in the Hammer of the Year award that season. He worked his nuts off every single week, and we respected that.*

**EX:** *The fact that Iain Dowie was runner-up in the HOTY shows you that you can be popular at West Ham by giving your all – which is something all players should know. There have been far more skilful and glamorous winners such as Moore, Di Canio and Tevez, but Dowie deserves his place amongst those names for the sheer effort he gave for the cause.*

**DAVE:** *A mid-table finish was unquestionably a successful season, and it was clear that Harry was starting to thrive as a manager. He made some fantastic signings, created a good camaraderie and was playing exciting, attacking football.*

*I couldn't wait to see what he would do in the summer to make us even better, and really kick on as a football club.*

## FA Premier League - 1995/96

| Date | Opponent | H/A | Score | Att. | Scorers |
|---|---|---|---|---|---|
| 19 August | Leeds United | H | 1–2 | 22,901 | Williamson |
| 23 August | Manchester United | A | 1–2 | 31,966 | Bruce (og) |
| 26 August | Nottingham Forest | A | 1–1 | 26,645 | Allen |
| 30 August | Tottenham Hotspur | H | 1–1 | 23,516 | Hutchison |
| 11 September | Chelsea | H | 1–3 | 19,228 | Hutchison |
| 16 September | Arsenal | A | 0–1 | 38,065 | |
| 23 September | Everton | H | 2–1 | 21,085 | Dicks (2 p) |
| 2 October | Southampton | A | 0–0 | 13,568 | |
| 16 October | Wimbledon | A | 1–0 | 9,411 | Cottee |
| 21 October | Blackburn Rovers | H | 1–1 | 21,776 | Dowie |
| 28 October | Sheffield Wed | A | 1–0 | 23,917 | Dowie |
| 4 November | Aston Villa | H | 1–4 | 23,637 | Dicks (p) |
| 18 November | Bolton Wanderers | A | 3–0 | 19,047 | Bishop, Cottee, Williamson |
| 22 November | Liverpool | H | 0–0 | 24,324 | |
| 25 November | QPR | H | 1–0 | 21,504 | Cottee |
| 2 December | Blackburn Rovers | A | 2–4 | 26,638 | Dicks (p), Slater |
| 11 December | Everton | A | 0–3 | 31,778 | |
| 16 December | Southampton | H | 2–1 | 18,501 | Cottee, Dowie |
| 23 December | Middlesbrough | A | 2–4 | 28,640 | Cottee, Dicks |
| 1 January | Manchester City | A | 1–2 | 26,024 | Dowie |
| 13 January | Leeds United | A | 0–2 | 30,658 | |
| 22 January | Manchester United | H | 0–1 | 24,197 | |
| 31 January | Coventry City | H | 3–2 | 18,884 | Cottee, Rieper, Dowie |
| 3 February | Nottingham Forest | H | 1–0 | 21,257 | Slater |
| 12 February | Tottenham Hotspur | A | 1–0 | 29,781 | Dani |
| 17 February | Chelsea | A | 2–1 | 25,252 | Dicks, Williamson |
| 21 February | Newcastle United | H | 2–0 | 23,843 | Williamson, Cottee |
| 24 February | Arsenal | H | 0–1 | 24,217 | |
| 2 March | Coventry City | A | 2–2 | 17,459 | Cottee, Rieper |
| 9 March | Middlesbrough | H | 2–0 | 23,850 | Dowie, Dicks (p) |
| 18 March | Newcastle United | A | 0–3 | 36,331 | |
| 23 March | Manchester City | H | 4–2 | 24,017 | Dowie (2), Dicks, Dani |
| 6 April | Wimbledon | H | 1–1 | 20,402 | Dicks |
| 8 April | Liverpool | A | 0–2 | 40,326 | |
| 13 April | Bolton Wanderers | H | 1–0 | 23,086 | Cottee |

| | | | | | |
|---|---|---|---|---|---|
| 17 April | Aston Villa | A | 1–1 | 26,768 | Cottee |
| 27 April | QPR | A | 0–3 | 18,828 | |
| 5 May | Sheffield Wed | H | 1–1 | 23,790 | Dicks |

## FA Cup

| | | | | | |
|---|---|---|---|---|---|
| 6 January R3 | Southend United | H | 2–0 | 23,284 | Moncur, Hughes |
| 7 February R4 | Grimsby Town | H | 1–1 | 22,030 | Dowie |
| 14 February R4R | Grimsby Town | A | 0–3 | 8,382 | |

## League Cup

| | | | | | |
|---|---|---|---|---|---|
| 20 Sept R2 1L | Bristol Rovers | A | 1–0 | 7,103 | Moncur |
| 4 October R2 2L | Bristol Rovers | H | 3–0 | 15,375 | Dicks (p), Bishop, Cottee |
| 25 October R3 | Southampton | A | 1–2 | 11,059 | Cottee |

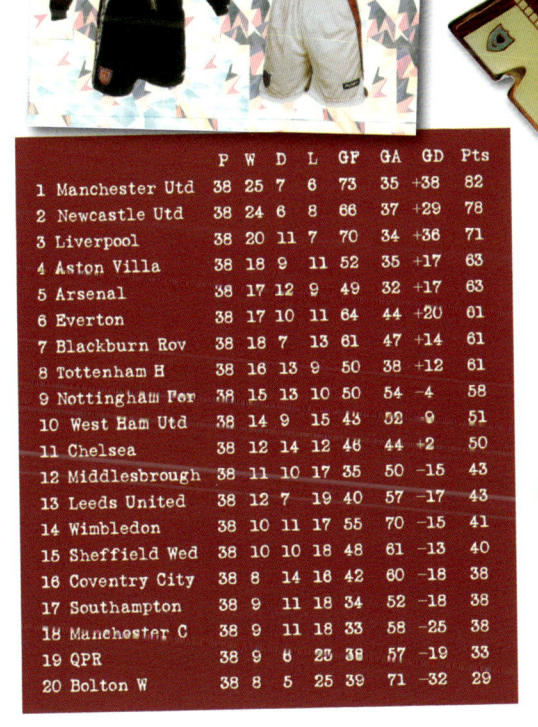

| | P | W | D | L | GF | GA | GD | Pts |
|---|---|---|---|---|---|---|---|---|
| 1 Manchester Utd | 38 | 25 | 7 | 6 | 73 | 35 | +38 | 82 |
| 2 Newcastle Utd | 38 | 24 | 6 | 8 | 66 | 37 | +29 | 78 |
| 3 Liverpool | 38 | 20 | 11 | 7 | 70 | 34 | +36 | 71 |
| 4 Aston Villa | 38 | 18 | 9 | 11 | 52 | 35 | +17 | 63 |
| 5 Arsenal | 38 | 17 | 12 | 9 | 49 | 32 | +17 | 63 |
| 6 Everton | 38 | 17 | 10 | 11 | 64 | 44 | +20 | 61 |
| 7 Blackburn Rov | 38 | 18 | 7 | 13 | 61 | 47 | +14 | 61 |
| 8 Tottenham H | 38 | 16 | 13 | 9 | 50 | 38 | +12 | 61 |
| 9 Nottingham For | 38 | 15 | 13 | 10 | 50 | 54 | -4 | 58 |
| 10 West Ham Utd | 38 | 14 | 9 | 15 | 43 | 52 | -9 | 51 |
| 11 Chelsea | 38 | 12 | 14 | 12 | 46 | 44 | +2 | 50 |
| 12 Middlesbrough | 38 | 11 | 10 | 17 | 35 | 50 | -15 | 43 |
| 13 Leeds United | 38 | 12 | 7 | 19 | 40 | 57 | -17 | 43 |
| 14 Wimbledon | 38 | 10 | 11 | 17 | 55 | 70 | -15 | 41 |
| 15 Sheffield Wed | 38 | 10 | 10 | 18 | 48 | 61 | -13 | 40 |
| 16 Coventry City | 38 | 8 | 14 | 16 | 42 | 60 | -18 | 38 |
| 17 Southampton | 38 | 9 | 11 | 18 | 34 | 52 | -18 | 38 |
| 18 Manchester C | 38 | 9 | 11 | 18 | 33 | 58 | -25 | 38 |
| 19 QPR | 38 | 9 | 6 | 23 | 38 | 57 | -19 | 33 |
| 20 Bolton W | 38 | 8 | 5 | 25 | 39 | 71 | -32 | 29 |

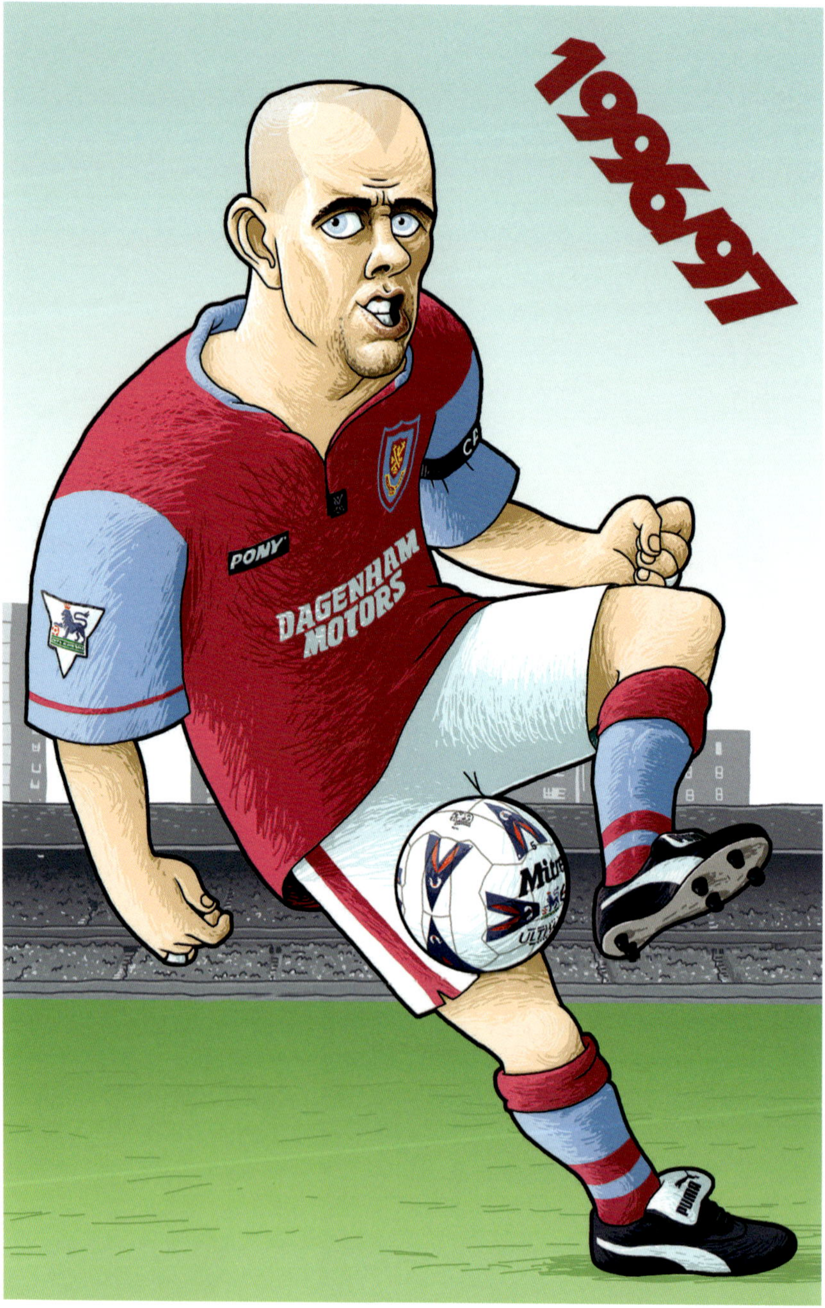
1996/97
PONY
DAGENHAM
MOTORS
PUMA

## Hammers Go Back to the Futre

In May 1987, Paulo Futre had the world at his feet. He had just inspired unfancied Porto to European Cup glory, defeating a brilliant Bayern Munich side that counted Brehme, Matthaus and Rummenigge in their ranks.

His virtuoso second-half showing had been one of the great individual performances in competition history. He was already a household name in his homeland – having inspired Porto to successive Primera Liga titles – but this made him a megastar. The way he had dropped a shoulder, then drifted past players at will, earned him comparisons with Diego Maradona

Fast forward nine years and Futre was in football's wilderness. That brilliance vs Bayern had earned him a money-spinning move to Atletico Madrid where his legendary left peg made him an instant hit… until the injuries took their toll.

The problem with players like Futre – and Maradona – was that their effortless talents made them easy targets for the hatchet men. It was an era when skilful players were offered little protection by referees. Defenders could commit the sort of atrocities that should have seen them hauled up in front of The Hague, only to escape with a ticking off from timid officials. Meanwhile, men like Futre were left to count their scars.

The knee injuries mounted up, and each time Futre returned he was a paler shadow of the star that had once shone so bright. After five seasons, it was painfully clear that his time had been and gone.

Stints in Italy followed. A spell with Reggiana – where flashes of brilliance were enough to convince the mighty Milan to offer him a contract – was about as good as it got. He made one solitary appearance at the San Siro before they cast him off into no-man's land.

That night against Bayern felt like a lifetime ago. Having barely played football in two years, he was now a football has-been. A crock. All set for football's unforgiving scrapheap.

Then along came Harry Redknapp.

How the Portuguese passed the medical at Chadwell Heath remains one of mankind's great mysteries – up there with Bigfoot, the Bermuda Triangle and Tony Adams' romancing of Caprice. Even West Ham's basic medical equipment, presumably bought second-hand from Viktor Frankenstein, surely noticed the gaping holes where his knee joints should have been.

Apparently not.

And so, on a July day in 1996, one of the most famous names in football was announced as a West Ham player, and – completely unaware that he hadn't kicked a ball for two years, or that his knees were held together by muscle fibre made of Alphabetti Spaghetti – I couldn't have been happier. That's the glory of transfers. It only takes one big name, one surge of adrenaline for you to abandon all reason.

Besides, it was high time we got in on the act. After the steady trickle of continental superstars arriving in the Premier League over recent years, the floodgates had officially opened. The country was riding the wave of a glorious summer of football. Despite England's typically agonising exit at the semi-final stage, Euro 96 had exceeded all expectations. June had been a blur of Britpop, alcopops and Karel Poborsky's lollipop finish. It felt like Italia 90 revisited, when a whole country had celebrated in the sunshine. English football was back at the top table of European football, not just a retirement home for some of the game's biggest names. Players in their pomp – with big reputations and even bigger paypackets – were arriving in their droves.

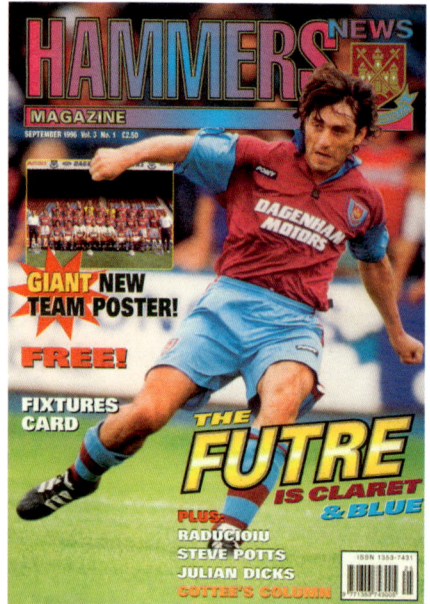

Czech sensation Poborsky signed for champions Manchester United, Chelsea brought in Roberto Di Matteo, Franck Leboeuf and the legendary Luca Vialli. And even Middlesbrough, unfashionable Middlesbrough, were in on the act. Fabrizio Ravanelli – a Champions League winner with Juventus the prior season – was on his way to Teesside for a reported 42 grand per week.

Now, after years of picking our way through the bargain basement, we were in on the act. This was West Ham's bright new Futre. And there was another big name on his way, too.

**EX:** *That summer of Euro 96 was one of the peak moments of my life. I was 15 at the time, starting to get some independence. Every day was boiling hot. And with the emergence of Blur, Oasis and even the Spice Girls, it felt like Britain ruled the music world. It was such a great time to be alive.*

*Paulo Futre was the first proper exotic signing I remember us making. He had long hair, which was the classic '90s trait of an exciting continental player, like*

Batistuta, Poborsky, Petit and Baggio. When the club announced the signing, I rushed out to get the latest edition of Hammers News, *which had exclusive pics of our new superstar signing.*

**DAVE:** *Signing Paulo was so exciting. I was naïve to his injury problems at the time because he had passed a medical at the club; but believing in that process was like believing in OJ Simpson's alibi. Futre had the superstar ego to match his talent as well. During pre-season, the boys would face a gruelling cross-country run at Hainault Forest and, on Paulo's first run, he arrived in a chauffeur-driven limousine! But his talent was undeniable, all on 20 Marlboro Lights a day! I wonder what he would have achieved with us without his injury issues? That said, if he never had those issues, would he have ever joined West Ham?!*

## Rad-ical Signing for Redknapp

My first sighting of Florin Raducioiu had been during that wonderful World Cup in the States two years prior. He'd been the focal point of the attack for Romania, and seemed to be a global superstar in the making.

When the Eastern Europeans returned to our screens at Euro 96 they were a huge disappointment. Gheorghe Hagi's left peg still had more magic than David Copperfield's coat pocket, but elsewhere the team flattered to deceive. Ilie Dumitrescu, who Harry Redknapp had fought so hard to get a work permit for back in February, hadn't been selected. The official reason was concerns about his fitness. The unofficial reason was he was rubbish.

And, up front, Raducioiu looked lively but also a little bit lightweight. Every time you walked past the telly he seemed to fall over. Nonetheless, he had scored Romania's only goal of a tournament in which they lost all three games.

He wasn't going to hold the ball up much and he wasn't going to run the channels. He seemed to be a proper penalty-box poacher. In that respect he reminded me of Tony Cottee. Which posed a problem, as we already had a Tony Cottee on our books. How the two would play together was a mystery for me – a mystery that was solved when TC was sensationally sold to Malaysian outfit Selangor for £750,000.

With Raducioiu and Futre joining the likes of Bilic, Rieper, Lazaridis and co., Redknapp's squad was christened the 'Foreign Legion' by the press. Though there were some more familiar faces amongst our new arrivals. The most curious of which was Stevie Jones, back from a spell at Bournemouth for around £200,000. His goal at White Hart Lane two years prior had sealed him legend status in my eyes, but 24 goals in 76 appearances on the south coast didn't suggest he'd turned into a top-class finisher overnight.

Mark Bowen, who had been part of Norwich's European adventures two seasons before, arrived on a free transfer to bolster the squad. I'd seen him play a lot and had never been able to work out what his best position was. In hindsight, it was probably the bench.

The most intriguing of the domestic transfers was Richard Hall, a tall and muscular centre-half from Southampton. Rumour had it he was on the radar of clubs like Liverpool and Spurs. So for us to secure his services for a £1.9 million fee felt like a great bit of business. This was a chance to right the wrong of Simon Webster, who was cruelly cut off in his prime, and had left the club after several aborted comebacks. Hall was 24 years old, Southampton's standout performer (behind the legendary Matt Le Tissier), an Under-21 international, and touted by many in the game as the future of England's backline.

It was an exciting time. We had two big names from European football joining us alongside a genuine Premier League prospect.

**DAVE:** *It wasn't just an exciting time for West Ham, it was an exciting time for the Premier League. These overseas players were really starting to take the division to another level. Florin was our marquee signing (or so I thought!) but it didn't take long for the bubble to burst. On his first day in training, Dicksy wanted to see what he was made of with some tough tackles. Very quickly, Julian had his answer... Playdoh. Florin had joined the most physical league in world football, and he just couldn't deal with it.*

**EX:** *I remember Raducioiu being quality at USA 94, but he got a real culture shock when he arrived in England – and it wasn't just Julian who was ready to test him out. We played a pre-season friendly at Torquay, who gave Florin a traditional lower-league welcome to English football. Rough, tough centre-half Jon Gittens nearly rearranged Florin's nose with an off-the-ball challenge. Looking back, I wonder if that immediately sowed seeds of doubt in Raducioiu's mind – was this really the sort of league he wanted to be a part of?*

*Mark Bowen was a pretty average signing at the end of his career, just a cheap addition to the squad. I always enjoyed watching Southampton because of Matt Le Tissier, so I was well aware of Richard Hall and was delighted when we signed him. But the curse of Simon Webster struck again and he was seriously injured before the ink dried on his contract. Classic West Ham – a promising career over before it started.*

**DAVE:** This club's luck with signings is absolutely diabolical. On paper, Futre, Raducioiu and Hall looked like some of the best business in the club's history. It was like a dream – one which didn't take long to fade and die.

## Paulo Goes from Zero to Hero

"F*** you, I no play."

The shirt was hurled back in the face of loyal kitman Eddie Gillam. His crime? He'd handed West Ham's new superstar a jersey with the number 16 on it. Short of Gillam defecating on his ancestor's graves, Futre could not comprehend a greater insult. Here he was, one of the beautiful game's most iconic number tens, being denied his shirt number... because of John Moncur?

Whilst Gillam faced an existential crisis, Harry Redknapp tried to defuse the situation.

"It's the first game of the season, Paulo. We've got Arsenal away. There's thousands of fans out there now, singing your name – and they're all wearing Futre 16 shirts on the back. We can't get them reprinted now. We're kicking off in half an hour. Come on, son. Get your boots on, we'll get this sorted next week."

"F**k you, I no play."

Peter Storrie had been summoned from the cosy confines of the director's box to mediate. But Futre could not be calmed. He changed into his civvies and f**ked off home. Meanwhile, the massed ranks of Hammers in the away end at Highbury, blissfully unaware of the shitstorm unfolding below ground, eagerly awaited their first glimpse of the Portuguese playmaker.

If that wasn't bad enough, Redknapp had bigger administrative problems on his hands. We'd been besieged by our traditional pre-season injury crisis, with seven first-teamers missing from the squad, including new signings Raducioiu, Bowen and Hall. The teams had already been submitted to the referee. By law, no changes could be made. Unless Futre got out of his limo and turned around, West Ham would be starting the new season with ten men on the pitch.

In his famous poem *If*, Rudyard Kipling wrote about the virtue of *"keeping your head when those around you are losing theirs,"* and perhaps that's what Redknapp had in mind as he sought to avert the crisis unfolding before his eyes.

Like any good leader, the West Ham boss marched into the referee's office to take charge of the situation. And like any good leader, he did the decent thing – blamed it on his assistant Frank Lampard Snr. Dear Old Frank, never the best of spellers, had forgotten his glasses. Instead of putting Stevie Jones (the workhorse forward from Billericay) on the team sheet, he's only gone and written down the name of Portugal's most famous footballer instead. It was an honest mistake.

Could have happened to anyone.

Thankfully, the referee accepted the unlikely excuse and West Ham were allowed to field eleven men, who duly rolled over and lost 2-0. The shirt situation was solved the following week when Futre, his legal team in tow, offered Moncur a tidy sum and a couple of weeks at his villa in the Algarve in exchange for the number ten.

Futre made his debut against perennial strugglers Coventry City. The Sky Blues had been in the top flight for what seemed like an eternity without anyone ever really noticing. My parents had an armchair like that once.

It was exactly the sort of game we needed after the false dawn of Highbury. At least it should have been. The first 45 minutes were dreadful. Two chaotic teams chasing a ball to all corners, to little effect. My parents had a cat like that once.

It took the introduction of Futre at half-time to inject some much-needed quality into proceedings. Even with kneecaps made of polystyrene, he was comfortably the best player on the pitch and helped us secure a point.

His second appearance in Claret and Blue was his most memorable. Buoyed by his cameo against Coventry, Redknapp granted his star man a starting berth against Southampton. And for one fine day in the east London sunshine, he looked like the Paulo Futre of old. It was like watching a Greatest Hits of him in his prime. There were dragbacks, nutmegs, driving runs from midfield. The opposition couldn't get near him, and when they did, they resorted to violence. Francis Benali tried to launch the Portuguese maestro into the Thames and was justifiably red-carded. The fans held their breath, but Futre hobbled back to his feet, as he had done so many times over the course of his career.

As the sun set on a thoroughly deserved 2-1 victory, John Motson lauded one of the finest individual performances this old stadium had seen in years.

The Upton Park faithful dared to dream.

The dream lasted 34 minutes. In the next home game, a typically robust tackle from Wimbledon's midfield folded Futre like an accordion. He lay prone on the turf clutching his knee, before hobbling off wearing the grimace of a man who knew he was finally done.

There were a couple of aborted attempts at a comeback, but he'd made his last meaningful appearance as a professional footballer. And to make matters worse, he'd been upstaged by Efan Ekoku, who powered the Dons to a 2-0 win.

Football can be a cruel, cruel mistress.

*EX: Futre was absolutely magical against Southampton. The team was insane: Dumitrescu, Raducioiu and Futre all in the first eleven. I remember John Motson* purring on Match of the Day. That's why I found it so hard to accept that we would never see Futre like this again. The Arsenal shirt incident is a classic West Ham moment, exactly the type of incident that wouldn't happen at any other professional football club. It was also the first time I realised the value foreign players put on the number ten shirt. It meant that you were the best player, the creative fulcrum of the team. Players like Maradona, Pele and Futre were legendary number tens. John Moncur maybe not so much...

**DAVE:** Of all the people to try and take the number ten shirt from, it had to be John Moncur, didn't it? I bet John had a field day with that! At least Moncs brokered a sweet little deal out of it, getting a free holiday in exchange. Paulo was a diva, and it was justified when he completely bossed the game against Southampton, a poetic performance. But for us fans, it was a Bullseye scenario - "let's see what you could have won" – because, sadly, we never saw it again. That performance seemed to be his swansong, but what a performance it was.

I can understand why Harry took a punt on him; what I can't understand is how Paulo (like many others that shouldn't have) passed a medical?! Did the medical team win a competition to work at West Ham or something? It seemed like unless you arrived in a hearse, you were signed off to play!

### Dowie Disaster

The loss of one Portuguese was counter-balanced by the arrival of another. Hugo Porfirio made his debut in a 2-1 loss to Liverpool. Like Dani, he was something of a young prodigy who had been tipped for stardom. He represented his country at Euro 96, and his arrival on loan from Sporting felt like the boost we needed following Futre's demise. Porfirio was a slight but speedy left winger, who scored his first goal for the club in a 4-1 thumping of Forest in the League Cup, followed by another in a 2-1 win over Blackburn Rovers that propelled us up to tenth in the table.

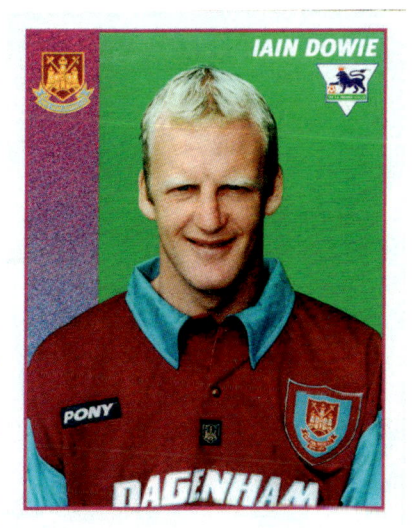

First impressions were positive. He was painfully one-footed – the primary occupation of his right was to admire his left – but his direct running and willingness to take players on brought something extra to a forward line that needed a lift.

The sale of Cottee – a man with proven experience at this level – was looking increasingly foolish. With Futre gone and Dumitrescu looking about as dangerous as a custard cream, goals were in short supply. Within the space of a few months Iain Dowie, who had probably expected to start the season as second fiddle behind the raft of new arrivals, was our main hope of goals. As dependencies go, that's a bit like relying on a dolphin for advice on a new pair of shoes.

And then there was the mystery of Florin Raducioiu. Rumours were rife that the Romanian was unfit, unhappy and unsettled. Whatever the case, sightings of him in first-team action were few and far between, much to my own frustration. By late November he'd made the grand total of six appearances: four starts (where he was substituted on each occasion) and two brief showings from the bench.

Our lack of potency up front was starting to affect results. Defensively, we were fairly solid with the likes of Bilic, Rieper and Dicks. But we couldn't kill teams off. After Blackburn, we could only muster four points – and four goals – from our next six League games.

Raducioiu had finally scored his first goal for the club with a smart finish in an otherwise dire draw at home to Stockport in the League Cup. And when he scored again (from the sub's bench) to help us come from 2-0 down to draw at home to Manchester United, it felt like he'd potentially turned a corner.

At least until he didn't turn up.

What happened next is, to this day, the stuff of rumour and innuendo. Redknapp maintains that the Romanian forward didn't show up for the replay at Stockport, opting instead to go shopping with his wife at Harvey Nichols. Raducioiu insists that he was already excluded from the team ahead of a pending return to Espanyol which Redknapp had himself negotiated. Whatever the case, there was no sign of Raducioiu when the bus turned up at Stockport for one of the most infamous nights in recent memory.

Mention Edgeley Park to any West Ham fan of a certain vintage and it provokes the sort of painful wince of a man being shown a video of his own vasectomy.

The evening had all the hallmarks of a giant-killing. The Sky cameras were in attendance. Stockport were a team on the up. There was the sort of biblical rainfall that made Noah get out his hammer and plywood. And, the most important ingredient of all, West Ham United were in town.

This was like Chum in the water for Richard Keys and co. If there was anyone that could conjure up an unlikely and undignified exit from cup competitions, it was us. And we didn't disappoint.

Leading 1-0 through Julian Dicks, Dowie took centre stage in the most extraordinary fashion. The Northern Irishman was in the midst of an absolutely stinking run of form, having scored twice in his past 25 games. Playing up front on his own, we needed him to quickly rediscover his scoring touch. And... bingo!

A cross came into the box, was flicked on at the near post and, despite the howling wind and torrential rain, Dowie somehow mustered enough physical force to power the ball past the keeper. It was one of the best headed goals of his career. The most textbook of textbook bullet headers. For any kids watching, it was a masterclass in heading a football, the perfect fusion of force and accuracy... except for one minor detail: it was also in the wrong f**king net.

That moment became the quintessential image of Iain Dowie in a West Ham shirt: stood there with his head in his hands, Ludo Miklosko speechless, Stockport fans delirious. Once again, West Ham United were making an inglorious exit from cup competition (Brett Angell scored the winner) and once again, we only had ourselves to blame.

We were out of the League Cup, sliding down the table after a two-month winless streak, and our star striker had apparently popped to the shops whilst we were getting pumped by Stockport.

What else could go wrong?

**EX:** *What a disaster of a day. First the story about Raducioiu came out on Sky before the game, and I was really pissed off with it. Then Iain Dowie does that. What was he thinking? It must have been muscle memory that went wrong, an instant reaction like driving your car on the other side of the road when you go abroad. It summed up the whole game. It was pissing down with rain, there was no roof on the away stand, and we were knocked out by a goal from Brett Angell – a classic carthorse forward from the lower leagues. Another cup catastrophe.*

**DAVE:** *I cannot tell you how many times I've watched Iain Dowie's own goal against Stockport, purely because I'm desperate to understand it! What was he trying to do? It was just bizarre. What a horrible night that replay was. Awful weather, awful pitch, awful performance. And an awful attitude from our marquee signing who would – allegedly – rather go shopping with his missus than play for West Ham. At least we still had the FA Cup to look forward to...*

## FA Cup Wrex-it

Remarkably, Florin Raducioiu was to make one more contribution to the side, scoring a slick solo effort from the subs' bench to secure a 2-0 win over

Sunderland. It was a welcome three points that kept our heads just above the dreaded drop zone.

It was to be his last act before his return to Spain became a reality, and he rejoined Espanyol. Any thoughts that he and Redknapp could mend their differences were dispelled when the boss drafted in veteran striker Mike Newell from Birmingham on an emergency loan. You could understand his frustration, nothing says "f**k off" better than losing your place to a man who's scored one goal in 15 games in the second tier.

Also on his way was countryman Ilie Dumitrescu, packed off to Mexico. A year earlier, Redknapp and Storrie had fought the Department of Employment tooth and nail to ensure the Romanian was granted a work permit. If Dumitrescu had shown similar determination then maybe he would have been a success at Upton Park. And, lastly, medical advice led Paulo Futre to retirement. Playing the game of football without kneecaps was a bit like playing a game of Guess Who? without eyeballs. Though he would later reverse that decision and try some predictably ill-fated comebacks elsewhere.

The FA Cup did its best to kick us while we were down by drawing us away to Wrexham, in perhaps the worst conditions since records began. There had been a furious flurry of snowfall in north Wales, leaving the pitch looking like Tony Montana had a sneezing fit. Incredibly, the referee allowed the game to begin on the proviso that both penalty areas were cleared – whilst the rest of the pitch was caked in the sort of heavy frosting that made Mr Kipling a household name.

It led to a ludicrous spectacle, and you had to feel for poor Hugo Porfirio. The Portuguese was making his FA Cup debut and had never seen snow before, let alone been expected to play football on it. Somehow, he managed to score a glorious left-foot chip that was enough to take the tie to a replay on a day when it seemed destined for us to be the victims of another giant-killing.

Meanwhile, we continued our alarming slide down the table. A creditable 0-0 at Anfield, which once again displayed our dogged defensive ability, was followed up by an insipid display at home to a fairly crap Leeds team on *Monday Night Football*. By now, the crowd's patience was wearing thin with our so-called strikeforce. For all their endeavour, the trio of Jones, Dowie and Newell had contributed zero goals in a combined total of 27 appearances. We'd have been more dangerous with Sooty, Sweep and Soo up front.

Dowie's fall from grace had made for painful viewing. The embarrassment of Edgeley Park was exacerbated by an injury that meant we hadn't seen him since. In his absence, Newell took a bit of stick for his contribution to the Leeds defeat. It's quite rare, and possibly a little unfair, for a loan player to be catcalled by his new fans – though at one stage I'm pretty certain Mike was outpaced by the linesman – so you could understand the frustration.

Things didn't improve with the visit of Wrexham for the FA Cup third-round replay. It should have been a chance for us to boost our fragile confidence by sticking a few goals past them. Instead, we produced another toothless performance, and when Kevin Russell smashed home a late winner, it was no less than the Welshmen deserved.

We'd been dumped out of both cups by lower-league opposition and were now 18th in the table, just above Southampton and Middlesbrough. The brave new dawn of the foreign legion had been replaced by the dark, familiar clouds of a relegation battle.

West Ham fans had seen us sleepwalk into this kind of situation before – and weren't about to go quietly into the night.

**EX:** *Mike Newell came with a decent CV. He'd won the league at Blackburn, and been a very decent top-division forward at Luton and Everton. But it was pretty obvious those days were long gone. He was absolutely terrible. When I look back at the worst forwards in West Ham history – and that's a long, long list – his name is right up there.*

*My dad and I went to that Wrexham game. We drove to the match and the whole way down there was speculation that game was likely to be called off. We had a dilemma as to whether to turn around. The roads were covered in snow and, as we went through the valleys, the conditions were getting worse. We stopped at a supermarket with loads of West Ham fans and asked a copper if the game was still on. He said yes, and the fans were cheering. The Racecourse was a real old-school ground. One of the stands was part built, and the wind was blowing snow right in our faces. Hugo Porfirio's goal made the trip worthwhile.*

**DAVE:** *I remember being relieved that we had Wrexham in the Cup because a win would give us a well-needed confidence boost. F\*\*k me, as it transpired we needed that fixture like a hole in the bollock! I will always remember that first game for Hugo's reaction to the snow. It reminded me of when my dog discovered sand the first time I ever took him to the beach! Hugo was the same (although he never took a shit at the Racecourse Ground, though it might have brightened the place up a bit). The fact that we were then in a replay was embarrassing enough, but to actually lose it at home to a last-minute winner was sickening. It had reached a stage where something drastic had to be done.*

## Double Deal

Rumour had it that Redknapp had offered his resignation to the board after the Wrexham defeat, an offer they rejected out of hand. But they knew something needed to change if they were to dodge the flak being sent their way.

Sensing the unrest on the terraces, businessman Michael Tabor had launched a PR campaign to announce a potential takeover of the club, and was promising a big cash injection to boost the team's flagging fortunes. The fans were restless, and fanzines were flooded with messages of support for the potential new owner.

The board knew they needed to invest. The problem was that Redknapp, who had discovered buried treasure for so long during his spell as manager, seemed to have lost his Midas touch. Particularly with forwards.

In the past two seasons, he'd signed Boogers, Dowie, Cottee, Dani, Jones, Dumitrescu, Futre and Raducioiu. It made for grim reading. Only Cottee and Dowie could be considered a success (though the Northern Irishman was now approaching a full calendar year without a League goal).

The next move had to be right. Our Premier League status depended on it. There were rumours of Pierre van Hooijdonk from Celtic, but his temperament was a concern. Then there was Wimbledon's Dean Holdsworth, whose goalscoring record was almost as impressive as his hair gel. But Wimbledon didn't want to sell a prized asset. Though Crewe's Dele Adebola was getting lots of attention in the First Division, there were question marks as to whether we could wait for someone to settle at Premier League level. We needed goals – fast.

The arrival of Paul Kitson from Newcastle in a £2.2 million deal felt like good business. He was quick, with a decent touch and intelligent movement. He'd scored plenty of goals at Derby before his big-money move to the North East, but spent most of his time playing second fiddle to the likes of Andy Cole, Peter Beardsley, Les Ferdinand and world-record signing Alan Shearer. There was no shame in that. It's like being dropped from your pub darts team because Phil Taylor's popped in for a pint and fancies loosening the old arm up. Sometimes there's nothing you can do. Hopefully he would see this as an opportunity to show he belonged at the top level.

Alongside him was John Hartson, a £3 million signing from Luton. The big Welshman was a familiar face to West Ham fans, having been part of the Hatters' squad that broke our hearts in 1994. More recently, he'd scored for Arsenal in our tame surrender at Highbury on the first day of the season. At 6'1" and topping 15 stone, he was quite the physical specimen – a far cry from Raducioiu, who looked like Bambi had stolen his dinner money.

The announcements of the new signings in a whirlwind 24 hours breathed new life into our season. Suddenly we had a brand new partnership to lead our attack.

The Hartson and Kitson era had begun.

**EX:** *I was convinced Dean Holdsworth was coming to us. He was a West Ham fan who went to school in nearby Woodbridge. He seemed destined to end up here at some point, and this felt like the perfect moment. This was his time.*

*When we signed Hartson, I was really surprised. We rarely signed players who were first-team regulars at top clubs. We always got players who were on the downsides of their career (like Mike Newell). Hartson was a first-teamer at Arsenal, an up-and-coming talent with loads of potential.*

*I knew about Paul Kitson from Derby and Newcastle. The Toon were the glamour side of the Premier League and became everyone's second team. Kitson was always in and around the matchday squad, even if he didn't start. So he clearly had the class to play at this level.*

**DAVE:** *When you're in a dogfight, you need character, determination and aggression. John Hartson ticked every box and also had the physicality and ability in front of goal to make a real difference. Paul Kitson was smart with his movement and had a decent goalscoring record. Harry Redknapp deserves so much credit for bringing these players to West Ham. He sold them on his plans to build a side around them, and made them feel a million dollars to get the deals done. They were outstanding signings who went on to become one of the best strike partnerships since Cottee and McAvennie in 1986.*

### The Resurrection

The new arrivals made their eagerly awaited home debuts on *Monday Night Football*, at home to Spurs. They were a classic little-and-large duo. Hartson, all massive shoulders and thighs, had the build of a prop forward rather than a professional footballer. Meanwhile Kitson, with his curtains and coy smile, resembled the former member of a boyband who left due to 'creative differences'.

The heavens opened that night at Upton Park. To this day, I can't remember worse conditions at the Boleyn. Torrential rain, puddles on the pitch and gale-force winds weren't conducive to free-flowing passing. This was exactly the sort of game that tested your heart and your strength of character. West Ham were equal to both.

We trailed to a Teddy Sheringham strike before a powerful Julian Dicks header brought us level. In an instant, the game turned. Stan Lazaridis forced a smart save from Ian Walker before the new boys made their mark. Lazaridis' corner was caught in the swirling wind and Kitson nodded into the net about two centimetres from goal. Darren Anderton's equaliser didn't derail us. Before half-time, a Dicks free-kick was met brilliantly by the diving head of Hartson, who had bullied Sol Campbell from the first minute. The Big Man celebrated by kissing the badge, to the delight of his new, adoring public.

Even when David Howells equalised with a smart finish after the break, still we believed. In the dying minutes, Hartson was brought down inside the penalty area and the referee pointed to the spot. Upton Park held its breath. The fate of the match, and potentially our season, rested on the shoulders of Julian Dicks.

It was never in doubt. The Terminator hit potentially the hardest penalty in the history of association football, cannoning of the crossbar past the terrified Spurs keeper. God only knows what would have happened if the net hadn't been there to stop the ball. It would probably be on NASA's radar as we speak, a lone Mitre Delta circling Earth's atmosphere and destroying everything in its path.

From then on, we were a completely different proposition. Our next home game was against Ruud Gullit's Chelsea. The Dutchman, who had tormented us the previous season, had taken over from new England boss Glenn Hoddle and spent big bucks to move Chelsea into the top six. A rare mistake from Ian Bishop allowed Gianfranco Zola to set up Gianluca Vialli for the opener, before another Julian Dicks penalty brought us level.

Then came a brief moment of redemption for Iain Dowie, drafted in as cover for the absent Hartson. A deft flick-on found Kitson steaming into space, and he smashed a left-foot shot in off the post to put us ahead. Sub Mark Hughes levelled in the second half and in injury-time we would have gladly settled for a point. With the seconds ticking down, Michael Hughes swung in a corner, Dowie rose like a salmon on a trampoline to power it goalwards, and there was Paul Kitson to nod it over the line. East London erupted in delight.

In the space of just three weeks we had turned our season on its head. We had gone from a timid, toothless team that looked relegation certainties, to a team scrapping for every bastard inch on the football pitch. And we had beaten two of our biggest rivals in the process.

Harry's big-money gamble on Hartson and Kitson had already worked wonders. But the defining image of the season so far was Julian Dicks, with his freshly shaven head and ripped shirt collar, screaming with delight after the last-minute winner against Chelsea.

This was the Terminator in his pomp. He couldn't be reasoned with. He couldn't be bargained with. He didn't feel pity, or remorse, or fear. And he wasn't going to stop until he'd dragged us out of the relegation dogfight.

The greatest of Great Escapes was well and truly on.

**EX:** *That 4-3 win over Spurs still ranks as one of my favourite ever games at Upton Park. I can still remember how cold and wet it was, but our new signings gave the whole place a lift. John Hartson kissing the badge after scoring his first goal for the club helped cement his status as a new hero.*

**DAVE:** *The intensity of that game against Tottenham will live with me forever, and that win was the turning point for us. Hartson and Kitson changed everything when they came in. Suddenly the players grew in self-belief, the fans were rejuvenated and, with goals back in the side, I genuinely felt that we would be safe that season. Our fortunes had changed overnight.*

**EX:** *That Chelsea team had Zola, who would become one of the all-time Premier League greats, but he was overshadowed by Julian Dicks that night. He summed up that bulldog spirit, never-say-die attitude that being club captain of West Ham is all about. Everyone at school knew Julian was my favourite player, and now they could see why. He was absolutely amazing, and this was when he should have won an England cap. The fact he didn't deprived the country of someone who could have been a cult hero.*

**DAVE:** *The win against Chelsea that followed was a big statement, and you just got the feeling that the black cloud was lifting. But not just temporarily. Potentially long term, if we could build on what we had now.*

## Five-star Showing

We followed up the win over Chelsea with worthy draws at Villa and Wimbledon. We still needed more wins on the board though and, even with our recent resurgence, a trip to Coventry didn't offer much hope. We hadn't won there since 1987. At times, it felt like you were more likely to bump into Halley's Comet browsing the soft furnishings in Debenhams than you were to witness a West Ham win at Highfield Road. When Dion Dublin nodded the home side in front, it felt like a familiar story.

Thankfully, our new strike partnership had other ideas. Kitson flicked on a John Moncur cross and Big John produced a smart finish to bring us level. Kitson was the provider again minutes later. Another cross, another flick-on, and this time Rio Ferdinand was there to prod the ball home. The teenager was making only his sixth League start for the club. At first glance, he didn't really look like a footballer. He was so skinny, he could dodge raindrops. But the youngster had impressed everyone in recent weeks with his positional awareness and his extraordinary composure on the ball. He had slotted in beautifully alongside Bilic and Rieper in the backline.

When Hartson slid home a third, the points were secured, and ten years of misery in the Midlands were all but forgotten.

April brought a first sighting of Richard Hall in Claret and Blue, making an impressive debut after eight months out with injury in a goalless home draw with Middlesbrough. And there was a first start too for new signing Steve Lomas, a £2.5 million arrival from Manchester City, brought in to give us some extra bite in the battle against relegation.

We did our best to shoot ourselves in the foot against Everton. Paul Kitson scored twice to put us in total control at the interval. Then midway through the second half we won a penalty. Designated taker Hartson threw the ball to his strike partner, who duly missed. When Duncan Ferguson salvaged a point for the visitors in the last minute, it felt like a killer blow to our survival chances.

Thankfully, amends were made in the following home game, where we produced a five-star display to hammer a very decent Sheffield Wednesday side. Again, it was our strike duo that did the damage. Hartson's aerial threat terrified the visitors' defence and we preyed on that from the first minute – producing more crosses than a Transylvanian timber yard. Kitson scored three and Hartson two as we smashed David Pleat's side 5-1. Between them, they'd contributed 13 goals since their arrival, a spell which saw us amass 19 points from eleven games.

Safety was officially secured in an entertaining 0-0 draw at home to Newcastle, who would again finish runners-up behind Manchester United in the championship race. We finished the season two points, but four places, clear of the drop as Sunderland, Middlesbrough (whose big spending backfired dramatically) and Nottingham Forest went down.

One of the most Jekyll-and-Hyde seasons in our history was at an end. We started with a side packed with expensive overseas talent and ended with an all-British strikeforce that saved our top-flight status. Amidst all the mayhem, one man had stayed constant. Julian Dicks was again named Hammer of the Year, despite missing the last few games with injury. His eight goals made him joint top scorer (alongside Kitson), and the strikes against Spurs and Chelsea further cemented his status as a West Ham legend.

**EX:** *You could tell instantly that Rio Ferdinand was going to be a top-class player. I'd heard so much about him for so many years before he made his debut. And when he did, he didn't disappoint. When he scored, there was still discussion as to whether he was a better forward or centre-back, which shows how talented he was. After that Coventry game, I met Rio in the car park. In the '90s, you used to be able to hang around by the bus after a game and get things signed. I remember Rio had such confidence, you knew his personality would take him far.*

**DAVE:** *The relief when we finally stayed up was incredible! It was such a mentally exhausting season with so many ups and downs. For me, I'll always remember it for the Hartson and Kitson partnership – we only lost three of our last 13 games once they arrived – and of course for the iconic performances from Julian Dicks. At times, he carried that side with his leadership, quality on the ball and goal contribution.*

*With the signing of Steve Lomas and the emergence of a young Rio Ferdinand, I was already looking forward to the following season. Then again, the captain of the* Titanic *was looking forward to America!*

**EX:** *Steve Lomas was a brilliant signing, and one that maybe is too easily forgotten. Over the years, Michael Hughes, Keith Rowland and Iain Dowie recommended him to Redknapp, and I'm glad they did. He had that Peter Butler-esque work ethic in centre midfield that we'd not really replaced, and he also brought leadership qualities to the team that were crucial during our escape from relegation.*

*Dave mentions the emotion of the 5-1 game, and it was doubly so for me as I lost the last of my grandparents that morning. On the morning of the game I went to see her at Whipps Cross Hospital in Leytonstone. One of the last things she said to me was: "Don't worry, I think West Ham are going to win big today." By the time we got to the game, my dad got a call to say she'd passed away. She knew somehow.*

## FA Premier League - 1996/97

| Date | Opponent | H/A | Score | Attendance | Scorers |
|---|---|---|---|---|---|
| 17 August | Arsenal | A | 0–2 | 38,056 | |
| 21 August | Coventry City | H | 1–1 | 21,580 | Rieper |
| 24 August | Southampton | H | 2–1 | 21,227 | M Hughes, Dicks (p) |
| 4 September | Middlesbrough | A | 1–4 | 30,060 | M Hughes |
| 8 September | Sunderland | A | 0–0 | 18,642 | |
| 15 September | Wimbledon | H | 0–2 | 21,294 | |
| 21 September | Nottingham Forest | A | 2–0 | 23,352 | Bowen, M Hughes |
| 29 September | Liverpool | H | 1–2 | 25,064 | Bilic |
| 12 October | Everton | A | 1–2 | 36,571 | Dicks (p) |
| 19 October | Leicester City | H | 1–0 | 22,285 | Moncur |
| 26 October | Blackburn Rovers | H | 2–1 | 23,947 | Berg (og), Porfírio |
| 2 November | Tottenham Hotspur | A | 0–1 | 32,999 | |
| 16 November | Newcastle United | A | 1–1 | 36,552 | Rowland |
| 23 November | Derby County | H | 1–1 | 24,576 | Bishop |
| 30 November | Sheffield W | A | 0–0 | 22,321 | |
| 4 December | Aston Villa | H | 0–2 | 19,105 | |
| 8 December | Manchester United | H | 2–2 | 25,045 | Raducioiu, Dicks (p) |
| 21 December | Chelsea | A | 1–3 | 28,315 | Porfírio |
| 28 December | Sunderland | H | 2–0 | 24,077 | Bilic, Raducioiu |
| 1 January | Nottingham Forest | H | 0–1 | 22,358 | |
| 11 January | Liverpool | A | 0–0 | 40,102 | |
| 20 January | Leeds United | H | 0–2 | 19,441 | |
| 29 January | Arsenal | H | 1–2 | 24,382 | Rose (og) |
| 1 February | Blackburn Rovers | A | 1–2 | 21,994 | Ferdinand |
| 15 February | Derby County | A | 0–1 | 18,057 | |
| 24 February | Tottenham Hotspur | H | 4–3 | 23,998 | Dicks (2, 1 p), Kitson, Hartson |
| 1 March | Leeds United | A | 0–1 | 30,575 | |
| 12 March | Chelsea | H | 3–2 | 24,502 | Dicks, Kitson (2) |
| 15 March | Aston Villa | A | 0–0 | 35,992 | |
| 18 March | Wimbledon | A | 1–1 | 15,771 | Lazaridis |
| 22 March | Coventry City | A | 3–1 | 22,291 | Hartson (2), Ferdinand |
| 9 April | Middlesbrough | H | 0–0 | 23,988 | |
| 12 April | Southampton | A | 0–2 | 15,244 | |
| 19 April | Everton | H | 2–2 | 24,525 | Kitson (2) |
| 23 April | Leicester City | A | 1–0 | 20,327 | Moncur |
| 3 May | Sheffield Wed | H | 5–1 | 24,960 | Kitson (3), Hartson (2) |

| 6 May | Newcastle United | H | 0–0 | 24,617 |  |
| 11 May | Manchester United | A | 0–2 | 55,249 |  |

## FA Cup

| 4 January R3 | Wrexham | A | 1–1 | 9,747 | Porfírio |
| 25 January R3R | Wrexham | H | 0–1 | 16,763 |  |

## League Cup

| 18 Sept R2 1L | Barnet | A | 1–1 | 3,849 | Cottee |
| 25 Sept R2 2L | Barnet | H | 1–0 | 15,264 | Bilic |
| 23 October R3 | Nottingham Forest | H | 4–1 | 19,402 | Dowie (2), Porfírio, Dicks (p) |
| 27 November R4 | Stockport County | H | 1–1 | 20,061 | Raducioiu |
| 18 Dec R4R | Stockport County | A | 1–2 | 9,834 | Dicks |

|  |  | P | W | D | L | GF | GA | GD | Pts |
|---|---|---|---|---|---|---|---|---|---|
| 1 | Manchester Utd | 38 | 21 | 12 | 5 | 76 | 44 | +32 | 75 |
| 2 | Newcastle Utd | 38 | 19 | 11 | 8 | 73 | 40 | +33 | 68 |
| 3 | Arsenal | 38 | 19 | 11 | 8 | 62 | 32 | +30 | 68 |
| 4 | Liverpool | 38 | 19 | 11 | 8 | 62 | 37 | +25 | 68 |
| 5 | Aston Villa | 38 | 17 | 10 | 11 | 47 | 34 | +13 | 61 |
| 6 | Chelsea | 38 | 16 | 11 | 11 | 58 | 55 | +3 | 59 |
| 7 | Sheffield Wed | 38 | 14 | 15 | 9 | 50 | 51 | –1 | 57 |
| 8 | Wimbledon | 38 | 15 | 11 | 12 | 49 | 46 | +3 | 56 |
| 9 | Leicester City | 38 | 12 | 11 | 15 | 46 | 54 | –8 | 47 |
| 10 | Tottenham H | 38 | 13 | 7 | 18 | 44 | 51 | –7 | 46 |
| 11 | Leeds United | 38 | 11 | 13 | 14 | 28 | 38 | –10 | 46 |
| 12 | Derby County | 38 | 11 | 13 | 14 | 45 | 58 | –13 | 46 |
| 13 | Blackburn Rov | 38 | 9 | 15 | 14 | 42 | 43 | –1 | 42 |
| 14 | West Ham Utd | 38 | 10 | 12 | 16 | 39 | 48 | –9 | 42 |
| 15 | Everton | 38 | 10 | 12 | 16 | 44 | 57 | –13 | 42 |
| 16 | Southampton | 38 | 10 | 11 | 17 | 50 | 56 | –6 | 41 |
| 17 | Coventry City | 38 | 9 | 14 | 15 | 38 | 54 | –16 | 41 |
| 18 | Sunderland | 38 | 10 | 10 | 18 | 35 | 53 | –18 | 40 |
| 19 | Middlesbrough | 38 | 10 | 12 | 16 | 51 | 60 | –9 | 39 |
| 20 | Nottingham For | 38 | 6 | 16 | 16 | 31 | 59 | –28 | 34 |

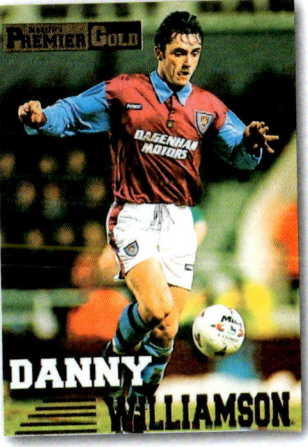

1997/98

## All Change

Barely had the ink dried on the story of our fairytale escape from relegation than the plot took a dramatic twist in the post-season.

Slaven Bilic, the man who had made himself a hero in these parts of London, was gone. There had been speculation that the Croatian was on the brink of a move to Everton on transfer deadline day two months prior, only for his conscience – and a rumoured loyalty payment of some 200 grand – to convince him to stay and help us fight relegation. But his head had been turned. Howard Kendall had returned to the Toffees and there were rumours of a £50 million war chest, with the likes of Fabrizio Ravanelli on their way for big money and big wages to bring the glory days back to Goodison.

For his part, Bilic was going to be coining in over £1 million a year on Merseyside, a hefty increase in wedge on his West Ham pay packet. Though I don't doubt he was sad to leave Upton Park, the fact he could wallpaper his whole house with £50 notes from his new employer probably softened the blow.

His departure felt like a real kick in the plums, so soon after the elation of the Great Escape. Bilic, Rieper and young Rio Ferdinand had formed potentially the strongest rearguard we'd seen in years, and already it was crumbling before our eyes. Bilic had packed his bags, meanwhile Rieper was in the last year of his contract and considering offers from elsewhere. Richard Hall, who had taken eight months to make his debut for us, was injured again in pre-season having made just seven outings since his £1.5 million move last summer. And with Julian Dicks' latest knee injury threatening to rule him out for the whole season, our defence suddenly had more gaps than Bobby Charlton's scalp. There were other departures in attack, too. Hugo Porfirio, whose pace and trickery had been integral to our late-season recovery, had left London for the sunny climes of Santander.

As usual, Harry wasted no time in shuffling the pack. The arrival of Eyal Berkovic from Maccabi Haifa allayed some of the fears about our creativity. The playmaker had spent the previous season on loan at Southampton. For years, the Saints had relied on the mercurial feet of Matt Le Tissier to keep them afloat, but evidently Berkovic had made quite the impact on the south coast. I hadn't seen much of him myself because the thought of watching Southampton play was about as appetising as watching a Margaret Thatcher striptease. But the general consensus was that this was a good piece of business, albeit one that probably signalled the end of Ian Bishop's status as our main playmaker.

The defence was strengthened by the signing of David Unsworth from Everton, who was exactly the sort of no-nonsense left-sided defender we needed in Julian's absence. However, the deal could only be financed as a part-exchange – which meant a farewell for Danny Williamson. The tidy midfielder had endured a bit of a stop-start career in Claret and Blue after that glorious goal at Bolton two seasons prior. Every time he got a run in the team, he picked up a knock. By now I was convinced that Millwall had land-mined the pitches at Chadwell Heath; it was the only possible explanation for the spate of serious injuries that befell us every year.

The loss of Williamson was a little deflating. Much like Stuart Slater's departure to Celtic, it felt like bad luck had robbed us of seeing a star shine in his prime. I just hoped he had better luck than Slater, whose career had tailed off dramatically since his departure thanks to his troublesome Achilles.

As ever, we felt drastically unprepared for the start of the season. The Unsworth deal hadn't been concluded and the fixture generator had awarded us an awayday at top-flight newcomers Barnsley. Trips to Yorkshire rarely brought success over the years, and facing a team riding high after promotion felt like a recipe for disaster.

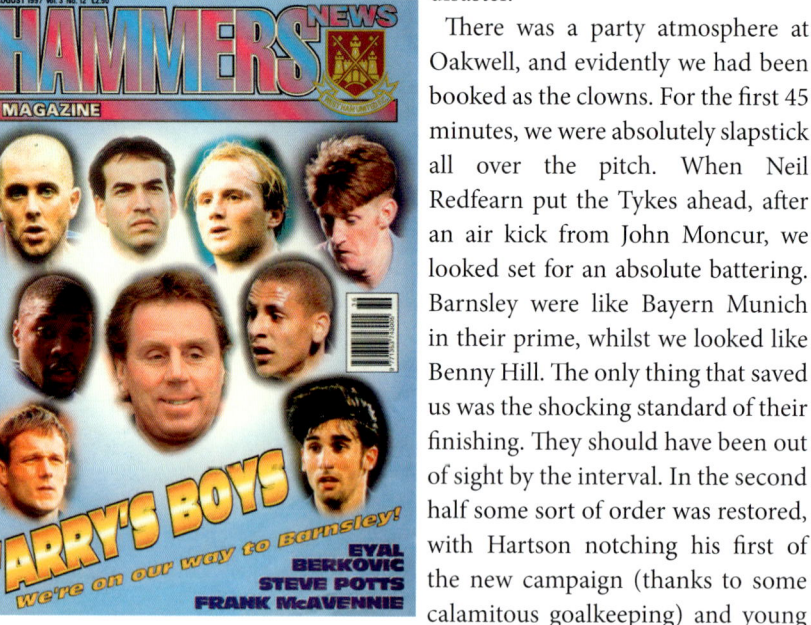

There was a party atmosphere at Oakwell, and evidently we had been booked as the clowns. For the first 45 minutes, we were absolutely slapstick all over the pitch. When Neil Redfearn put the Tykes ahead, after an air kick from John Moncur, we looked set for an absolute battering. Barnsley were like Bayern Munich in their prime, whilst we looked like Benny Hill. The only thing that saved us was the shocking standard of their finishing. They should have been out of sight by the interval. In the second half some sort of order was restored, with Hartson notching his first of the new campaign (thanks to some calamitous goalkeeping) and young sub Frank Lampard slotting home a totally undeserved late winner.

Our makeshift side had bowled into Barnsley wearing balaclavas and stolen three points. But after the upheaval in pre-season, it was a relief to start with a win and keep up the momentum from last year.

The question was whether it was a false dawn. Was this a new West Ham United, one that could win ugly, or would we slip back into old habits?

**DAVE:** *Not only was I gutted about losing Slav, but I was gutted about the way he handled it. His comments essentially suggested that he was bigger and better than the club and that he had more chance of winning trophies at Everton? As it transpired, he didn't. It annoyed me that we had plucked him from oblivion, gave him a platform to shine, then at the first opportunity he dropped us like a sack of shit! I felt that he had used West Ham and disrespected the club in the process.*

**EX:** *It was a huge disappointment. There was nothing to suggest Everton were in a better position than West Ham, either. Every year, they were mooching about either near the relegation zone or in mid table. Slav left for the money, not to win things like he claimed. That's fine because it's his career and a short one, and everyone knew it. Losing him hurt even more because Julian's latest injury looked like it was going to be the end. We now had a hole in the team for two massive personalities.*

**DAVE:** *I had such an overwhelming amount of trust in Harry's eye for a player that I felt excited by anyone that was coming in, not just Slav's replacement. I only ever saw glimpses of Eyal on* Match of the Day *but he looked decent. And let's not forget, he turned down a move to Tottenham to come to east London, which instantly made him a hero in my eyes!*

**EX:** *It was sad to see Danny Williamson go – he seemed to disappear off the face of the Earth after this – but in David Unsworth, Harry was buying someone who was solid, reliable and experienced. I listened to the Barnsley game in the car on the way back from holiday. The atmosphere sounded incredible, and when they went one up I thought we were in real trouble, only for Frank Lampard Jnr to score the winner. Who would have known this would be the start of a journey that would lead him to 100-plus England caps and runner-up position in the Ballon d'Or?*

## Eyal Be There for You

We followed up the win at Barnsley with a midweek home game against Spurs. Unlike Oakwell, we were at it from the first whistle. Lazaridis laid on the opener for Hartson with barely three minutes on the clock and we held our own in a closely contested encounter. This wasn't the emotional cauldron of five months prior. We weren't being carried by the crowd. We were competing with Spurs on the quality of our play. And at the heart of it was Berkovic. The Israeli – who had turned down a move to White Hart Lane in favour of us over the summer – ran the midfield from the offset. With Moncur and Lomas doing the spit and sawdust work behind him, he was free to prowl around the pitch, prodding and probing the visitors' defence at will.

He got the goal his performance deserved, twisting and turning Ramon Vega like he was reading an Agatha Christie novel, before firing past Ian Walker. There was still time for Les Ferdinand to score what felt like his 1000th goal against us in all competitions, but we saw out the game comfortably enough. We had two wins from two, the perfect setup for a game at Goodison and a quick reunion with Slaven Bilic.

Slav was greeted like Judas Escariot at a Disciples reunion by the thousands of visiting fans. The air was bluer than his new shirt, and the former Hammers hero was absolutely rattled. He was booked for a mad challenge early in the game and could have seen red, were it not for some generous officiating. Unfortunately, despite taking an early lead, we lost 2-1 to a sloppy goal. Some things never change.

A decent draw at Coventry was followed up with a 3-1 win over Wimbledon at Upton Park. The South London spoilers, who had booted us all over the pitch for large parts of the decade, were dispatched in routine fashion. They couldn't live with our passing and movement, and they couldn't handle Hartson up front as he notched his third goal in five League games. By now his partnership with Berkovic was really blossoming. The Israeli playmaker was fast becoming the creative fulcrum of the whole team. Despite the Dons' midfield doing their best to launch him into orbit, they couldn't find a way to stop him. Hartson was grabbing all the headlines, but it was Berkovic who was the unsung hero of the season so far. When he was on the ball, there was a rumble of excitement in the crowd. Already, he seemed like a brilliant bit of business.

**DAVE:** *Eyal Berkovic. To this day, I think he had the best final ball I have ever seen at West Ham. His passing was intelligent, weighted and incredibly accurate. He was basically a striker's dream! If you made the right run, you were getting it on a plate. This little Israeli, who I'd only ever seen snippets of thanks to Des Lynam on a Saturday night, was showing similar qualities in the final third to that of the mighty Trevor Brooking. That's how good he was.*

**EX:** *That's so true. And looking back, he's probably not talked about enough in terms of the impact he made at Upton Park. He was the best creator of chances West Ham have had in my lifetime. Through-ball after through-ball. It was like he* was constantly pressing the triangle button on FIFA, and nobody could stop him.

**DAVE:** When Tottenham came to Upton Park, I remember David Unsworth being revealed to the fans and there was such a buzz, such an air of confidence going into that game. What a win that was, and one that belonged to Eyal, who scored his first goal for the club.

We were unlucky not to make it three straight wins at Goodison, that would have been sweet given the way Slav had treated us. He left to win trophies in Merseyside, f\*\*kinell there was more chance of Julian Dicks winning trophies in ballet!

## Home and Away

Our season was developing a noticeable Jekyll-and-Hyde pattern. At home we played fast, free-flowing football that was a delight to behold. We attacked teams from the first minute to the last, creating chances aplenty against the best defences in the League, and built a buzz of genuine excitement on Saturday afternoons that Upton Park hadn't felt since the heady days of 1986.

Away from home, we attacked teams from the first minute to the last, conceded chances aplenty against the worst attacks in the League, and created a buzz of genuine excitement on Saturday afternoons at stadiums across the land as we rolled over and gifted the opposition three points. It was utterly bizarre viewing.

We followed up the win over Wimbledon with a 2-1 defeat at Old Trafford, where United hit the bar twice and kept Ludo Miklosko busier than a wasp at a picnic. Incredibly, we could have snatched a point were it not for two terrible misses from Paul Kitson, whose shooting boots looked like they'd been replaced by a pair of high heels. We then lost 1-0 at home to Newcastle and got panned 4-0 by Arsenal as our performances lurched from brilliant to bollocks on a week-to-week basis. It was chaos.

In an effort to make changes and bring more consistency, Redknapp had gone into transfer overdrive, chopping his personnel quicker than Henry VIII's executioner. Michael Hughes was sold to Wimbledon and Marc Rieper was shipped off to Celtic. Their replacements were Andy Impey from QPR and Ian Pearce from Blackburn.

I was fairly indifferent to the signing of Impey. I'd seen him plenty of times from a distance and never really thought he was worth taking a closer look – which is how I still feel every time I walk past WH Smith. But he was fast and direct, and gave us options on either flank.

On the other hand, Pearce brought back bad memories of springtime 1994, when the Ewood outfit came down to Upton Park on the hunt for a European place. One of the joys of being a football fan is that you're allowed to make instant judgments on players you've never seen before and relay them with supreme confidence, despite having precisely zero f**king knowledge on the subject matter.

As he trotted gingerly on to the pitch, Pearce had looked like the typical centre-halves of the era: big frame, slightly ungainly, turning speed of a fridge in treacle. And then something unusual happened. Instead of heading towards his natural habitat of the back four, Pearce made a beeline up front to provide a makeshift foil for the hottest striking property in English football: Alan Shearer. This seemed like the most unlikely duo since He-Man texted Skeletor and asked if he fancied popping out for a cheeky pint after work.

Nonetheless, in the space of a few seconds, I'd seen all I needed to compile a comprehensive scouting report for the West Stand: *Not much to fear here, fellas. I've seen forklift trucks with better technique than him.*

Sixty seconds later, Shearer got the ball deep and set Pearce through on goal. His first touch gave him a shooting angle, the second rifled a winner into the bottom corner from fully 20 yards past an utterly confused Ludo Miklosko. Since then, Pearce had won a Premier League title and established himself as a very decent operator at this level. *So much for the forklift truck.*

Both Impey (who was playing as an attacking wing-back in our balls-to-the-wall 3-4-1-2 formation) and Pearce played their part in a sensational 2-1 win against Liverpool, where the dream team of Hartson and Berkovic were both on the scoresheet again. The victory lifted us to seventh in the table.

**EX:** *It was sad to see Hughes and Rieper go, they had both performed really well for us and helped us to progress from a side that was constantly looking over our shoulder, sat in the relegation zone. But we were getting used to the merry-go-round of players at the club as Harry constantly tinkered with the squad to keep progressing.*

**DAVE:** *During this period, I think Redknapp knew he had the foundations of a really good side but he needed some more versatility, which is what he got from Impey and Pearce. This would also allow for more of a Plan B if it was going tits-up on some of these head-scratching away days.*

*Of course, Ian Pearce also brought his trademark goal celebration with him, where he always looked like he had just hit one of those boxing machines you find in arcades to measure the power of your punch!*

**EX:** *Ian Pearce actually became one of my favourite players. People didn't realise how quick he was. He looked like a pub player, but in reality he had a really impressive turn of pace when he needed it. He was also one of those bizarre '90s players – like Paul Warhurst or Ian Marshall – that could play centre-back or centre-forward, sometimes in the same game! That doesn't happen any more.*

## Young Guns

Whilst Redknapp continued to reshape the squad with established Premier League experience, some of our homegrown talents were beginning to blossom.

In the absence of Bilic, Rio Ferdinand was proving a more than able deputy. Alongside the physical specimens of Unsworth and Pearce, his supreme elegance and composure gave us the right mix of steel and sex appeal at the back.

He was unlike any other central defender in the country, capable of committing players and dribbling out of dangerous areas. There was no such thing as Row Z for Rio, he was a Rolls-Royce of a player. It was no surprise when he caught the eye of England boss Glenn Hoddle, who rewarded him with his first cap against Cameroon. There was even talk of him making the World Cup squad as a deputy for the likes of Tony Adams – who was experiencing a revival under the Arsène Wenger revolution at Arsenal – Sol Campbell and Gareth Southgate. Rio was already better on the ball than all of those players, and he seemed certain to become an England regular.

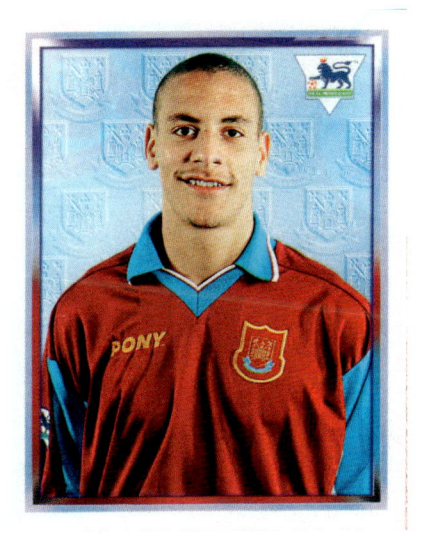

What made Rio's meteoric rise all the more enjoyable was that Slaven Bilic's career was already circling the khazi. The good times at Goodison had failed to materialise – as did the raft of new signings. The Ravanelli deal fell through when the Italian demanded that Everton pay his gas and electricity bills alongside his whopping 50-grand-a-week wages. Hence the Toffees were largely stuck with the same crap players they had the prior season – and were hovering above the relegation zone.

Meanwhile, in midfield, Frank Lampard Jnr was making his mark. Being the son of a *bona fide* West Ham legend (and assistant manager) and the nephew of the current manager can't have been an easy burden for him to bear, particularly in the bearpit of a first-team dressing room. He'd made a dozen or so appearances, mainly as substitute, the previous season without really catching the eye in the same way Rio had.

Nonetheless, the opening day winner at Barnsley seemed to have boosted Lampard's stature no end. He was difficult to define as a player. He didn't put his foot in like Moncur or Lomas, and whilst he was tidy enough on the ball, he didn't dictate play like Berkovic. But whenever a cross went into the box he seemed to be there. He scored in a 3-0 League Cup demolition of Villa at Upton Park (Hartson notched two), and then got a hat-trick in the next round against Walsall, before hitting the net again in a 3-1 reverse at Elland Road. He reminded me a little of Alan Dickens, which was no bad thing. We hadn't had a reliable source of goals from midfield since the John Lyall era.

With Ferdinand and Lampard alongside Hartson, Unsworth and Lomas, the spine of the team was in their early or mid 20s. We weren't foraging around for free transfers or older pros looking for one last payday. Instead, we were a young and exciting team. It meant we were naïve at times, as the away form showed, but we were always entertaining.

**DAVE:** *Personally, one of the most deflating things about being a West Ham fan is when you have an absolute gem of a player, you find yourself worrying about how long they'll be with us for! This was the case with Rio, especially – because he was practically world-class from the moment he made his debut.*

**EX:** *Rio was a quick learner, too. Because he was so confident in his own ability on the ball, he did have the odd error in him during his early days, but he matured quickly and cut those out soon enough.*

**DAVE:** *In relation to Frank, to this day I will never understand why he was given such a hard time. Was he a world beater from day one? No. Did he contribute to the side and show signs of being a promising player? Yes. But for some reason that wasn't good enough for some people. He was one of our own. As a kid, he would never be seen without a West Ham shirt, yet the treatment by some fans took that love away from him. He said a few things when he left, but you can't really blame him after the way he was treated. No wonder his old man has nothing to do with West Ham any more. It's a sad situation, really.*

**EX:** *Frank had this great knack for being in right place at right times, but didn't* seem to offer much else. At the time I wasn't really sure what his role was in the team. If he didn't score, you weren't sure what he'd done – which is mad, because goals win games. Maybe we hadn't adjusted to a different type of central midfielder. He was very attacking and focused on getting in the box, whereas we had always had playmakers like Ian Bishop, or ball-winners like John Moncur. Whatever the reason, in hindsight he deserved better treatment.

### King of Our Harts

Hartson was soon on his third partner of the season. With Paul Kitson sidelined by injury, a scenario that would become depressingly familiar for the rest of his West Ham career, Iain Dowie had been drafted in to do the donkey work up front – a task that he took quite literally. The Big Man's confidence had been shattered by that night in Stockport. He now had the same sort of relationship with the net as a stubborn koi carp. He hadn't scored a League goal for 18 months and was on the brink of asking Steve Potts for some shooting tips.

The latest incumbent was Samassi Abou, a £250,000 signing from Cannes whose name was exotic enough to provoke instant excitement. First glances of him were mixed. He had quick feet and a couple of nice flicks and tricks, but then again so did Fred Astaire. The Ivory Coast striker definitely had something, though it might take him a while to come to terms with English football.

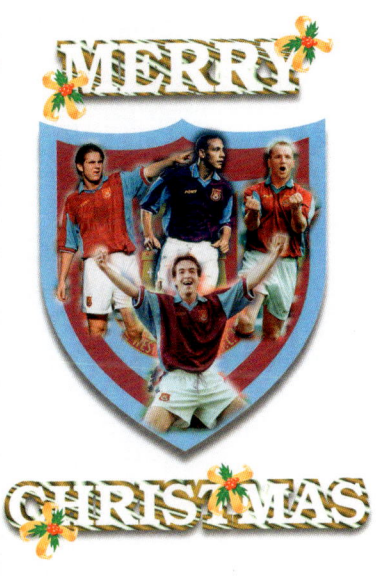

No matter who was alongside him, Hartson's form remained remarkable. He had blossomed into one of the deadliest strikers in the Premier League, allying his physical gifts with an excellent touch and intelligent link-up play – particularly with Berkovic. The little Israeli may have only weighed about nine stone soaking wet and looked like he'd lose an arm-wrestle with Basil Brush. But his brilliant football brain matched with Big John's brawn was proving too much for even the division's most accomplished defences – especially at Fortress Upton Park.

The Welshman scored both goals in a 2-1 win over Villa that showcased his supreme confidence. The first was a tremendous technical finish, drifting past two players with a touch that was softer than a peck on your nan's cheek. The second was a 20-yard fizzer into the bottom corner. He was much more than the big target man we'd bargained for.

Hartson scored again as we walloped Crystal Palace 4-1 in a game rearranged after a bizarre floodlight failure caused the earlier fixture to be abandoned. Berkovic was on the scoresheet too, and there were first goals in Claret and Blue for Unsworth and Lomas on another evening of high-octane entertainment under the lights at Upton Park.

In December, Paul Kitson made a welcome return to first-team action – and to goalscoring duty – with winners against Sheffield Wednesday, Coventry and Wimbledon (our first away win since the opening day of the season).

By the turn of the year, we were eighth in the League, whilst Spurs and Slaven Bilic's Everton were mired in the bottom three. It was an extraordinary turnaround from 12 months earlier when we looked destined for relegation. The dark days of Mike Newell were long gone. Now we had one of the top flight's top marksmen, and we were easily one of the most entertaining sides in the country.

After the disastrous overseas dalliances of 1996, Harry Redknapp had firmly rediscovered his transfer market mojo. He was building a team of primarily young British talent, with a sprinkling of overseas flair, and in the early days of 1998 he made one of his most important signings yet.

**DAVE:** *What a signing Super Johnny Hartson was proving to be. As a striker, you are only as good as the service you are given – and what a partnership he had with Berkovic. Has there been a better duo in the final third at West Ham since? I don't think so. They were just a pleasure to watch, and every time we broke forward you just felt something was going to happen.*

**EX:** *It's a shame Kitson was injured so much, as I'd have loved to have seen them play more together. I was there at Chelsea away when we got a glimpse of Abou for the first time. As he started warming up down the touchline all the fans all fans shouted "ABOOOOOOOOOUUUUU" – and he looked totally confused.*

**DAVE:** *Apparently, Samassi was sitting in the changing room, staring at the floor looking quite downhearted. Harry pulled him to one side, asked him what was wrong, and in broken English Samassi replied, "Why are the fans booing me?" Harry said, "You silly sod. They're not booing you, they're singing your name!"*

**EX:** *The floodlights failed just as Lampard had scored an equaliser vs Palace,* *and there were the usual jokes about someone forgetting to put 50p in the meter; but it later emerged the game was linked to a shady Far East betting syndicate. It made me wonder what else I'd seen that might have been manipulated to suit betting markets. Was someone betting on Iain Dowie to score that bullet header at Stockport? Maybe we finally had an answer, after all.*

## Harry's Clever Trevor Deal

There's no denying Harry Redknapp's charm. Whether he's having a cosy chat with a journalist or with Z-list celebrities in the jungle, he's always been one of English football's great talkers. He has an uncanny ability to communicate with anyone and everyone, making them feel like they're being listened to. And, most importantly, make them feel like he'd do anything to help.

It was this skillset that made him such an arch negotiator in the '90s. He could seemingly ring up any manager in the lower leagues, pilfer their best player for peanuts, and make them feel like he was doing THEM a favour.

Even so, quite how he managed to pull off this illusion during a phone call with QPR boss Ray Harford in January 1998 remains a mystery to this very day. Harford had been sacked by Blackburn Rovers following a dreadful defence of their title in 1995, then had a fairly dismal spell at West Brom before arriving at Loftus Road to try and reinvigorate their promotion charge. With little money to invest in the squad, he had to do some wheeling and dealing – which was music to Harry Redknapp's ears.

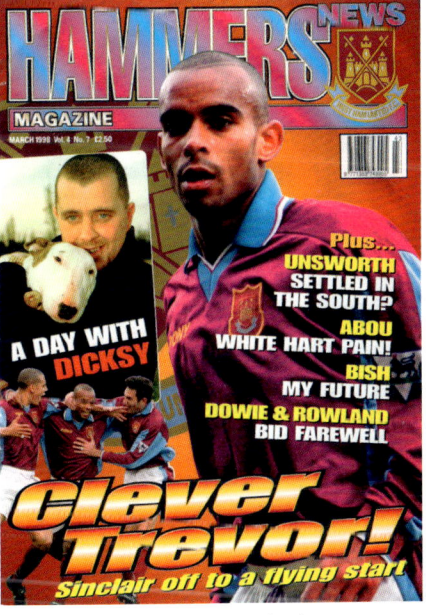

Not only did Harry offer up "two proven Premier League professionals" to help Harford get Rangers back in the Promised Land, but he'd also heard Ray was having a spot of bother with Trevor Sinclair. The winger had at one time been considered one of the most exciting young prospects in the top flight. He'd joined Rangers in 1993 from Blackpool and won England Under-21 honours. As the Hoops started to sell off their prize treasures such as Les Ferdinand and Andy Sinton, and slid into the second tier, it seemed only a matter of time before they'd cash in on Sinclair. Every season he was linked with a move to one of the top six, but for some reason no one pulled the trigger on the deal. Now a career that was once red-hot was now at risk of going off the boil. He'd been at Loftus Road too long. He was way too good for that level and needed an exit route from the club... fast.

And so, on January 29th it was announced that QPR had made two big signings from West Ham, with their wantaway forward going in the opposite direction. It was an incredible deal. Somehow Redknapp had persuaded Harford to take Keith Rowland and Iain Dowie in part exchange for Trevor Sinclair. It's like convincing James Bond to trade in his Aston Martin for a Ford Fiesta.

We needed strengthening in forward positions. Paul Kitson's goalscoring return had been cut short by another injury, whilst Paolo Alves had been and gone on loan from Sporting Lisbon without anyone really noticing. Abou, meanwhile, had shown in flashes that he was starting to adjust to his new surroundings. He'd scored a brilliant hat-trick against Barnsley to inspire us to a 6-0 win and complete the double over the Tykes. But this was Barnsley after all, the worst defence in the League. You'd have fancied Mother Theresa to nick a goal against them.

Sinclair's versatility was potentially a huge asset for us. He could be wide on either flank in a midfield four, he would potentially operate as wing-back in Redknapp's beloved back-three system, or he could play up front as a pacy partner for Hartson. And, indeed, that's where he made his debut.

Any concerns that he wasn't the player of old were instantly dismissed when he scored with a neat header from a corner to put us ahead. Nick Barmby equalised, and then Sinclair showed the skill that had once made him such hot property. Jinking between defenders, he played a one-two with Berkovic and then struck the ball into the bottom corner. It was a brilliant bit of improvisation. Even a late Everton equaliser didn't take too much shine off the day. There was a new star at Upton Park.

When Stan Lazaridis scored the thunderbastard of all thunderbastards at St James' Park a week later to seal a rare win on Tyneside, we were absolutely flying.

**DAVE:** *I cannot tell you how excited I was when we signed Trevor Sinclair. What a player. He was quick, strong, skilful, tenacious, versatile and could score goals. Plus, he had scored probably the best overhead kick in the history of the game (against Barnsley in the FA Cup). In fact, I was really surprised he hadn't been snapped up by another club. Any concerns over whether he still had it were rubbish. The only thing missing was his dreads! I remember that debut against Everton, it was a* *fantastic performance. How Ray Harford didn't get sacked on the spot for agreeing to that deal is a mystery to me.*

**EX:** *I remember Sinclair was one of that group of players that girls would have posters of on their walls. He always seemed to be in teen magazines, at a time when footballers were actually becoming heart-throbs (well, some of them).*

*The deal for Dowie and Rowland was an incredible bit of business. And the Lazaridis strike at St James' Park was an incredible bit of skill. I still think it's one of the most underrated goals in Premier League history. He was basically in the car park when he hit it, absolutely miles out.*

**DAVE:** *I think if Shearer or Cantona would have scored the goal 'Skippy' did at Newcastle, Sky Sports would still be gushing over it to this day! It doesn't get the credit it deserves. It's one of the best goals I've ever seen from a West Ham player.*

## Heavy Hart

There was something disconcerting about John Hartson. You always worry about young players and how they'll handle the media spotlight. With great fame comes great temptation. Paul Merson's descent into drink and drugs was a sombre lesson about the spoils of fame.

In Hartson's case, there was less concern about Class A drugs as there was about his waistline. By March, he looked like he'd been snorting Cadbury's Creme Eggs. To put it into perspective, he'd scored 17 goals in his first 20 games of the season across all competitions. That was a ludicrous stretch of form that had Pele reaching for his abacus. The drop-off, at least in terms of goal outputs, was alarming. He'd since notched two in 14 and seemed noticeably frustrated by his form in front of goal. He was still a handful for any centre-half on a Saturday afternoon, but the sharpness and surprising movement of early season wasn't quite there. He was reduced to running physical battles with the opposition, which didn't seem the most effective use of his energy.

The frustration boiled over at Bolton where Big John was dismissed for a stupid swipe at Per Frandsen in the first half. Incredibly, a smart finish from Trevor Sinclair nearly earned us all three points, only for Nathan Blake to net a late equaliser for the basement strugglers.

We needed Hartson fit and focused for a stretch of games that would define our season. We were still in the FA Cup and duking it out with the likes of Leicester, Derby and Leeds for the European places. As much as Europe sounded exciting, the FA Cup was my priority. After years of being booted out unceremoniously by lower-league opposition, it felt like we had a genuine chance of getting to Wembley. In some respects, we were a classic cup team. We were a bag of Revels – you never quite knew what you were getting from one week to the next. If the draw was kind to us, I fancied there was a real chance of getting to Wembley.

We'd overcome two banana skins already with a win over non-League Emley and another 2-1 win away at Manchester City. The fifth round drew us against a resurgent Blackburn, fifth in the Premier League under new boss Roy Hodgson. After a 0-0 draw sent us up to Ewood for the replay, it seemed like we might have blown our best chance.

But Big (or Slightly Bigger) John was back in business, scoring with a neat finish after some clever work from Abou to give us the lead in extra-time. We looked set to dig in for the win in horrendous conditions, only for Stuart Ripley to send the tie to penalties. With the shootout level at 4-4, Craig Forrest stuck out a leg to deny Colin Hendry, and then Steve Lomas drilled home the deciding spot-kick to send us into the quarter-finals for the first time in seven years.

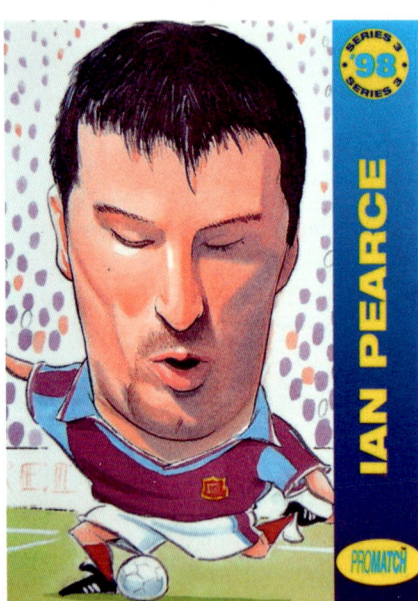

That set us up for what seemed to be a daunting tie at Arsenal. The Gunners were absolutely firing. After a dodgy pre-Christmas period when they lost four in six games and the media were quick to decry the wisdom of appointing a man christened 'Arsène Who?', Wenger's French Revolution was now in full effect. The team, which married the English fight of Keown, Adams, Dixon and co. with the foreign flair of new arrivals Petit, Overmars and Anelka, were hot on the heels of Manchester United in the title race.

We managed a well-deserved 0-0 draw in the League before our Cup trip to Highbury, where Arsenal's Alex Manninger was beaten all ends up by a left-foot screamer from Ian Pearce after just 12 minutes. It was the Big Fella's first goal for his boyhood club and a reminder that appearances can be utterly deceiving. Pearce was worth every penny of his £2.3 million fee. What marked Pearce out immediately was his adaptability. In fairness, I thought the same when I first saw him that night in 1994. *This lad could conceivably be a Premier League defender, a bailiff or a bare-knuckle boxer.* Never did I imagine he'd become one of our most important signings of the season.

Within passages of the same game Pearce could be a dominant aerial presence, a cultured libero striding into midfield or a full-back flying forward down the flanks. Hartson, Berkovic and Ferdinand had stolen the headlines so far this season, but Pearce's consistency was at the heart of our transformation from basement dwellers into an established top-ten outfit. Unfortunately, within 15 minutes he'd gone from hero to zero in North London as a rare mistake resulted in a Dennis Bergkamp penalty to level the tie.

There was a buzz in the air for the replay under the lights at Upton Park. It was our third meeting with the Gooners in as many weeks, and we'd given them as good a game as anyone in the country. The fans could sense an upset in the air, and when Bergkamp was red-carded for a rogue elbow in the first half, it felt like the semi-final was in reach – only for a sizzling strike from Nicolas Anelka to put the ten men in front. When Hartson buried a brilliant leveller after half-time, the dream was still alive. Despite our best efforts, that fabled Arsenal back four held firm and we headed to the lottery of a penalty shootout.

Of course, this being West Ham United, this was no ordinary penalty shootout. Our hopes relied on on-loan goalkeeper Bernard Lama, who'd arrived a few weeks earlier from PSG. The Frenchman had something of a controversial reputation in his homeland, having received a lengthy suspension for smoking cannabis. He'd have been forgiven for thinking he was still under the influence as the spot-kick drama unfolded.

For once, the odds seemed to be weighted in our favour. There was no Bergkamp (obviously), whilst Overmars, Anelka and Petit had been substituted as the Gunners defended with their lives in extra-time. Meanwhile, reserve keeper Alex Manninger in goal was a significant downgrade on David Seaman. *We could do this.*

When Christopher Wreh missed Arsenal's second kick, the pendulum seemed to swing in our favour, only for John Hartson to hammer one off the post. Then, with the scores level at 2-2 after six kicks, Remi Garde hit another one wide, only for Eyal Berkovic, who had been so brilliant all season long, to see his effort saved by Manninger.

Ultimately, the shootout went to sudden death, and there was an air of disbelief in the Boleyn as Tony Adams strode forward. The idea of a man who had spent his career permanently appealing for offside taking a crucial penalty seemed utterly ludicrous. Unsurprisingly, his effort from the spot may be one of the single worst since records began. The big centre-half bounded forward to seemingly strike the ball with all his might, only for it to bobble apologetically down the centre of the goal. Incredibly, Bernard Lama had committed himself approximately 1.5 centimetres to his right and could not adjust his footwork in the five minutes it took for the ball to dribble over the line. *I do not believe it.* I'd have backed f**king Victor Meldrew to save that.

We had to score to stay in the competition. Samassi Abou, who'd been a handful for Martin Keown all evening, struck the post and we'd shot ourselves in the foot once again. The FA Cup dream would fade and die for another year.

**EX:** *Hartson wasn't quite the same player in the New Year. He seemed a bit more static, a bit heavier and maybe he'd just got a bit over-confident after his explosive first half of the season, and wasn't quite dedicating himself as much. As a fan, you're not privy to what's going on in the dressing room or at the training ground, so it was hard to work out what was going on.*

*Nonetheless, when he scored that equaliser against Arsenal, I really thought we were in with a chance. We'd had a good Cup run. We'd overcome a proverbial banana skin against Emley, who did a lap of honour round Upton Park after the game. We'd won at Maine Road, where Georgi Kinkladze scored an amazing goal (I always thought he'd have been brilliant in our midfield alongside Berkovic) and then beaten Blackburn. Now we were up against ten-man Arsenal and the semi-final was in sight.*

**DAVE:** *Sadly, our history is littered with missed opportunities, and the quarter-final replay against Arsenal was one of them. This one hurt, big time. So did my eyes after watching the penalties through a cloud of cigarette smoke in the Bobby Moore Lower! I remember I didn't say a single word to anyone on the way home, I was absolutely gutted. The majority of my mates at school were Arsenal as well, so for weeks all I got from them was "ABOOOOUUU." Painful.*

### European Tour-ture

We quickly brushed off the disappointment by dispatching Leeds under the Monday-night lights again at Upton Park. Hartson scored his first League goal for two months; Abou – who was becoming something of a cult hero by virtue of his name alone – got on the scoresheet, and Ian Pearce's latest audition for *Stars in Their Eyes* continued in front of a live TV audience. *Tonight, Matthew, I'm going to be 1970s buccaneering Brazilian defender Carlos Alberto.* The Big Man notched the third in a 3-0 win when we could have scored six.

The win put us into the coveted seventh spot, which meant a UEFA Cup place.

For years it seemed our best chance of getting into Europe was on a stag do to Benidorm. Now, rather than mixing spirits in Lineker's Bar, we were potentially going to mix it with the continent's finest football teams. We had eight games left to hold on.

Two points from our next three matches didn't help. We lost 2-0 at Villa, our main rivals for European football, then John Hartson kiboshed our home game against Derby by giving Igor Stimac a straightener and earning an instant red card. We held on for a draw despite playing for over an hour with ten men, but the Welshman was rightly roasted by Harry Redknapp afterwards for resorting to such stupidity.

Thankfully, we weren't the only ones fluffing our lines. None of our main rivals could string a series of results together. Derby, Villa and Leicester were all treating the prospect of European football like an acute case of gonorrhoea. Hartson's last meaningful act of a frustrating second-half of the season was to net twice against Blackburn (the first courtesy of what felt like Eyal Berkovic's 5000th assist of the season) to give us our first win in four games.

Even after an absolutely appalling showing at Liverpool, where we were 4-0 down at half-time and Lama played like the Invisible Man, we still had a sniff of glory. Our fortunes were dependent on our final two fixtures – a sojourn across the capital to Selhurst Park and then a final game at home to Leicester.

The Palace game should have been a formality. They'd endured the sort of batshit crazy season which had become *de rigueur* at Upton Park. They'd started the season in a blaze of publicity after the frankly ludicrous signing of Attilio Lombardo from Juventus. The Italian had inspired them to mid table by November but since then they'd been in freefall. Steve Coppell had resigned, Lombardo had taken over as caretaker player-manager (with a rather rotund Tomas Brolin as his unlikely assistant) before the duo resigned after relegation was confirmed, leaving Ray Lewington in charge. If that wasn't bad enough, they'd been taken over by IT guru Mark Goldberg, who was unwittingly on his way to bankrupting the club. And on-loan midfielder Sasa Curcic, who had been booted out of Aston Villa after sordid rumours about hiring a double-decker bus and filling it with strippers and booze, was on the pitch protesting at NATO's bombing of Yugoslavia. *Que sera, sera and all that.*

Now they were rooted to the bottom of the League and set for the second tier alongside Barnsley and Bolton. Their players would surely have their minds on the beach by the time kick-off came around. When Lombardo put them 3-1 up, it was us who were all at sea. Our awayday curse had struck again. We were making the worst team in the League look like Cruyff's Oranje side of the late '70s.

With very few options at his disposal, Harry Redknapp used all those years of managerial nous and pressed the panic button. He sent on substitute striker Manny Omoyinmi, an unproven youth teamer whose last name looked like your worst nightmare of a Countdown Conundrum. Like most of our young players, I'd read about his exploits in matchday programmes, but long since learned not to believe the hype. On this occasion, and on this night, the hype was real. Omoyinmi scored two clinical left-foot finishes to earn us a point and keep us in the European hunt.

Aston Villa were in the driving seat and faced a final day at home to champions Arsenal, who had sealed the silverware with a 4-0 hammering of Everton (Slaven Bilic scored an own-goal) a week prior. Since then, Arsène Wenger's men had been walloped at Anfield in midweek, suggesting that their focus would be on the FA Cup final against Newcastle, and a potential Double. It seemed unlikely that the Gooners would do us a favour. They'd knock us out of the League Cup, the FA Cup, and if they lost at Villa Park, they'd inadvertently knock us out of the UEFA Cup running, too.

With half an hour gone, we had one foot in passport control. Two superb strikes from Lampard and Abou had put us in charge against the Foxes, whilst word was spreading around the ground that Villa had been reduced to ten men against Arsenal. Maybe our London brethren would do us a solid after all.

That goodwill towards the Gunners lasted all of seven minutes, by which time they'd conceded a penalty and inexplicably gone into the interval a goal down. As the minutes ticked by in the second half, our nerves started to jitter. Tony Cottee, who was back in England after his bizarre move to Malaysia turned predictably sour, pulled a goal back. Then Trevor Sinclair and Emile Heskey traded strikes as the drama reached new heights. When Abou notched his second we felt sure the game was ours, only for Cottee again to show why Redknapp was wrong to ship him out during that ridiculous summer of Raducioiu two years prior.

The last ten minutes were spent in some kind of Premier League purgatory. We were pleading with the referee to blow the whistle before Leicester snatched an equaliser, whilst simultaneously hoping that the official would allow anywhere up to three hours of injury time in the Midlands to force Arsenal to salvage a point.

In the end, our prayers were in vain. We held on to finish the campaign with three more points on another day of high drama at Upton Park. But Arsenal's feeble surrender, despite their numerical superiority, meant seventh spot went to Villa by a single point.

It was hard to feel too disappointed. Twelve months before, we'd been clinging on to our top-flight status. And now here we were, on the brink of the UEFA Cup. Harry Redknapp had turned us around from basement strugglers to one of the most batshit bonkers sides in the country. A seven-goal thriller on the final day felt like a poetic end to a season that was never predictable, but always entertaining.

**EX:** *That comeback at Palace was ridiculous. When we looked down at the touchline and saw Omoyinmi was coming on, most of us were scratching our heads. He was so tiny, he looked like one of the mascots. Then he goes and gets two goals to save us a point. It wouldn't be his only significant contribution to West Ham folklore.*

*The final game of the season was brilliant, but the Monday at school was a disaster. My class was absolutely crawling with Arsenal fans and they couldn't wait to remind me that they'd not only knocked us out of both cups, but they also stopped us qualifying for Europe by losing to ten-man Aston Villa. Still, it wasn't going to ruin my enjoyment of what was otherwise a brilliant season.*

**DAVE:** *It was such a good season for West Ham, considering we were fighting relegation 12 months prior. Our final League finish was a credit to the fantastic job Harry was doing at the club. Now felt like the perfect time to push on. If we could keep our best players and add that little bit of extra quality to the squad, then we could genuinely achieve the dream of European football.*

## FA Premier League - 1997/98

| Date | Opponent | H/A | Score | Att. | Scorers |
|---|---|---|---|---|---|
| 9 August | Barnsley | A | 2–1 | 18,667 | Hartson, Lampard |
| 13 August | Tottenham Hotspur | H | 2–1 | 25,354 | Hartson, Berkovic |
| 23 August | Everton | A | 1–2 | 34,356 | Watson (og) |
| 27 August | Coventry City | A | 1–1 | 18,289 | Kitson |
| 30 August | Wimbledon | H | 3–1 | 24,516 | Hartson, Rieper, Berkovic |
| 13 September | Manchester United | A | 1–2 | 55,068 | Hartson |
| 20 September | Newcastle United | H | 0–1 | 25,884 | |
| 24 September | Arsenal | A | 0–4 | 38,012 | |
| 27 September | Liverpool | H | 2–1 | 25,908 | Hartson, Berkovic |
| 4 October | Southampton | A | 0–3 | 15,212 | |
| 18 October | Bolton Wanderers | H | 3–0 | 24,864 | Berkovic, Hartson (2) |
| 27 October | Leicester City | A | 1–2 | 20,201 | Berkovic |
| 9 November | Chelsea | A | 1–2 | 34,382 | Hartson (p) |
| 23 November | Leeds United | A | 1–3 | 30,031 | Lampard |
| 29 November | Aston Villa | H | 2–1 | 24,976 | Hartson (2) |
| 3 December | Crystal Palace | H | 4–1 | 23,335 | Hartson, Berkovic, Unsworth, Lomas |
| 6 December | Derby County | A | 0–2 | 29,300 | |
| 13 December | Sheffield Wed | H | 1–0 | 24,344 | Kitson |
| 20 December | Blackburn Rovers | A | 0–3 | 21,653 | |
| 26 December | Coventry City | H | 1–0 | 24,532 | Kitson |
| 28 December | Wimbledon | A | 2–1 | 22,087 | Kimble (og), Kitson |
| 10 January | Barnsley | H | 6–0 | 23,714 | Lampard, Abou (2), Moncur, Hartson, Lazaridis |
| 17 January | Tottenham Hotspur | A | 0–1 | 30,284 | |
| 31 January | Everton | H | 2–2 | 25,909 | Sinclair (2) |
| 7 February | Newcastle United | A | 1–0 | 36,736 | Lazaridis |
| 21 February | Bolton Wanderers | A | 1–1 | 25,000 | Sinclair |
| 2 March | Arsenal | H | 0–0 | 25,717 | |
| 11 March | Manchester United | H | 1–1 | 25,892 | Sinclair |
| 14 March | Chelsea | H | 2–1 | 25,829 | Sinclair, Unsworth |
| 30 March | Leeds United | H | 3–0 | 24,107 | Hartson, Abou, Pearce |
| 4 April | Aston Villa | A | 0–2 | 39,372 | |
| 11 April | Derby County | H | 0–0 | 25,155 | |
| 13 April | Sheffield Wed | A | 1–1 | 28,036 | Berkovic |
| 18 April | Blackburn Rovers | H | 2–1 | 24,733 | Hartson (2) |
| 25 April | Southampton | H | 2–4 | 25,878 | Sinclair, Lomas |

| 2 May | Liverpool | A | 0–5 | 44,414 | |
| 5 May | Crystal Palace | A | 3–3 | 19,129 | Lampard, Omoyinmi (2) |
| 10 May | Leicester City | H | 4–3 | 25,781 | Lampard, Abou (2), Sinclair |

**FA Cup**

| 3 January R3 | Emley | H | 2–1 | 18,629 | Lampard, Hartson |
| 24 January R4 | Manchester City | A | 2–1 | 26,495 | Berkovic, Lomas |
| 14 February R5 | Blackburn Rovers | H | 2–2 | 25,729 | Kitson, Berkovic |
| 25 February R5R | Blackburn Rovers | A | 1–1 | 21,972 | Hartson (5–4 on pens) |
| 8 March QF | Arsenal | A | 1–1 | 38,077 | Pearce |
| 17 March QFR | Arsenal | H | 1–1 | 25,859 | Hartson (3–4 on pens) |

**League Cup**

| 16 Sept R2 1L | Huddersfield Town | A | 0–1 | 8,525 | |
| 20 Sept R2 2L | Huddersfield Town | H | 3–0 | 16,137 | Hartson (3) |
| 15 October R3 | Aston Villa | H | 3–0 | 20,300 | Hartson (2), Lampard |
| 19 November R4 | Walsall | H | 4–1 | 17,463 | Lampard (3), Hartson |
| 6 January QF | Arsenal | H | 1–2 | 24,770 | Abou |

| | P | W | D | L | GF | GA | GD | Pts |
|---|---|---|---|---|---|---|---|---|
| 1 Arsenal | 38 | 23 | 9 | 6 | 68 | 33 | +35 | 78 |
| 2 Manchester Utd | 38 | 23 | 8 | 7 | 73 | 26 | +47 | 77 |
| 3 Liverpool | 38 | 18 | 11 | 9 | 68 | 42 | +26 | 65 |
| 4 Chelsea | 38 | 20 | 3 | 15 | 71 | 43 | +28 | 63 |
| 5 Leeds United | 38 | 17 | 8 | 13 | 57 | 46 | +11 | 59 |
| 6 Blackburn Rov | 38 | 16 | 10 | 12 | 57 | 52 | +5 | 58 |
| 7 Aston Villa | 38 | 17 | 6 | 15 | 49 | 48 | +1 | 57 |
| 8 West Ham Utd | 38 | 16 | 8 | 14 | 56 | 57 | –1 | 56 |
| 9 Derby County | 38 | 16 | 7 | 15 | 52 | 49 | +3 | 55 |
| 10 Leicester City | 38 | 13 | 14 | 11 | 51 | 41 | +10 | 53 |
| 11 Coventry City | 38 | 12 | 16 | 10 | 46 | 44 | +2 | 52 |
| 12 Southampton | 38 | 14 | 6 | 18 | 50 | 55 | –5 | 48 |
| 13 Newcastle Utd | 38 | 11 | 11 | 16 | 35 | 44 | –9 | 44 |
| 14 Tottenham H | 38 | 11 | 11 | 16 | 44 | 56 | –12 | 44 |
| 15 Wimbledon | 38 | 10 | 14 | 14 | 34 | 46 | –12 | 44 |
| 16 Sheffield Wed | 38 | 12 | 8 | 18 | 52 | 67 | –15 | 44 |
| 17 Everton | 38 | 9 | 13 | 16 | 41 | 56 | –15 | 40 |
| 18 Bolton W | 38 | 9 | 13 | 16 | 41 | 61 | –20 | 40 |
| 19 Barnsley | 38 | 10 | 5 | 23 | 37 | 82 | –45 | 35 |
| 20 Crystal Palace | 38 | 8 | 9 | 21 | 37 | 71 | –34 | 33 |

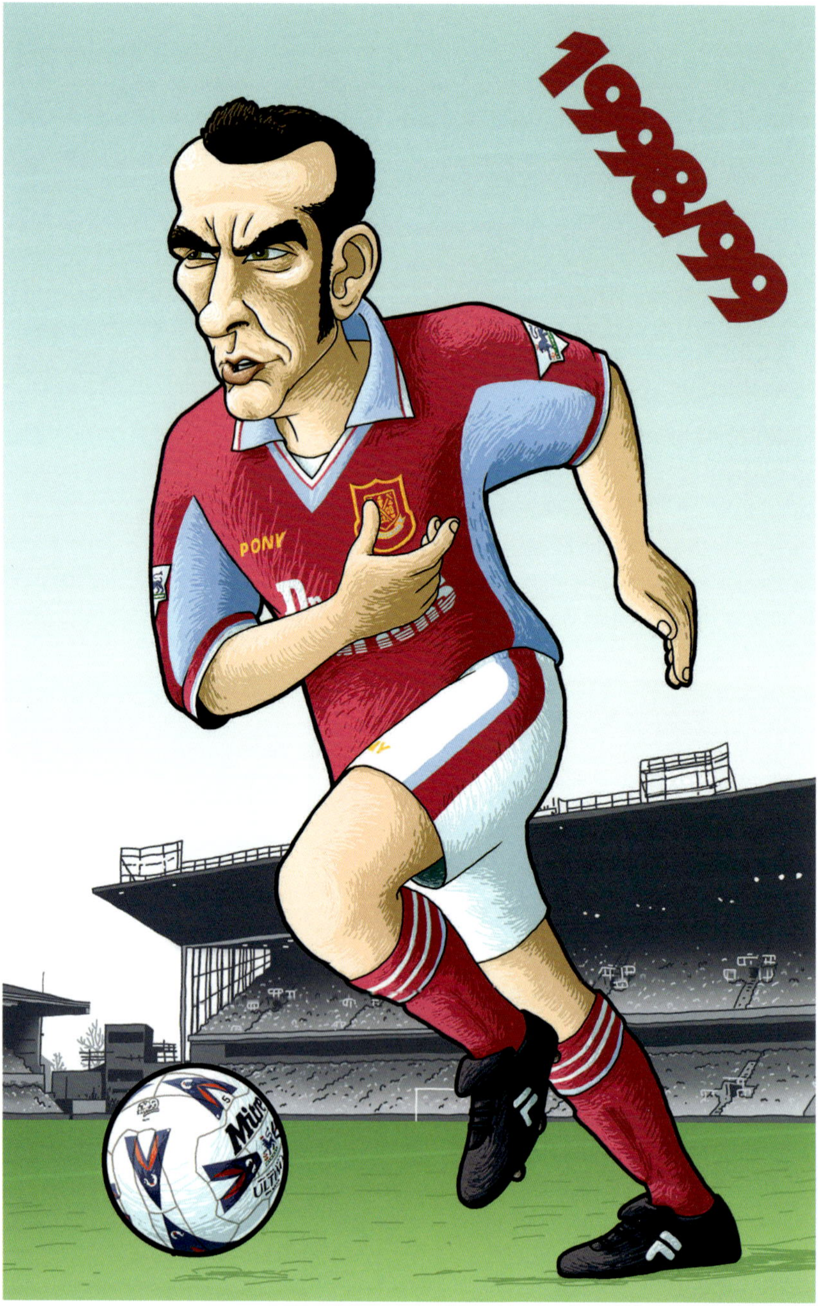
1998/99
PONY

## Harry Finds Mr Wright

Pre-season began with the now traditional search for a new striker. John Hartson had a fabulous first full season in Claret and Blue, but when his form dropped alarmingly after Christmas, we were short of goals elsewhere. Those goals could have helped us earn that precious European place.

During the '90s the headline 'HAMMERS IN STRIKER SEARCH' on the Teletext ClubCall page was enough to send an icy shiver through your veins. Our file on rubbish summer signings was thicker than a submarine door. If we were serious about moving to the much-hyped next level, then there could be no more costly mistakes like Boogers, Futre, Raducioiu or Dumitrescu.

We needed someone with proven quality. And we got him.

When news broke that Ian Wright was signing for West Ham, it felt like I was living in a fever dream. This couldn't be happening. THE IAN WRIGHT? The England international? The former Golden Boot winner? Arsenal's all-time record goalscorer? That Ian Wright was moving to Upton Park? Surely not.

In fairness, the livewire striker probably felt quite at home in his new surroundings. Our defence had spent the decade making him feel comfortable on a Saturday afternoon. Cup of tea, Mr Wright? And how about five yards of space in the penalty area? He terrorised us every season. Of the 185 goals he scored for the Gunners, it felt like he'd scored roughly 184 of them against us.

His last year at Highbury hadn't hit the heights of his previous years, as he was slowly moved to the sidelines in favour of the prodigious Nicolas Anelka. And he was now branching out into the world of TV, hosting his own show *Friday Night's All Wright*, where he interviewed a range of guests from Janet Jackson to Frankie Dettori, who both seemed more plausible West Ham purchases than one of the top flight's greatest ever goalscorers. Indeed, if you'd told me a charismatic chat-show host was signing for us, I'd have assumed it was Jerry Springer.

Once again, Harry Redknapp's silver tongue had worked its magic. Wright could have moved elsewhere, but the chance to work with Harry was too good to turn down. As was the two-year contract – pretty good going for a 34-year-old.

The age was the only doubt in my mind. Our record with players in their twilight years wasn't exactly stellar. Paulo Futre had turned up without his kneecaps, whilst Mike Newell looked like he'd lose a footrace with Bagpuss.

But Wright had still been scoring at domestic and international level. He'd notched a creditable eleven goals in 28 appearances in his final year in north London, whilst also playing an influential role in England's qualification for World Cup 98 – only to miss the tournament through injury. There was life in those shooting boots yet. And I couldn't wait to see him in a West Ham shirt.

**DAVE:** To this day, Ian's press conference is the best I've ever seen from a new signing at West Ham. Any concerns over his age, enthusiasm and loyalty to Arsenal was squashed immediately. Peter Storrie said that it took about 30 seconds to agree personal terms with him, then Wrighty said his first ever kit as a child was a West Ham one, and as a professional footballer, it will be his last. He was saying all the right things, as was Harry who had worked his magic again. He was spot-on when he said that signing a player of Ian's stature was a sign of how far the club had come. I couldn't wait to sing "Ian Wright, Wright, Wright" in the Bobby Moore Lower!

**EX:** For years, I had sung "Ian Wank, Wank, Wank," and now I was actually going to sing the correct version. I couldn't believe that my arch-nemesis, who always seemed to score against us for the team most of my friends supported, was going to join us. He was one of the first players I remember hearing about as one of the League's top strikers, alongside the likes of Gary Lineker and Ian Rush, and now he was going to be playing for my club, after all these years.

## Big Deals

Wright wasn't the only big signing over the summer. We had a new goalkeeper in the sizeable shape of Shaka Hislop, a free signing from Newcastle. Goalkeeper had been a bit of a problem area for us. The ever-loyal Ludo Miklosko was ready to pick up his pipe and slippers, whilst Craig Forrest had been solid, if a little unspectacular between the sticks. Hislop, a 6'4" Trinidadian international had the presence and the persona to give the back line more authority.

That back line would include another familiar face in Neil Ruddock, who arrived for £100,000 from Anfield. 'Razor' had been one of the Premier League's biggest personalities since its inception, clocking up over 150 appearances for Spurs and Liverpool. His career at the latter had ended with the arrival of Gerard Houllier, a move by the Merseyside hierarchy to signal the end of the much-maligned 'Spice Boys' era, where players like Ruddock, Robbie Fowler, Steve McManaman, Jamie Redknapp, Jason McAteer and David James were accused of focusing on fame rather than football.

Razor's inclusion in that list had always seemed a little bizarre. He was hardly a heart-throb, and these days if there was any fragrance he was more commonly associated with, it was probably a chicken korma. The defender's weight and disciplinary issues had been well documented. Quite how he was going to buck that trend at Chadwell Heath, where training sessions sometimes had the same intensity as a game of rock, paper, scissors, was yet to be determined.

The last signing of the summer was perhaps the most exotic, if unexpected. A

World Cup summer is an excuse for football fans to gaze wistfully at the planet's best players and picture them in their own club shirt. France 98 had been no exception, and whilst Zinedine Zidane wasn't on his way to England anytime soon, a host of other high-profile names were.

Big-spending Chelsea led the way with the announcements of World Cup winner Marcel Desailly, Danish winger Brian Laudrup and Italian striker Pierluigi Casiraghi. Manchester United, looking to wrench the title back from Arsenal's grasp, had brought in Dutchman Jaap Stam and Swede Jesper Blomqvist (alongside the £12.5 million signature of Dwight Yorke from Aston Villa). Whilst the champions had signed a Swede of their own in the shape of attacking midfielder Freddie Ljungberg.

With the country still basking in the glow of football fever (even England's acrimonious exit to Argentina hadn't taken the shine off a glorious summer of tournament football), West Ham United entered the World Cup Sweepstake with the announcement of... Javier Margas.

Until June, the Chilean centre-half could have wandered through Green Street completely unnoticed, but his appearances in France had earned him a global spotlight. His superstition of dying his hair the same colour as the team he represented was just the sort of gimmick any diligent TV director was looking for. And as such, Margas received plenty of TV time during Chile's fixtures. He looked fairly solid in a team spearheaded by superstars Ivan Zamorano and Marcelo Salas, though in truth I was more impressed by his efforts at Wembley a few months prior when he kept England's debut boy Michael Owen quiet.

A fee of £1 million was agreed, which seemed a bargain for a man with his international record. And even if he was a bit of a gamble, the other new recruits had proven Premier League pedigree. We'd hoped for a solid summer of transfer activity and we'd got it. The season couldn't start soon enough.

**EX:** *Hislop would be a very good signing for us, over two separate spells at the club. I was pleased as I thought he was great for Newcastle, and a really big presence between the sticks. Neil Ruddock was an icon of the game. His physique looked like he played for a pub team, but he had been consistent in the top flight for years. He was a massive performer in every sense. He'd need to be a big character. As a former Millwall and Spurs player, he was going to have to work hard to win over the crowd.*

**DAVE:** *With Shaka, it's funny what you remember because I can still visualise his untucked shirt when he played for Newcastle, and it was so baggy that he always looked like he was having a duvet day on the sofa! I thought he was a great signing.*

*Harry was clearly trying to add experience to a young squad, and wanted some big characters in the dressing room. Wrighty and Razor ticked both of those boxes.*

*I didn't know much about Javier other than his outrageous hairstyles, but when someone has a reputation at international level, you can't help get excited by what they could bring to West Ham (other than a load of aggravation when he eventually climbed out of his hotel window and flew back to Chile without permission!)*

## Wright on Time

We kicked off with an opening-day trip to Hillsborough, never a happy hunting ground for the Hammers in my lifetime. Margas was unavailable, but there were debuts for Hislop, Ruddock and Wright in the sizzling Sheffield sunshine.

At least I thought it was Ian Wright. From the first whistle, West Ham's new number 14 was absolutely wretched. He hustled and harried but couldn't get into the game at all. At one stage, I thought the ball had taken out a restraining order against him, such was the distance between them.

This wasn't exactly the hero I'd hoped for. And as the clock ticked down, the doubts of old resurfaced. *Had we signed another star whose light had finally dimmed? Had his legs gone? Was the Curse of Newell real, after all?*

On 84 minutes of a truly terrible game, I got my answer. In the blink of an eye, Wright lost his marker, split Wednesday's offside trap and slotted nonchalantly past Kevin Pressman. From zero to hero in an instant. What really struck me was his celebration. This was the man who'd made history at Arsenal and led the line for England on a glorious night in Rome, yet he celebrated that strike – during a stinker at Hillsborough – like he'd just won the World Cup.

That was the essence of Wright. A man determined to enjoy every second of his career on and off the pitch. And why shouldn't he? We'd gone to Yorkshire, where we were typically about as successful as garlic bread, and got three points.

The early-season optimism continued with a goalless draw at home to Manchester United, Big Shaka endearing himself with an excellent performance. A decent point (and successive clean sheet) at Coventry, where Javier Margas appeared in trademark Claret and Blue hair dye, kept our unbeaten start to the season going as we headed into a midweek fixture at home to Wimbledon.

By 26 minutes, we were three up thanks to Hartson and Wright – skipper for the evening – who scored two predatory finishes to open his official tally on home soil as a West Ham player. Even a consolation from Marcus Gayle couldn't dampen the half-time enthusiasm. We were unbeaten, playing some brilliant football, and cruising into the top three of the Premier League.

What happened in the next 45 minutes is the stuff of infamy. Few structures have crumbled so seismically, and so shamefully, as the West Ham defence that September evening. The Berlin Wall had put up more resistance than this. As the Dons threw up a succession of hopeful high balls into the box, we lost our heads completely. Margas looked more nervous than a long-tailed cat in a room full of rocking chairs as he, and others, were bullied by Gayle, Euell and Ekoku. Somehow we contrived to lose 4-3 in a game that proved the old adage 'You can lead a horse to water, but you can't make him defend a 3-0 lead against Joe Kinnear's f\*\*king Wimbledon'.

If Ian Wright was wondering what sort of insanity he'd walked into, he got his answer three days later when we hosted unbeaten Liverpool. John Hartson, whose battle with the scales was still looking decidedly one-sided, proved he was the big frame for the big occasion, scoring one and assisting Eyal Berkovic as we ran out 2-1 winners.

The calamitous second-half showing vs Wimbledon aside, we'd made a sensational start to the season. With Wright, Berkovic and Hartson on song, the Good Ship West Ham was setting sail for European waters.

Until one swing of the boot kicked us dramatically off course.

**EX:** I remember being on my way back from a family holiday in our caravan. It was a long journey, made all the better by listening to the Sheffield Wednesday game. It was a brilliant result, and you just knew Wright would score the winner.

**DAVE:** The win at Hillsborough was a fantastic start to the season. What a start to the season this was; but that game against Wimbledon will live with me forever. It was just bizarre. Upton Park was absolutely rocking at 3-0, and there were even chants of "We want four" going around the ground. Ultimately, we got our wish, just for the wrong f\*\*king team! We absolutely capitulated, and I was still in shock walking down the Barking Road at full time. It was as if the back four went for a pint in Queens after half an hour. We needed to bounce back against Liverpool, and bounce back we did with a quality performance. The bubbles were flying high!

**EX:** *How can you be 3-0 up after 26 minutes and lose the game 4-3? We all know that West Ham can achieve the impossible, especially when it comes to spectacular f\*\*k-ups, but this was inexplicable.*

## Hart Loses His Head

Socrates once said, "The hottest love has the coldest end," and if the fabled philosopher had been there on a fateful day at Chadwell Heath in late September 1998, he would doubtless have had a rueful grin on his face.

It took a week for the full story to emerge, but when it did, the details were explosive. A few days earlier we'd beaten Southampton 1-0 (Wright notching again), and Eyal Berkovic was subbed at half-time after an off-colour performance.

The headline in the *Mirror* screamed 'HEADCASE', and underneath it the explanation: 'Hartson's Hammer horror training-ground attack on Berkovic'. The pictures inside spared no detail. Evidently, there had been a bad tackle, a crossed word between the two, before Big John unleashed a fearsome boot to the face that sent poor Eyal halfway down the A12. In an instant, the love affair was over.

Somehow, the club thought they could keep a lid on the situation, which had occurred 24 hours before the win over Southampton. Quite what inspired their faith in a PR department that had more leaks than the hull on the *Mary Rose* was open to question. After all, the club had spent the entire decade conducting our business almost exclusively in the public eye, whether it was Morley's stabbing, Boogers' disappearance or Raducioiu's Christmas shopping. Asking anyone at West Ham to keep a secret was akin to asking Bruce Banner to take an anger management course.

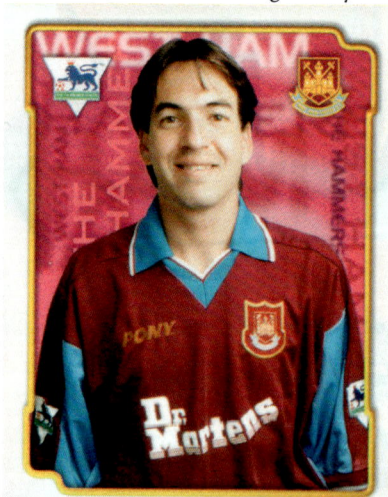

Unsurprisingly, within days, a combination of Berkovic, the FA and the press had blown the bloody doors off. Any hope that this could be shrugged off as 'one of those things' was long gone. Berkovic's father said he wanted Hartson arrested, whilst the FA was weighing up an investigation and a misconduct charge. Unsurprisingly, there were rumours that Berkovic had asked for a transfer – only for Hartson himself to suggest that the fracas was being used as a convenient excuse for the Israeli to engineer a move out of the club. The

Welshman was under attack from all corners, being unfairly depicted as a violent thug by the papers. Mind you, it didn't help that in the same month he'd given an interview to *Total Sport* saying 'he'd fight anyone', and was also appearing in front of a magistrate for damaging some hanging baskets at a local pub.

Amidst the chaos, Harry Redknapp was doing his best Rudyard Kipling impression, and trying to keep his head whilst all around were losing theirs. He did what any decent manager would do – supported his players and blamed Sky TV instead. If their reporters hadn't been there, none of this would have been such a big deal. Perhaps Jaws felt the same way. After all, if it wasn't for Spielberg and his f**king cameras, then no one would have given two shits about a few dead swimmers on Amity Island.

It was an almighty mess, and there seemed no obvious solution that didn't involve one of the two protagonists leaving the club. Thankfully, the international break gave everyone a little time to cool off.

**DAVE:** *It's just so typical, for everything to be going well at West Ham, only for something unpredictably shocking to derail us. Whilst this wasn't great from John, any player will tell you that this kind of thing happens every day in training. It just so happens that this was caught on camera, and the media being the media were hell-bent on making a mountain out of a molehill. The headlines being a prime example! You would have thought John attacked him with a bloody chainsaw!*

**EX:** *As I've learnt about football, I've understood that incidents like this were part of life at training grounds and often went unreported. Typically, we were the club who were put under the microscope by the media. We've had the pleasure of interviewing John and he says it was, understandably, the worst moment of his career. He knew he'd made a mistake. The reaction in the papers was out of all proportion.*

**DAVE:** *My immediate concern was for Eyal's future. I absolutely loved him, and it would have broken my heart to have lost him over something like this. I was praying for that cliché media appearance with their arms wrapped around each other, telling everyone they're the best of friends, so we could all move on.*

## Julian's Judgement Day

There was some good news, at least. Prior to the win over the Saints, we got an unexpected surprise when Julian Dicks made his first appearance in 18 long months in the League Cup second leg against Northampton. Trailing 2-0 from the first leg, after a typically dismal showing against lower-league opposition, there was a buzz of excitement around the 25,000 in attendance.

It felt like an astonishing achievement that Dicks had dragged himself back, through sheer force of will, to any kind of fitness. The toll that injuries had taken on his body was catastrophic. And though no one dared say it aloud, fans had long since consigned themselves to the fact that they may never see him don a Claret and Blue shirt again. In some ways, it was a reality that I'd become comfortable with. If my last sight of Julian was in that heroic '96/97 escape from relegation, then that was as good a way to remember him as any.

Against Northampton, Dicks was cheered every time he touched the ball, and even more so when he picked up his customary booking. Understandably, he lacked sharpness, but there were touches of class on the ball to suggest he had lost none of his quality in possession in a 1-0 win that wasn't enough to stop us exiting the competition on aggregate.

The real test would be when he returned to Premier League duty. How would his injury-ravaged limbs hold up against top-quality opposition? A few days later, we got our answer. A 3-0 walloping at Blackburn was made worse by the way Dicks was tormented by Stuart Ripley, the sort of winger he'd decimated in previous years. A similar showing at Charlton, in a demoralising 4-2 defeat, suggested the comeback might not be the fairy tale we were hoping for. The mind was willing, but the body wasn't. He would only make a handful more appearances before calling time on his magnificent service for this football club.

**DAVE:** *There are many iconic, long-awaited comeback appearances in history: Nelson Mandela in 1990, Terry Waite in 1991 and Julian Dicks in 1998. Dicksy is my all-time number one – the Bobby Moore or Billy Bonds of my era – so seeing him back in the shirt after 18 months of pining for him was a special moment for me. However, it was bittersweet because despite allowing some time for match fitness, it was obvious he wasn't the same player. I was gutted. Gutted for him more than anyone else, because he knew he was finished.*

*I remember his testimonial a couple of years later, I had tears running down my face. The word 'legend' is used too freely these days, but that's what Julian is, and will always be, to this football club.*

**EX:** *Julian's return was a sad insight into how badly injuries had affected his career, probably not helped by some inconsistent diagnoses and treatment. I was at the defeat to Charlton and remember a young Danny Mills tearing him apart. It was so sad to see. I wanted to run on and kick Mills into the stand to protect my hero. It was at that point that I knew his legendary career in Claret and Blue was over.*

### Top Dogs

If the '90s had taught us anything, it's that West Ham United had its finger constantly hovering over the self-destruct button. Having your two best players at war felt like the perfect opportunity for our season to go right down the khazi.

Neither Berkovic nor Hartson made the starting eleven for the trip to Newcastle, which despite all the gloom surrounding the club, produced one of our most stellar performances in recent memory. Newcastle boss Ruud Gullit, who had sauntered on to Tyneside promising sexy football, got exactly what he wanted. We stuffed them 3-0, Ian Wright rolling back the years with two clinical bits of finishing, either side of a goal from Trevor Sinclair.

Berkovic was back for the 1-1 draw at home to big-spending Chelsea, where Neil Ruddock put us ahead with a delightful free-kick. Razor had become something of a folk hero in these parts. He lacked the physique of an elite athlete but was a capable performer at this level. His no-nonsense defending complemented the craft of Rio Ferdinand. And given time on the ball, he could still produce one hell of a diagonal pass. He'd already repaid that paltry £100,000 fee many times over.

Quite how Redknapp was keeping the dressing room in check was a mystery. He had the likes of Ruddock, Wright, Moncur, Dicks and Hartson to contend with – enough to give anyone sleepless nights. Nonetheless, our form in early winter was positively dreamy. We beat Leicester 3-2 and then dominated Derby at Pride Park, in a game where Hartson marked his return to the starting line-up – alongside the brilliant Berkovic – with a superbly taken opener. Even that goal was eclipsed by a second-half screamer from Marc Keller. The unassuming Frenchman, whose arrival from Karlsruhe in the summer had gone somewhat unnoticed amidst the flurry of other deals, had made himself a starter on the left flank at the expense of Andy Impey (shortly to leave for Leicester). Keller had quality on either foot, and was proving to be another brilliant bit of business.

We ended November with a 2-1 win over Spurs. The star of the show this time was Trevor Sinclair, whose goals from wide positions had been key to our resurgence in form. An outrageous outside-of-the-boot effort proved the difference between the two teams.

Three months, and 15 games, into a tumultuous season, we were sitting second in the table. We were never going to be title contenders, but European football was now a distinct priority – even if it was going to be harder than ever before. Perhaps fearful of the Claret and Blue running amok at Roma or Real Madrid with our own brand of champagne football, UEFA had changed the qualifying requirements for the continent's showpiece competitions. Now only the top four teams were guaranteed a spot. The fifth-placed side would still be able to reach the UEFA Cup, by virtue of winning the little-known InterToto Cup.

The way we were playing, fifth position felt like a realistic possibility. All we needed was a bit of consistency.

**DAVE:** *This period for West Ham epitomised everything that was special about that season. Exciting, attacking football, a team of great players, big characters and outstanding performances that saw some memorable results. How many times have we needed an iron lung after climbing 15,000 stairs at St James' Park, ultimately leaving the North East pointless and potless? That 3-0 win was a statement of intent, followed by a run of good results, including that win against Spurs. As a fan, it was probably the most content I had ever felt in my life at that point. I was too young to remember the '86 season, so it felt like this was my version of that. There was such a buzz, home and away. We went into every game believing we could win it.*

**EX:** *I actually saw us do the double over Spurs that year. Later in the season, my dad managed to get us tickets in the corporate boxes at White Hart Lane, sitting amongst the Spurs fans. Wright's goal was so far out, it felt like he was in the car park. Then when Keller scored an absolute screamer, it took every bit of self-restraint not to join in with the noise from the away end. Somehow I managed to hide my smile as the Spurs fans drifted towards the Tube station.*

## Dear John

Obviously, we lost five out of our next seven games and tumbled down to ninth position. The run started with a 4-0 thumping at Leeds which saw the unlikely return of Javier Margas to first-team duty. The Chilean was last seen during that second-half schmozzle against Wimbledon, and it was only an injury to Rio Ferdinand that necessitated his call-up. Any hope that he might have recovered from that early crisis of confidence during his West Ham career soon disappeared. Poor Javier showed all the courage of a kitten going scuba diving, though he was by no means our only bad performer. We were caught in possession more often than George Michael, and were lucky to only concede four.

Once again, our away form was becoming problematic. Losses followed at Boro and Arsenal, before our traditional tonking at treble-chasing Man United.

Meanwhile, the Hartson Affair had resurfaced. The striker had received a hefty fine, but the FA had launched an investigation and the Welshman would be called to face a misconduct charge in the New Year. Even a letter from Eyal Berkovic – insisting that the incident had been forgotten and was essentially a waste of everybody's time – wasn't enough to deter the busybodies of Soho Square. The game's governance committee, who typically showed the urgency of a snail on a sunbed, weren't going to be put off by protests of procrastination. They would be the ones to decide if it was a waste of time, thank you very much. And they were going to spend as much time as they liked thinking about it.

Sensing the moment to strike, Wimbledon boss Joe Kinnear launched a £7.5 million bid for the Welshman's services out of the blue. It was a move right out of the Harry Redknapp textbook – and the West Ham boss was persuaded to sell.

It felt like a serious risk to discard a striker who had netted 25 goals the season before. But Hartson had been indifferent for the past 12 months, his form blighted by indiscipline and inconsistency. Passing him off to someone – for a hefty increase on his purchase price – meant Redknapp could spend less time worrying about legal ramifications and more on reinforcements to the squad.

The first of which was Scott Minto. The former Charlton and Chelsea defender joined from Benfica to a collective shrug from the fanbase. He was a serviceable full-back, but Hartson's exit left a gaping hole in attack that needed filling.

With Kitson injured (again), and top scorer Ian Wright also facing a spell on the sidelines, the unlikely strikeforce of Samassi Abou and Trevor Sinclair took to the field for the home game with Sheffield Wednesday. We were smashed 4-0 on a day when little Italian Benny Carbone ran riot, often at the expense of Scott Minto, whose debut was more horrific than Freddy Krueger's.

If we were going to have any hope of salvaging the season, we needed a striker – and we needed one quickly.

**DAVE:** *I literally couldn't believe our luck. We were flying at one point, then everything seemed to go down the khazi after that training-ground incident. This ultimately saw us lose John Hartson, and I know the Big Fella hadn't performed to the same level as he did during his first season, but given his age and the fact that he now had better players around him, I thought he still had something to offer.*

**EX:** *John Hartson's massive drop in form was a real mystery. He had gone from a Welsh wizard who was topping the scoring charts to a player hopelessly out of form. His magic touch had deserted him, and you didn't really know where his next goal was coming from. I thought the £7.5 million fee was a great deal. And I was surprised Wimbledon were prepared to spend such a massive amount of cash, especially when they seemed destined for relegation.*

**DAVE:** *John was a record signing for West Ham when he joined, and became a record signing for Wimbledon when he left. I was really sad to see him go. Yet again,*

*Harry needed to work some magic in the market because, with Hartson gone and injuries elsewhere, goals were going to be a problem for us.*

### Di Canio – Friend or Foe?

With Hartson gone, and the club in desperate need of some kind of stability, Harry Redknapp signed English football's Public Enemy Number One.

Paolo Di Canio had been the pantomime villain for the press since a game at Hillsborough in October. The Sheffield Wednesday-Arsenal fixture had pitted Di Canio against Patrick Vieira, two men whose tempers made the Incredible Hulk look like a UN diplomat. It didn't take long for proceedings to boil over.

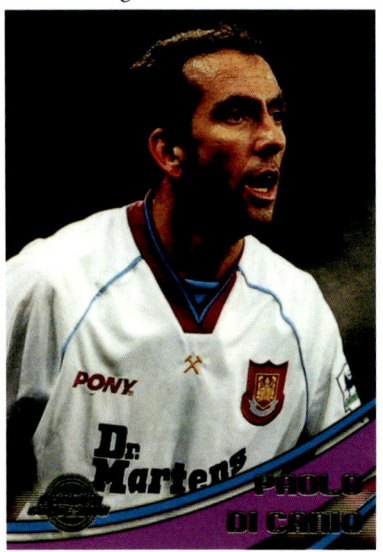

The irate Italian took exception to Vieira's ample aggression, Martin Keown swung him round by the collar, and chaos ensued. Keown and Di Canio were expelled. Meanwhile Vieira, at the hub of all the aggro, sheepishly whistled 'La Marseillaise' and headed back to centre midfield.

Di Canio, owner of the keenest sense of injustice in football, shoved referee Paul Alcock in disgust, albeit with the sort of contact that wouldn't have toppled Miss Marple. Nonetheless, Alcock stumbled to the floor like Charlie Chaplin after six pints and a kebab. It was slapstick stuff.

Di Canio had copped a £10,000 fine and an eleven-game ban. His time at Wednesday was over and he seemed destined to return to his homeland, until Harry Redknapp offered him an alternative escape route.

I'd seen plenty of Di Canio at Celtic and Sheffield Wednesday. He'd become a cult hero during his sole season in Glasgow with his long sideburns, short shorts and gold boots. His highlight reel was something to behold, and was recognised by his award as SPFA Player of the Year. He'd carried on that form at Hillsborough, top scoring in his first season with the club before falling out with Danny Wilson. The Wednesday boss couldn't wait to offload him, and accepted a ludicrously low £1.5 million bid from Redknapp. At least now he was someone else's problem.

Di Canio wasn't the only new face on show for the photographers. Marc-Vivien Foé, a defensive midfielder from French champions Lens, arrived for £3.4 million. All I had for info on the Cameroon international was his profile on Championship

Manager, which marked him out as a powerful force in the middle of the park. Mind you, the same CM database essentially depicted Ibrahima Bakayoko as the lovechild of Pele and Diego Maradona. The Ivorian was a legend on my laptop, but I'd seen him play for Everton and he was absolutely shite.

**DAVE:** *Cometh the hour, cometh the man! I was a big fan of Paolo as a player but, due to the constant toxic negativity from the mainstream media at the time, I remember feeling a bit concerned about his character and whether he could potentially disrupt the rest of the squad. Then I saw the photo of his arms wrapped around Marc-Vivien Foé with that beaming smile, and thought I'd give him the benefit of the doubt. In hindsight, I don't think any of us could have called just how good that signing would prove to be.*

**EX:** *What we didn't know at the time was that the signing of Di Canio would prove to be a significant moment in the club's history. It felt like a huge gamble, given all the negative headlines, but the maverick Italian would eventually become a Claret and Blue legend. He would go on to join Julian Dicks and Tony Cottee in my all-time top three, such was the incredible impact he had on the team and the terraces.*

**DAVE:** *It's easy to forget that we signed Marc-Vivien Foé that same day. I remember looking at him and thinking, "Blimey, this fella is an absolute unit." The fact that he was also a defensive midfielder instantly drew comparisons with Patrick Vieira. It was a brilliant double signing and gave everyone the boost we needed.*

**EX:** *We had beaten a lot of competition to sign the Cameroon international, and he felt like another coup on Harry Redknapp's part. He was a gentle giant off the pitch, but on it he was exactly the kind of presence we needed in midfield.*

### Paolo Power

The home game with Arsenal was one of firsts and lasts. It was our first glimpse of Foé and Di Canio and, sadly, our last sightings of Breacker and Dicks on first-team duty – neither of whom deserved the cruel twist of their final appearance in a West Ham shirt being an ignominious 4-0 defeat against the Gunners.

Whilst Dicks would always be a legend, Breacker was something of an unsung hero. For nine seasons he'd patrolled that touchline, bombing forward to put in a dangerous cross, scampering back to make a last-gasp tackle. Players like Breacker don't make headlines, don't make trouble. They just put on their boots on a Saturday afternoon and get stuck in. Amidst a decade of chaos, he had been a constant. Mr Reliable on the right flank. Within a few days he'd joined QPR, where he linked up with Ludo, Keith Rowland and Iain Dowie. There was no final flourish. Just a quick handshake with Harry and a "see ya later." In a strange way, it seemed typical of a man who'd gone about his business without any fanfare.

One player who did command the limelight was Di Canio. The Arsenal abomination on debut was quickly wiped from memory as the Italian put in an inspired performance at home to Forest. His white-booted wizardry was at the heart of a much-improved display which saw us sweep past the struggling Midlanders with goals from Pearce and Lampard, whose late runs into the box had been a feature of the season to date.

Lampard was at it again at Anfield, converting coolly from the spot in front of the Kop in a deserved 2-2 draw. In fact, we would have won the game but for a late miss from teenage debutant Gavin Holligan. The surprise sub, a £100,000 signing from Kingstonian, hit a one-on-one straight at the keeper when it might have been easier to square to an unmarked Marc Keller. It was to be Holligan's one and only first-team appearance. What might have been.

Di Canio dazzled in the next home game against basement dwellers Blackburn, setting up the opener for Pearce with a pinpoint cross and then netting the second after sensational build-up play between him, Berkovic and Sinclair. Paolo was quickly proving himself to be exactly the sort of entertainer that West Ham fans adored. He was like a mixture of all of our heroes. He had the sublime skill of a Devonshire, the vision of a Brooking and the star power of a McAvennie.

It didn't matter where he was meant to be playing, he was always in the centre of the action. One moment he would be skipping past a hapless full-back, the next twisting and turning in the penalty area to fire a shot at goal. He demanded the ball and demanded more of others around him, including new strike partner Paul Kitson. The latter scored the winner at Stamford Bridge, and the duo were both on the scoresheet in a 2-0 victory over Newcastle that owed just as much to another standout performance from Shaka Hislop. With six games to go we were fifth in the table, in pole position for European football.

Could we hold on?

**EX:** *It was sad to see Tim Breacker go. Vastly underrated by other clubs, he had been a constant during my time supporting the club. He was the first signing I remember as a season-ticket holder, and he lasted to the end of the decade. It really was incredible service he gave to West Ham. Meanwhile, Paolo was already making himself a Hammers hero. When I was younger, I remember the buzz of expectation when Stuart Slater had the ball at his feet. You could hear the noise of seats slapping* *shut as people to stood to watch him in full flight. It was the same with Di Canio. Every time he got the ball something happened, something you didn't expect, something that made you glad you'd bought a ticket to watch a player of his quality.*

**DAVE:** *I always say that to have really appreciated Paolo in all his glory, you had to watch him week in, week out; a lot of the jaw-dropping skill, exquisite touches and outrageous flair wasn't always shown on* Match of the Day *unless it led to a goal. Paolo was pure poetry. He was just so entertaining to watch, but what also made him an instant hit with the fans was his passion. He had a winning mentality, and when we lost, he hurt as much we did. Harry had signed one hell of a player and absolutely nicked him for £1.5 million. That superb bit of business had given us the best possible chance to qualify for Europe, and we were daring to dream!*

### Goals Galore and a European Tour

A goalless draw at Leicester saw us lose the spot to Aston Villa. A win over Derby, one point and one place behind us with a game in hand, was essential.

It was the sort of occasion that Di Canio relished. Within half an hour, he'd scored the opener and set up Berkovic for a second. When the returning Wright netted his eighth of the season, Upton Park was in raptures. Yet there was more to come. Ruddock nodded in a fourth from a Sinclair cross, and then a buccaneering run from Steve Lomas, who'd made a sterling effort as a makeshift right-back in recent weeks, supplied Sinclair with the fifth.

We marched on to White Hart Lane on a high. Ian Wright, who was given the sort of reception a Cornish pastie gets at a WeightWatchers convention, stuffed his abusers' criticism back down their throats with a sensational 30-yard lob on five minutes. When Marc Keller struck a second, we were reaching for our passports. Even a late David Ginola screamer couldn't dampen our enthusiasm.

We were one point behind Villa with three games to play. As ever, the fixture computer hadn't done us any favours. A home game against fourth-place Leeds, a trip to relegation-haunted Everton, and a home finale against Boro in seventh.

Villa's run-in wasn't much better. I couldn't see them getting much out of a trip to Manchester United, but they could easily beat Charlton at home. Incredibly, the final-day fixture was Arsenal – this time at Highbury – which meant our European aspirations were reliant on our London rivals. This time, at least, there would be no easing off. The title race was going right to the wire. Arsenal would need a win on the final day to deny United the first trophy of a potential Treble.

My instincts told me they'd get three points from three games. Their superior goal difference meant we'd need two wins to secure fifth.

It took all of 20 seconds to realise we weren't going to get anything against Leeds, as Jimmy Floyd Hasselbaink took advantage of some generous defending to slot the visitors in front. Things went rapidly downhill from there. Ian Wright – who was so amped up, you wondered if someone had injected raw Duracell into his bloodstream – received two yellow cards for reckless tackles. Leeds scored again and we went into the interval trailing by one man and two goals.

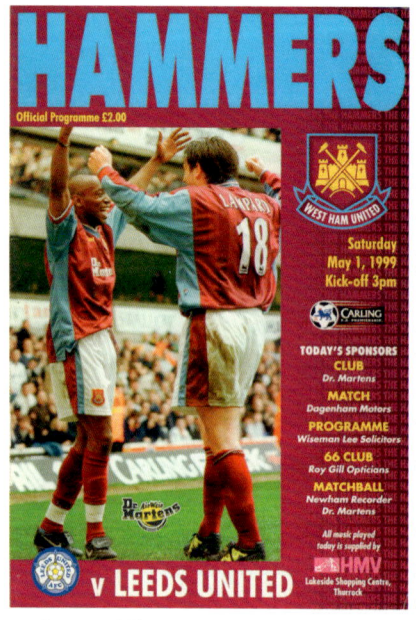

When Di Canio scored a smart finish to bring us back into the game soon after the restart, the crowd roared and we poured forward. A clever Leeds counter resulted in a professional foul by Hislop and another sending-off. The final score was 5-1, and the final player tally was 11-8 as Lomas saw red in injury time. The only consolation was that Villa had done their bit and lost at Old Trafford.

The less said about the game at Goodison, the better. We were absolutely rancid from the first whistle. Memories came flooding back of that rainswept night at Oldham nine years earlier, when a team in blue zipped around us like were a set of training cones. Everton scored six (it could have been 16) and in the space of two games we'd accrued a total of zero points and -10 goal difference.

Incredibly, the only team playing worse than us was our nearest rival. Villa conceded a last-minute winner in 4-3 home defeat to struggling Charlton, which meant that we entered the final day knowing we needed to beat Boro while hoping Villa didn't get a result at Highbury.

A year on from the game against Leicester, the atmosphere felt different. Despite the chaos that had gone before, this was a better team than the one that had taken the field 12 months prior. Shaka Hislop was rightly awarded Hammer of the Year. Rio Ferdinand had matured into one of the best central defenders in the country. Frank Lampard had been a source of vital goals from midfield. Trevor Sinclair was fabulous in full flight. And in Eyal Berkovic and Paolo Di Canio, we had two of the most gifted ball players that this famous old stadium had ever seen.

In glorious sunshine, we put on a sizzling display to silence any doubter of our continental credentials. A Lampard long-ranger set the tone, before a Keller tap-in put us in complete control. Two strikes from Trevor Sinclair, either side of a goal for Arsenal at Highbury, meant that we'd secured the InterToto spot in style.

It felt like the right end to a rollercoaster season. Legends had come and gone. Headlines had been made for all the wrong reasons. Yet this team had played some breathtaking football. We finished fifth in the League, our highest position since those heady days of 1986, with a -7 goal difference. It was utter madness.

But we didn't care. We'd started the '90s slumming in the second tier. We ended it with the mighty West Ham United on a European tour. What a time to be alive.

COYI.

**DAVE:** *I don't think I had a fingernail left that day. The smokers in the stands must have done about 20 fags in 90 minutes! Even the stewards neglected their duties to watch every kick of the ball. Everyone was desperate for that fifth-place finish and, to be fair to the lads, it's what they deserved. We were superb, that season. When the full-time whistle blew, the collective euphoria was something that money can't buy, it was a carnival atmosphere. I remember the players doing a lap of honour, and when Wrighty approached the Bobby Moore Lower he stood still, looked to the sky, closed his eyes, put both hands in the air and out of nowhere Razor crept up behind him and pulled his shorts down. It was a comedy end to a chaotic season.*

**EX:** *This season, I went to as many games as physically possible (only missing the trips to Newcastle and Blackburn). It was an absolute rollercoaster of a campaign. You never knew what was going to happen next. We could be like Real Madrid one week, the Dog & Duck the next. We actually finished with a negative goal difference, which is ridiculous for a team finishing in fifth position.*

**DAVE:** *I didn't realise it then, but the importance of the memories created that season would mean even more to me all these years later, because I created them with my dad. Side by side, week after week, watching the best football I'd ever seen at Upton Park. I thank West Ham, and that squad of players, for that.*

**EX:** *All the absurdity of the decade – Torquay, Oldham, Stockport – had led to this moment: West Ham United in Europe. I was 17 years old, without a care in the world, travelling up and down the country on a Saturday afternoon to watch some of the most entertaining football I would ever see in my lifetime. I would relive it all over again in a heartbeat.*

## FA Premier League - 1998/99

| Date | Opponent | H/A | Score | Attendance | Scorers |
|---|---|---|---|---|---|
| 15 August | Sheffield Wed | A | 1–0 | 30,236 | Wright |
| 22 August | Manchester United | H | 0–0 | 26,039 | |
| 29 August | Coventry City | A | 0–0 | 20,818 | |
| 9 September | Wimbledon | H | 3–4 | 25,311 | Hartson, Wright (2) |
| 12 September | Liverpool | H | 2–1 | 26,029 | Hartson, Berkovic |
| 19 September | Nottingham Forest | A | 0–0 | 26,463 | |
| 28 September | Southampton | H | 1–0 | 23,153 | Wright |
| 3 October | Blackburn Rovers | A | 0–3 | 25,213 | |
| 17 October | Aston Villa | H | 0–0 | 26,002 | |
| 24 October | Charlton Athletic | A | 2–4 | 20,043 | Rufus (og), Berkovic |
| 31 October | Newcastle United | A | 3–0 | 36,744 | Wright (2), Sinclair |
| 8 November | Chelsea | H | 1–1 | 26,023 | Ruddock |
| 14 November | Leicester City | H | 3–2 | 25,642 | Kitson, Lomas, Lampard |
| 22 November | Derby County | A | 2–0 | 31,366 | Hartson, Keller |
| 28 November | Tottenham Hotspur | H | 2–1 | 26,044 | Sinclair (2) |
| 5 December | Leeds United | A | 0–4 | 36,320 | |
| 12 December | Middlesbrough | A | 0–1 | 34,623 | |
| 19 December | Everton | H | 2–1 | 25,998 | Keller, Sinclair |
| 26 December | Arsenal | A | 0–1 | 38,098 | |
| 28 December | Coventry City | H | 2–0 | 25,662 | Wright, Hartson |
| 10 January | Manchester United | A | 1–4 | 55,180 | Lampard |
| 16 January | Sheffield Wed | H | 0–4 | 25,642 | |
| 30 January | Wimbledon | A | 0–0 | 23,035 | |
| 6 February | Arsenal | H | 0–4 | 26,042 | |
| 13 February | Nottingham Forest | H | 2–1 | 25,458 | Pearce, Lampard |
| 20 February | Liverpool | A | 2–2 | 44,511 | Lampard (p), Keller |
| 27 February | Blackburn Rovers | H | 2–0 | 25,529 | Pearce, Di Canio |
| 6 March | Southampton | A | 0–1 | 15,240 | |
| 13 March | Chelsea | A | 1–0 | 34,765 | Kitson |
| 20 March | Newcastle United | H | 2–0 | 25,997 | Di Canio, Kitson |
| 2 April | Aston Villa | A | 0–0 | 36,813 | |
| 5 April | Charlton Athletic | H | 0–1 | 26,041 | |
| 10 April | Leicester City | A | 0–0 | 20,402 | |
| 17 April | Derby County | H | 5–1 | 25,485 | Di Canio, Berkovic, Wright, Ruddock, Sinclair |
| 24 April | Tottenham Hotspur | A | 2–1 | 36,089 | Wright, Keller |
| 1 May | Leeds United | H | 1–5 | 25,997 | Di Canio |

| 8 May  |    | Everton       | A | 0–6 | 40,049 |                                  |
|--------|----|---------------|---|-----|--------|----------------------------------|
| 16 May |    | Middlesbrough | H | 4–0 | 25,902 | Lampard, Keller, Sinclair, Di Canio |

## FA Cup

| 2 January  | R3  | Swansea City | H | 1–1 | 26,039 | Dicks |
| 13 January | R3R | Swansea City | A | 0–1 | 10,116 |       |

## League Cup

| 15 Sept | R2 1L | Northampton Town | A | 0–2 | 7,254  |         |
| 22 Sept | R2 2L | Northampton Town | H | 1–0 | 25,435 | Lampard |

|    |                | P  | W  | D  | L  | GF | GA | GD  | Pts |
|----|----------------|----|----|----|----|----|----|-----|-----|
| 1  | Manchester Utd | 38 | 22 | 13 | 3  | 80 | 37 | +43 | 79  |
| 2  | Arsenal        | 38 | 22 | 12 | 4  | 59 | 17 | +42 | 78  |
| 3  | Chelsea        | 38 | 20 | 15 | 3  | 57 | 30 | +27 | 75  |
| 4  | Leeds United   | 38 | 18 | 13 | 7  | 62 | 34 | +28 | 67  |
| 5  | West Ham Utd   | 38 | 16 | 9  | 13 | 46 | 53 | −7  | 57  |
| 6  | Aston Villa    | 38 | 15 | 10 | 13 | 51 | 46 | +5  | 55  |
| 7  | Liverpool      | 38 | 15 | 9  | 14 | 68 | 49 | +19 | 54  |
| 8  | Derby County   | 38 | 13 | 13 | 12 | 40 | 45 | −5  | 52  |
| 9  | Middlesbrough  | 38 | 12 | 15 | 11 | 48 | 54 | −6  | 51  |
| 10 | Leicester City | 38 | 12 | 13 | 13 | 40 | 46 | −6  | 49  |
| 11 | Tottenham H    | 38 | 11 | 14 | 13 | 47 | 50 | −3  | 47  |
| 12 | Sheffield Wed  | 38 | 13 | 7  | 18 | 41 | 42 | −1  | 46  |
| 13 | Newcastle Utd  | 38 | 11 | 13 | 14 | 48 | 54 | −6  | 46  |
| 14 | Everton        | 38 | 11 | 10 | 17 | 42 | 47 | −5  | 43  |
| 15 | Coventry City  | 38 | 11 | 9  | 18 | 39 | 51 | −12 | 42  |
| 16 | Wimbledon      | 38 | 10 | 12 | 16 | 40 | 63 | −23 | 42  |
| 17 | Southampton    | 38 | 11 | 8  | 19 | 37 | 64 | −27 | 41  |
| 18 | Charlton Ath   | 38 | 8  | 12 | 18 | 41 | 56 | −15 | 36  |
| 19 | Blackburn Rov  | 38 | 7  | 14 | 17 | 38 | 52 | −14 | 35  |
| 20 | Nottingham For | 38 | 7  | 9  | 22 | 35 | 69 | −34 | 30  |

# Epilogue

And so a decade that had included three managers, two relegations, two promotions, an FA Cup semi-final and – ultimately – European qualification, came to an end.

In some ways it was the perfect encapsulation of life supporting West Ham United. A club that can lurch from calm to crisis in the blink of an eye. A club that can take you from the height of ecstasy to the depths of despair with a single kick of a football. If the '90s taught us anything, it's that nothing about this club is predictable.

Maybe that's why football means so much to us. We spend so much of our lives purely *existing*. We work, we pay our bills, we take the kids to school, we work, we pay our bills… and the cycle continues. There are days when you put your head on the pillow and you wake up four weeks later. Life has just passed you by.

To support West Ham is to live at the extremes of human emotion. The song 'Bubbles' encapsulates this club so perfectly. Moments of joy can be so fleeting that you have to savour every second of them, before your hope bursts under the inevitable cloud of impending doom. I've learned to cherish the chinks of light in the darkness. When I think of my favourite West Ham moments, they're when we've come out swinging whilst adversity surrounds us: Julian Dicks hammering home that penalty in the 4-3 win over Spurs, Tevez silencing Old Trafford and, more recently, Yarmolenko stroking home the winner against Chelsea. In those split seconds, I've never felt so alive.

You might be wondering why the book stops here. Why not include the '99/00 season and our assault on the InterToto Cup? Well, we started this adventure in 1989, and we'll start the next one in 1999 when we look back at life at the Boleyn during the '00s. A decade that included six managers, one relegation, one promotion, Play-off heartbreak, Play-off elation, one FA Cup final, one costly case of third-party ownership, and a takeover from an Icelandic billionaire biscuit baron whose entire fortune crumbled overnight during a global economic crisis.

New decade, same old West Ham.

# AUTHORS

Sid Lambert is a viral sensation, running his nostalgic Twitter account It's A Funny Old Game which celebrates '80s, '90s and '00s football with over 180,000 followers. His unique humour has featured on Planet Football and Mundial, and he is co-author of *Can We Not Knock It? A Celebration of '90s Football* with Chris Scull. A Claret & Blue fan since 1986, Sid now relives all those ups and downs in his column in the West Ham United programme, and on The West Ham Way. **Follow @sid_lambert.**

Dave Walker, a lifelong West Ham fan, arrived on the scene with his popular online fanzine *Sex, Drugs & Carlton Cole*. After creating some impressive content, Ex asked to meet him at the Queens pub on Green Street with a view to collaborating on The West Ham Way. Dave is the host and producer of the successful podcast, and co-creator of The West Ham Way pre-match event in Leytonstone (and Las Vegas!). He has also worked with many national media outlets as a pundit and presenter. **Follow @DaveWalkerWHU.**

In 2012, ExWHUEmployee created a Twitter account aiming to become the most reliable source of West Ham news, thanks to his various sources. He has since written for a number of West Ham-related websites, and has made many national podcast and media appearances. In 2016 came The West Ham Way, launched with close friend Dave Walker. Ex is a four-time nominee for the Best Social Media Account at the Football Content Awards, the TWHW podcast also being nominated twice. **Follow @ExWHUEmployee**

# THE WEST HAM WAY

Together, Dave and Ex created the highly popular The West Ham Way Patreon, offering fans a wealth of exclusive content, valuable insight and tight-knit community. It represents great value for any West Ham fan. Here are just some of the features you get for only £5 per month:
- Full access to TWHW Podcast with Dave Walker and ExWHUEmployee
- Weekly interviews with former players
- 'Mad Dog Bites' show with Martin Allen
- 'Wacka's World' with Jimmy Walker
- 'You Irons' podcast – Sam Delaney & co.
- Exclusive breaking news from Ex
- Expert pre-match opposition analysis from Dan Woffenden
- TWHWUSA Podcast – Brawley & Nick
- Discounts on pre-match events and merchandise
- Quarterly virtual events with former players
- Monthly column written by Tony Cottee
- Full access to TWHW Telegram platform

All of this, and much more, is accessible at: **www.patreon.com/thewesthamway**
Please do also check out the engaging and informative website at: **www.thewesthamway.com**

# ACKNOWLEDGEMENTS

Special thanks to Julian Dicks and Tony Cottee for their introductory notes. Illustrations: Simon Smith; photos Dave Morcom Photography; memorabilia Steve Marsh theyflysohigh.co.uk.
Also thanks to the West Ham United Statistics website, a treasure trove of useful information.

# TEAMWORK

Grateful thanks to everyone who subscribed in advance to Highs, Lows & Di Canios...

John Brooks | Scott MacKenzie | Dominic Murray | Adam Jones | Rod Evans
Rory Shipton | Charlotte Rayner | Nick Shepherd | Paul Suett | Nikki Vincent
James Hughes | Joe Bearman | Paul Adderson | Lewis Scanlan
Brett & Dylan Miller | Rob Hawkins | Dave Marlow | Noah Beckell | Paul Agar
Richard Menzies | Gary West | Brian Mundstock | Daniel Halton
Daniel Robert Black | Jamie Miller | Gary Donovan | Keith Evans
Hutch | Paul Cleavely | Steve Harris | Gavin Stevens | Andy Mason
Mathew Winter & Lina Budakova | Kyle Griffith | Paul Goody | Josh Ballard
Michael Pocklington | Paul Palmer | Kevin Peyton | Mark Woffenden
Virginia Black | Dan Baptiste | Bradley Taylor-Hicks | Shane Kelly
Jason Barron | Jonathan Lowe | Peter Beach | Brawley Darbon | Paul Duhig
Scott Goodman | Phillip T Hughes | Martin Huxley | Alfie Huxley
Ravi Sabharwal | Chris Skinner | Tim Skinner | Christopher Powell
Robert Jackson | Scott Hubbard | Nick Poole | Paul Haseltine | Freddie Hill
Vladimír Hebert | Steve Knight | Paul Valentine | Andrew Turl | Daniel Hand
Chris Ash | Paul Morgan | David Sandys | John Brooks | Steven Wills
Gary Portugal | Peter & Lucas Mc Shane | David Webster | Martin Taylor
Andy O'Toole | Luke Russell | Nick Ford | Steve Harris | Gerry McConnell
Paul Roberts | Max Cornely | Peter Jennings | Mark Davies | Jeff Marchant
Jeffrey Joyner | Neil & Mason Coles | Phillip Jensen | Paul Kimble
Marcus Johns | Dave Bell | Graham Chipperfield | Thorsten Zipfl
Ashley Pearce | Peter Glass | Neil Jepson | Peter Ferrigno | Adam Bender
Ken Pritchard | Andy Relton | Scott Wood | Nick Armstrong | Tom Clover
Roxanne Challinor | Nick Bessis | Cole Wood | Simon Rickman | Jon Foster
Matt Pasterfield | R.I.P. Dad, Love Laura, Kirk and Kira x | Abs Singh
Chris Jordan | Steve Hardy | Mark Rutherford | Mike Povey | Lyla Povey
Will Leaning | Simon Wells | Josh Harris | Ben Harris
Anthony Ferguson | Gavin Dunstan | Richard Salmon | Del Howard
Louie | Mark Walker | Gary & James Smithurst - Nottingham Hammers
Johnny Tutton | Craig Apps | Toby Revell | Graham Cox | James Williams
Andrew Phipps | Josh | Andrew Judge | Mark Speller | Mark Taylor
Symon Piddington | Darran Atrooshi | Luke Collins | Richard Collins
Matthew Sharkey | James Knight | Paul Griffiths | David LaPointe | Ulf Berg
Arild Østbø | Paul Renwick | Shay Dineen | Graham Hack | Jamie Smith

Carl Lumber | Michael Hayward | Melvyn Goulty | Lee Tysoe | Eli Love
Jamie Shears | Simon Wellington | Tom Smith | Charles Gadsdon
Blake Sloane | Ian & Tom Tricerri | Neil & Harry Shemmings | Ponny
James Lindsay | John Moore | John Reisenbuchler | Richard Smith | Rio Wray
Rob Andrew | Tim Mansfield | Ric Francis | John Price | Andrew Barker
Malcolm Atkins | Paul Taylor | Rick Elliott | Sam Kinnaird | David Matters
MJ Green | Andy Grist | Rob Kipling | Gianni Assirati | Andy Brooker
Vic & Rob Lindsell | Kevin Penny | Marcus Killick | Nathan Davey | Tom Wain
Tony Gibson | Paul Sheehan | Tom Ellam | Chas Sturton | Mark Fletcher
Oliver Wilton | Daniel Fallon | Graham Brailey | Mark Robertson
Kevin & Tom White | Ryan Ullman | Colin Goode | Stuart Power | Mads Furu
Mark Edwards | David Fulcher | Stuart Kipling | Sarah Langton | Tim Audin
Russell Garnham | Martin Douch | Peter Slade | Dave Shepherd | David Knox
Darren & Kyle Mollan | Joshua Dawkins Charlton | Andy Colley | Rayboy
Peter Goulding | John Cavanagh | Steven Cavanagh | Vicky Beautyman
James Burns | Ian Glander | John Brinsden | Mark Radford | Gregory Jock
Charlie Scrivener | Chris Scrivener | Ian Trayford | Brian Ikegami | Even Boge
Dominic Ryder | Brett Peake | Geoff Harrison | David Neck | Alan Frost
Paul Copeman | Harry Huhulski | Daniel Church | Dave Barnes | Robert Lane
Aaron Chapman | Victor Morgan | Zack Zvosecz | Terry Sidney | Jonas Eklöf
Paul Kirkwood | Callum May | Michael Bond | Terry Knight | Steve Barnard
Gareth James | Ashley Barton | Jon Williams | Jason Lloyd | Sue Skinner
Steve Davison | Mark Vickers | Mark Wilcox | Susan Clark | Darren Rao
Robin Cane | David Bale | Warren Celiz | Darren Scates | Ali Blundell
Gary Lock | Keith Evans | Matt Hayes | Michael Kinane | Lee Huckle
Thomas Nordahl Pedersen | Jim Oakman | Tobias Carlsson | John Zarri
Gérard Jakimavicius | Jon Yewman | Richard Gibson | Mikey Saunders
Paul Ruzzaman | John Murrell | James Regan | Iain Croll | Jeff Harling
Andrew Phillips | Alan Hicks | Patrick Hutt | Roslyn Groom | Callum Weaver
Barry Drake | Leon Shearing | Harry Aujla | John Chapman | Gary Thompson
Jim Humphreys | Brad Morgan | Matt Hammar | Sawn Sussams | Adam Celiz
Andy Connacher | James Hopkins | Tony Holdway | Nathan Weygood
Ed White | David Clements | John Angel | Paul Ewin | Johnny Heilbron
Lucian Mattison | Scott Crossland | Gary Bragg | Rob Taylor | Garry
Shaun Garman | Matthew Williamson | Sam Greenwood | Paul Friel
Mario Santangelo | Mark Constable